60 SEASONS

Also by Joey Monteleone

I'll be Tennessean Ya'
A History...His Story, Some Fish Tales and Tips

60 SEASONS

a fishing guide

JOEY MONTELEONE

WordCrafts

60 Seasons
Copyright © 2021
Joey Monteleono

ISBN: 978-1-952474-91-0

All rights reserved. No part of this book may be reproduced, stored in a retrieval system, or transmitted in any form or by any means—electronic, mechanical, photocopy, recording or otherwise—without the prior written permission of the publisher. The only exception is brief quotations for review purposes.

Published by WordCrafts Press
Cody, Wyoming 82414
www.wordcrafts.net

*To my fathers, heavenly and earthly,
who have guided me on this joyous journey,
gave my dreams and wings,
and continue to inspire me.*

Contents

Foreword xi
There's Magic In Moving Water 1
Bass Fishing Beginner? Hand 'em a Spinner 6
Finding Big Bass 9
Bass Patterns 12
Why I Love / Hate Crankbaits 14
The Misunderstood Strike Zone 17
Bass Feeding Factors 21
Crappie Class—Lessons Learned 25
Finding Fish 101 30
Jig Tips: Turn the Beginner into a Bragger 33
Simply Smallmouth 36
Beyond Bass 39
Why You Don't Catch Good fish on Bad Casts 42
Love at First Bite 46
The Bountiful Bluegill 50
Bass Techniques That Really Work 53
Big Bass Secrets 57
Family Fishing 72
Simple System for Cool Water Crappie 76
Ten of My Favorite Fishing Facts 79
More Big Bass Secrets 84
Game of Throws 89
Spinnerbaits—Spinner Bites 92
Ten Essential Kayak Bass Fishing Tips 96

The One(s) That Got Away 101
Bass Without Borders 105
Natural Clues to Stream Health 108
Making a Hard Case for Soft Plastics 111
Advanced Topwater Tips 115
Big Bass Secrets 119
Between and a Dock and a Hard Place 123
Until Depth Do Us Part 127
Master Muddy Water 131
A Big Fishing Challenge—New Spots 134
Smallmouth Bass—Why and How to Catch 'em 137
Get Right to the Point 141
Spring Statistical Strategy 145
Night Stalkers—The Night Bite 148
Fishing Apps—Common Sense Clues For Big Bass 151
The Shallow Bite in Deep Summer 155
Speed Trap 158
How To FIND and FOOL Late Spring Bass. 162
Seeing Red 166
Follow the Leader 168
Low Tech Catch 171
The Right Bite 175
The ABCs of Catching and Playing Fish 179
Plan for Soft Plastics 181
The Hot Rods...and Reels 185
The Five Things I Always Do 188
Urban Angling 191
The Tackle Box Test 194
The Science of Bass Fishing...and Catching 199
That 10% 203
The Underwater World of Fish 207
Continuous Improvement 210
The Moment of Truth—The Hook Set 214
The Rules of Fishing 219

Look, No Batteries Needed	223
The Three Best Baits	227
What About Winter	231
What Does It Weigh?	234
Why the Fly	236
Summer Midnight Monsters	240
Ultimate Organization	244
Keys to Kayak Crappie	247
Working the Weeds	251
What's All the Buzz About?	254
Catching Fish on the Crossover	258
Shad-Oh	261
Weather or Not	265
Stream Secrets	269
Trophy Bass Tackle Box	272
Kayak Casting Accuracy	276
Submerged Secrets	278
Acknowledgments	281

Foreword

60 *Seasons* is the memorialization of years of experience and knowledge gathered by one of America's most treasured professional fishermen. It doesn't matter if you fish for bass, walleye, crappie or any other species of freshwater fish, this book is a masterclass. One's level of experience is irrelevant as well. Everyone who enjoys sport fishing knows there is always so much more to learn. If you are a novice, just having picked up a rod and reel for the first time, or a seasoned, experienced fisherman looking to up your game, *60 Seasons* is the next step towards accomplishing your goal. This read is like having your own personal guide in the boat with you.

I know a guy! Once you read *60 Seasons* so will you. And you will come to know him as a personable, approachable, funny, gracious man, a professional in every sense of the word. A professional who loves mother nature, respects her, has spent as much time with her as any student has spent with his/her master. His discipline as a master of the martial arts has helped him become so focused on her that he understands her better than you and I do. Whatever it is besides the time this student has spent on the water as a competitor, a guide, a television, and radio host, he has become the consummate expert fisherman. Mother nature should give out awards to those who come this close to her, but perhaps that is the award in and of itself.

One might ask himself/herself why a guy as busy as Joey is would take the time, energy and effort to reduce all his experience to pen and paper. He surely doesn't need the fame or attention. He could just sit back and enjoy the rest of his days on the water. But he's not that kind of man. Knowing him personally for several years, I know Joey derives as much pleasure from watching one of his friends take his advice and catch fish as he does catching it himself. That's more than a rare quality in any professional in any profession. He is not the guy that will hide his favorite spot from you; he'll take you there because your joy in catching fish is his joy as well. He is not going to bury his rods, reels and lures in his locker so you can't see what he's doing. They are out there on the deck so anyone who asks can see for themselves what he's been up to.

Joey Monteleone is a treasure to have as a friend and brother. I can call upon him at any time to ask his opinion, get advice or the answer to a question I have about the sport we both love. Now you can too. Let me introduce you to Joey Monteleone, one of the greatest men I've ever known and the greatest fisherman I've ever had the pleasure of knowing.

Come along, you are about to join a master class of 60 Seasons on the water with Joey Monteleone!

Michael J. Vines
Fisherman/Author
President, The VCM Media Group

1

There's Magic In Moving Water

Here's a true, unbelievable, once in a lifetime story.

Imagine a fishing hole that you discovered almost accidentally, close to home, accessible and full of fish, giant fish. This place would be magical, diverse, clean and have nothing but wild fish. Think of this place as a virgin fishery, managed naturally, it received minimal pressure and that was by people of limited resources and skills. This dream spot was seemingly to be untouched by the human hand, had an assortment of cover and conditions, and promised unbelievable catches for decades.

Does this sound mythical?

I found a place like this. It looked like many spots I had seen before but gave no clue to the future it offered below the surface. It was bordered by country roads, history, and fertile farm land. Its secrets and stories would be revealed slowly. Unintentional success came as unexpectedly as the days, weeks, months, and years drifted like its current. Changes to the area, the banks, and to the life forms occurred organically, tragically, and sometimes drastically but always my mistress bounced back.

At times the river water was more like my life blood flowing through my veins. It saw me through many difficult times—I went there to confess my sins, to celebrate my life, and to find my balance. The river never lied to me, was always available, kept all its promises, and comforted me during hard times. In return I protected her secrets, worked to keep her clean, and honored her. Not to be outdone she delivered big fish and big memories. I spent days learning all I could about her and her *friends*. I was introduced to foxes, beavers, muskrats, osprey, several types of snakes, herons, owls, coyotes, deer, quail, turkeys, ducks, geese, and yes, multiple species of fish—oh, the fish!

At first they came as surprise. What? A crappie—in this fishing hole? Then came a few bluegill, and eventually a bass—a good one, probably 2 ½ pounds. I could have never imagined how this place would change my life nor the lessons I would learn in the most basic boats and through every season.

My river reflections include invasions by people, progress, and lack of respect for the resource. I'd foolishly thought, maybe hoped, it would always be sustainable and maintained by the gate keepers who would learn to love her to like I did. I saw the dark side of the river as it claimed lives of those who challenged it and disrespected its power. I watched helplessly as it was abused in every possible way, even as I worked to maintain it.

In private moments I often recall my introduction—an older gentleman sitting on the banks—who always built a small fire—sat on one bucket and had one close by to hold his catch. I recall seeing other people bringing their kids to the shoreline, with a blue bait cup full of worms and the excitement for the possibilities of a catch. Large numbers of fair-weather fishermen in the spring—numbers that dwindled in the summer and many were non-existent in the fall and winter. Few recognizable faces consistently visited, and none worshiped the river like I did. All along I wondered how long this love affair would last. I agonized over seeing people pulling stringers of fish out of the water. I tried not to think about the people who were raping *my* river. Trash, over-harvest, abuse of the resource—it was too painful to watch.

There were occasional reminders of how the river could heal itself—a giant autumn fish, proof that this one made it through the season and might spawn again.

Countless hours were spent learning the lessons that were given up begrudgingly by the river. This place became a living laboratory. The definition of scientific experiment contains these elements; observation, asking questions, forming a hypothesis, making a prediction, testing and forming a hypothesis based off results. I had a certain degree of control over my environment, I was looking (fishing) for repeatable results and then coming to a conclusion from the measured results. Now in English: I could fish a specific spot using techniques that I understood and then log results to determine what and how fish reacted to every aspect of my approach. Sounds dry right? Now imagine pitching jigs to fish that had never seen one. Further consider the places were small but full of cover and food sources, and the environment was ideal for producing quality fish—kind of a fishing heaven.

When I studied weather and water conditions, catches became more predictable. Each different access spot on the river offered a microcosm of any water almost anywhere. There were many forms of aquatic vegetation, tree lined shore and submerged stumps and fallen trees, creek channels, bottom contours, a few man-made boats slips, docks, points, gravel bars, chunk rock, bridge pilings, secondary creeks entering, and current. The balance of fish was ideal—all three major species of bass, largemouth, smallmouth, and the spotted Kentucky bass, bluegill, flathead catfish, carp, red eye, and crappie also inhabited this place.

The introduction of new lures and techniques were exciting, so exciting often times I couldn't sleep the night before in anticipation of the fish that would be fooled by something they had never seen before. There were several locations and access points that were simple and some that required my turtle imitation, namely hauling a green boat on my back a quarter of a mile in order to slide it into secret spot. My means of propulsion was a marine battery and a trolling motor. It was an adventure casting a jig into waters teeming with big bass that had not seen this swimming, hopping, darting crawfish imitating creature before—they couldn't wait to *taste* it. If you were willing to do the work to reach spots for a rough, physical launch, you could sling a buzzbait around cover and be assured of at least one five-pound bass.

Oh, there were a few people who would make their way in but tried to force the fish to take the standard minnow rig or tight line a live red wiggler worm, but they tired of the game. People had minimal success when they began to try to imitate what they saw me doing. The word spread about this guy catching big fish in this unlikely looking place. I foolishly sought notoriety for my catches and sent photos to the local newspaper and to the *bragging boards* of sporting goods stores and TV stations. This made it difficult to remain anonymous around a small town loaded with outdoorsmen.

The more I learned the more I became obsessed with the river and the fish. Five-pound bass became common. Rarely did I even test myself against the other species—this bass mecca was intoxicating. With the heavy hits I was getting, a five-pounder was almost anticlimactic, a disappointment.

The smallmouth began to disappear due to the loss of habitat, slow-moving waters, and the increase on water temperatures. Their spawning and lifestyle weren't really suited to these changes. The *spots* were a nuisance even though they put on an aerial display after being hooked. Largemouth bass from six to eight pounds started to show up regularly. Then a few nine pound bass were added to my journal of catches.

One unusually mild December day I pushed off the bank and headed to a secret underwater bass magnet—a long, slow, tapering point. The first cast of a spinnerbait was greeted with a solid jolt, and my hook set revealed a lot of weight at the business end of the line.

The cold water bass gave a good account of herself, but surrendered quickly, almost like she knew I would release her back soon. A landline call to my wife was followed by a request for her presence accompanied by a camera and two rolls of film. After several posed pictures, I took my trophy for a ride in a cooler full of river water to a small market with a meat scale. Ten pounds and seven ounces—a new personal best bass. Four more time I would top ten pounds. A seven-pound smallmouth, a four-pound spot, and a crappie that would scale at just under four pounds all came from the secret river waters.

It would be impossible to place a value on the lessons I learned in thirty years fishing this incredible place. What I learned translated to being able to duplicate my success all across North America. I transcribed my thoughts to the pages of magazines, made outline notes to use doing seminars, prepared radio scripts to instruct others, and occasionally brought TV cameras to my honey hole while insisting no shoreline shots were allowed that might reveal our location. Fish behavior, seasonal migration, lifestyle, feeding preferences, and predictable location all became second nature to me.

I watched as farm fields gave way to parking lots and apartments. Word of upstream chemical spills would create panic until I could check the impact of the interruption. There was no question the river was paying the price for progress—they were raping my river. In time I'll tell of the eventual fate of the river.

I haven't been back to this place for almost two years. I'm afraid. I'm afraid to go back because I fear that the place I came to love will no longer love me back or be the same—that I'll be disappointed. Is it possible that the progeny of the fish I released will reward me with a big bite? Will it spoil the memories I have of a safe haven—a place that shaped and saved my life?

Oh, in time I'll go back, face my fear, and maybe realize the memories can't be tarnished by a poor day fishing or a less than perfect experience. Will the magic still be there? We'll have to wait and see.

2

Bass Fishing Beginner? Hand 'em a Spinner

When faced with the problem of taking someone fishing that was new to the sport of bass fishing, I tried to decide what would be the best bait to position them for success. Whether I was just taking a casual trip or guiding it seemed to be the easiest way to guarantee some action for the novice bass angler—hand 'em a spinnerbait. With lots of possibilities the safety pin style spinner has proven to be the best bet for new bass hopefuls in any boat or kayak, wading or walking the bank. Many factors *weigh in* as to choosing the whirling, skirted versatile spinnerbait. In-line spinners can also be very effective for bass and most game fish. The in-line spinner is virtually forgotten by most fishermen. A long straight body, a feather dressed treble hook and a single willow type blade revolves around the in-line bait and is best utilized in a more open water environment and catches almost anything that swims.

First a spinner can be cast on any type of standard rod and reel. At home being launched toward largemouth on spincasting outfits, employed by a lot of starters, on the *open faced* spinning reels with the free flying, looping line or power fishing with a stout rod and baitcasting reels geared to winch bass and bigger baits back to the angler. Lightweight spinners even those smaller in size can even be used on fly rods. Suffice to say, anything short of a cane pole can be used to cast and retrieve spinnerbaits.

Safe and Successful—Spinnerbaits are safe due to the fact that they have only a single hook. Some models come with a *stinger* hook or trailer hook for short striking fish. The second hook can be added by sliding the eye of the trailer hook over the point and barb of the main hook but isn't necessary much of the time. When bass are striking short a quick clip and shortening of the skirt can solve the problem. Reducing the size of the skirt is just one of the many adjustments and altering of the spinner. Another plus for the kayak angler regardless of experience level is the spinnerbaits can be cast, worked, and ultimately bring fish to your grip from the sitting or standing model kayaks.

*(Always wear your life jacket on the water.)

Busting Out the Blades—Size, shape, color and more are all qualities of spinnerbait blades. Each offers difference performance capabilities and can be used to boat more bass under specific conditions. There are other odd ball blades but for the most part the Colorado (round), Indiana (tear drop), and willow leaf (because it resemble the leaf from a willow tree) are the most widely used. Combinations, colors, and finishes are also considerations. All this being said, you can imagine there are literally thousands of possibilities. The Colorado excels at creating dynamic water displacement aiding in increased wire arm vibration and a minimum of flash. That's right, the arm—not the blade—vibrates. The Indiana creates less vibration and a bit more flash than the Colorado. The willow leaf, based off shape, gives a maximum amount of flash and a minimum of vibration. Best bet, a mix of color, blade type, and size.

A #5 ½ willow trailing a #3 Colorado on a 3/8ths ounce frame is universal in its appeal and fish fooling. Single blades, double blades, some baits are equipped with four blades. Black blades for night fishing and other colors for other angling applications. One of the most successful spinnerbait tricks for me has been the altering on a ½ ounce double willow leaf spinner. Removing the front blade (closest to the head) allows for a more weedless, different visual presentation, and effective bait when bass are feeding heavily on shad—a common occurrence. The double willow model is still a great bait for very murky to muddy water.

Retrieve Tricks—The magic of spinnerbaits are they can be cast out and cranked back and catch fish. Pretty simple. Add a few wrinkles and more fish will come to the kayak. A *stop and go* retrieve makes the blades appear to flash and disappear like a fleeing minnow or bait fish. The bait is said to be *waking* when retrieved just under the surface and calling bass to investigate and attack the surface intruder. *Killing* a spinner is when the bait is coming back, and an abrupt stop makes the falling bait blade helicopter down simulating a dying shad. Bumping the stump (or any cover) creates a deflection / reaction strike to fish hugging objects and sense the bait is injured or disoriented. As you can imagine presentation is not just a cast and catch proposition.

Spinner Spots—Working year round spinnerbaits like other artificial lures do produce better at certain times. If there is open water (no ice over) a single-bladed Colorado is the choice of many winter bass anglers. As water warms, surface temperatures ranging from 55 to 65F, in spring bass feed heavily preparing for the spawn. Summer post-spawn fish are recovering from the exhausting spawn and ready to reload, and spinners looking like baitfish, minnows, bluegill, and more are gobbled up. As fall approaches and surface temperature drops, and days grow shorter, the natural reaction of a bass is to feed heavily in anticipation of the winter layoff. Spinnerbait spots include bur are not limited to shorelines, submerged stump fields, boat docks, bridge pilings, aquatic weed beds, creek channel, on points and around submerged wood. Quite a list and gives the impression that essentially anywhere a bass lives it will strike a spinnerbait.

Experiment with weights, blade configurations, and by all means each time out have one attached to the end of a medium heavy action rod and tied to 12-pound test line. Learn to recognize spinnerbait water and conditions, and the payoff is a consistent bass catcher, seasoned angler or novice, spinners are winners.

3

Finding Big Bass

After years of chasing bass, I said, "Little fish are liars, big fish hold the secrets." Of primary concern is, does the body of water you kayak in actually have big bass? Word of mouth, pictures, and a history of producing trophy size bass are all good indicators. Prior to the development of electronics, dedicated bass fishermen learned to *read* their waters by studying the shoreline and mostly common sense applications. The sun rises in the east and sets in the west; this makes the northwest side of your fishing hole get the longest exposure to the sun and makes it a few degrees warmer—a huge advantage in the late winter and early spring. The goal is to find fish quickly and efficiently and replicate results.

If you gaze at most old artificial baits, they were mostly made to fish topwater. Some in-line spinners and a small assortment of lipped lures were available, and all artificial baits were held dear by the owners. Eventually technology yielded tools for the ardent anglers anxious to apply new-fangled *sonar* devices to help determine the bottom contours, depth, and even little hump like figures indicating fish. With the advent of crystal clear images and marking waypoints with GPS, fishermen can easily navigate to within mere feet of spots that have previously produced fish. Hopefully when choosing and using your electronics you do not fall into the trap of separating yourself from your senses.

When a body of water gets an inordinate amount of boating

and fishing pressure, the bass adjust by moving to the next offshore cover, finding a more remote area or even changing their feeding habits and possibly go nocturnal. It is generally believed that fish in more than eight feet of water are not affected by boat traffic. In conjunction with this theory, my records indicate the majority of my trophy fish catches come from the magic depth of three to eight feet.

One flaw of the trophy hunting bass anglers is to establish what I refer to as a *milk run*. They return to the same spots, on the same body of water, throw the same baits, and wonder why they never catch any large fish. There are many flaws with this habit. What does convince folks to use this approach is the almost accidental success of catching the occasional big bass. Sorry, but this is explained as *lucky cast, lucky catch*. It doesn't diminish the achievement, but if you want to consistently catch lunker bass, adjustments are required.

Eric Jackson's explained his approach to finding bass. "I struggle to get myself to fish areas or types of cover where I am not already catching fish. Once I have caught a few fish and am ready to catch big fish, I tend to focus on the best spots only and stop pounding the banks, or smaller cover locations without a break."

Fish location is dictated by water temperature, food sources, and what I term the four bass factors. Bass want / need oxygen, food, cover, and deep water close by. Oxygen speaks for itself. If you can't breathe, very little else matters. Water within flowing creeks, aquatic vegetation, moving waters, springs, areas below dams, and the windy side of the specific body of water all are highly oxygenated. It's also likely an abundant food supply will be there for the same reason. Largemouth bass are object-oriented creatures (cover). Smallmouth relate to deep water like a largemouth relates to objects. Don't try to force largemouth tactics on smallmouth. Largemouths are ambush and chase predators. Cover offers the opportunity for both, concealing themselves and darting out to catch their prey is how they catch the majority of their meals. Target weeds and wood, both types of cover are bass magnets. Besides being cover, wood grows algae and brings baitfish in, and weeds provide oxygen so necessary to the lifestyle of the largemouth.

What do bass eat? A big bass will eat anything that fits in their cavernous mouths and comes within range—that's how they get and stay big. Always remember another of my frequently used quotes—"All creatures are slaves to their stomachs." Find the food = find the fish.

The last factor, deep water only matters because it gives the fish the comfort of an escape route—a very common trait among many other wild creatures. Secondary cover has the potential to produce that one huge bass. Mental note—find a compact area that serves all these needs, and you can drop the anchor, put the Power Pole down or just start saturating the water with lures, and begin your quest for Mr. Big. These types of places will consistently produce monster bass.

Your approach in the hopes of catching a big fish cannot be stressed enough. My term for this is *ninja stealth mode*. Fitting in and becoming part of the entire scenario is critical. Look for natural signs. Herons and fish-eating birds are there for a reason. Minimize noise, fish with the sun in your face to not cast a shadow on the fish you are trying to catch, let the wind drift you into the zone, pitch cast underhanded to make the least amount of splash and create a silent entry of the bait. Consider even dressing to match the background of the place you are fishing. Bass relate to any kind of an edge—this is the shoreline, the bottom, the surface. Bass can push bait and school of shad to edges and gorge themselves. Think edge! Don't discount that sixth sense, the intuitive feeling that you are in the right place at the right time. The great anglers have this.

Trophy Tip: Start by using the quietest baits that you have the most confidence in first. Then move up each time you change lures in size and sound. For example, try the plastic worm, jig, spinnerbait, crankbait and then topwater noisemaker. If the bass are spooky you increase the odds of hooking and catching the biggest fish in the area using this trick.

4

Bass Patterns

Catch one bass it's luck, catch two it's a clue, catch a third you have a pattern. Many people who fish don't look for the tip-off that the fish are in fact doing some similar things. Developing a pattern can be species specific—same kind of cover, similar depth, or even something that the fisherman is consciously (or unconsciously) doing differently. Often there is a pattern inside a pattern. I recall a day on a local fishing hole trying to catch crappie with another person along. There was a submerged tree, a very common crappie hideout, and it normally held numbers of white and black crappie—notorious schooling fish. We were casting the same pearl colored curly tail grub on spinning equipment. I was catching fish on almost every cast. My partner—zero. The pattern—fishing a submerged tree top in slightly stained water using a horizontal presentation and a medium slow retrieve. Why was I catching fish and my partner wasn't? Every time my soft plastic lure *ticked* the branches on the tree I got a reaction strike from the fish suspended in the openings of the branches. A pattern inside a pattern.

More specifically with bass, another example would be a similar situation. The popularity of square-billed crankbaits has risen to previously unimagined popularity. While the action of these baits will draw strike from open water bass, they excel when cast around heavy cover in the form of wood, dock pilings, and rock. Again the deflection triggers bites from bass of all sizes. Last fall I hooked back to back six-pound bass. They were schooled up on a secondary off-shore log jam. Cast past the target, crank the bait down, as it bounced off the wood, the strike predictably came.

Isolated instance? Nope—a pattern inside a pattern.

More recently while fishing a small lake, a wind-blown back, on a full moon, waters heavily stained by recent rains, and a thick weed edge extending out to five to eight feet of water, I picked up a jig rod. Most people cast from the middle of the body of water to the cover and work the lure back. While this works, when fish are staged along an edge, many time paralleling the edge draws more strikes. When there is a specific target, buck bushes, downed trees, or a boat dock on the weed edge I paddled out and worked those pitching from the middle and working the jig back, swimming it slowly while keeping full contact. Both techniques worked to the tune of eleven bass—two topping six pounds. Again a pattern inside a pattern.

Spinnerbaits are also pattern type lures. Casting to cover, blade configurations, retrieve nuances all play into the pattern. All this being said, there are times when you must make adjustments. Early in the day bass often swim around openly, covering water, looking for food. Once the bright sun rises the same fish seek overhead cover to use as an ambush point. The same baits sometimes work, but a different presentation might be in order. As the day and conditions change, so do the patterns that produce bass. Bait changes, retrieve speeds, along with colors, size, and sound makers are all considerations.

Make mental notes, commit to memory the patterns, adjustments and the seasonality of baits, presentations, depths, cover, conditions. Each of these helps to create a menu of patterns that are repeatable and lead to consistent catches.

5

Why I Love / Hate Crankbaits

A quote from Hall of Fame baseball player Yogi Berra, "I feel strongly both ways." That's my stance on crankbaits. I love the crankbait bite, but there are problems associated with these lures. Crankbaits in one form or another have been around for decades. A look at an old 1947 catalog shows "underwater" baits proclaiming they'll "dive a foot or two deep when retrieving." This lure was available in three colors and could be yours for 59 cents. A recent catalog advertises 68 colors, a much deeper dive, and over 10 times the price.

I love crankbaits because they are search lures. You can cover a fair amount of water casting and cranking—a plus for the tournament fisherman. The more casts you make there's an increased possibility you'll put that bait in front of a fish.

I hate crankbaits because they are a chore to repeatedly cast and retrieve. A full day of cranking almost guarantees you'll be hungry and most assuredly tired at the end of your trip. The bigger the bill of the bait, the deeper it dives and the more exhausted you're going to be.

I love the crankbait "bite." You feel the flow of the lure on its return, and all of a sudden it just stops cold. It sometimes is described as "knocking slack in your line." When the cranking bite is good it's as fun as any other method.

I hate the crankbait when the fish are really deep or locked down and suspended way off the bank. The suspended fish for me are usually the toughest to catch. If there's a cold front, you get a lot of casting practice and sore shoulders.

I love the crankbait when bass are around isolated cover. A submerged stump, a boat dock rock piles or any object call for a square billed crankbait. The bill, by virtue of the name, looks squared off. The bait will deflect off any object and causes a unique hit I refer to as a deflection bite. I refer to this scenario as *between a dock and a hard place*. It's almost predictable and fun when it's right.

I hate the crankbait because it is generally equipped with a pair of treble hooks, not affectionately known more likely as *trouble* hooks. Two hooks, six hook points and if they hooked fish as securely as they hooked your clothes, anchor ropes, truck seats, carpet and your skin that would be awesome. Once imbedded in underwater obstructions it can be frustrating. I draw my line tight and plink it like a banjo string first. If that doesn't work I get directly over the bait and push the rod down and turn it in a circle, then reverse the circle. No luck still, I go past the bait and change the direction trying to dislodge the lure. Still stuck, I cuss and pull (prepared to duck) and then just wait for the snapping sound of my line breaking.

I love the crankbait because the same troublesome hooks will keep the fish secured if they are sharp, the rod has some give and your knot is good. Sometimes they, the fish, get both hooks and stay *buttoned up*.

I hate the crankbait because landing a feisty bass, especially smallmouths, can quickly turn into a trip to the emergency room to get the previously mentioned hook—or hooks—professionally removed. I have grippers positioned on each side of my kayak for safely securing the crankbait hooked fish. I also advocate the use of a rubberized net for purposes of landing my multi-hook baits. Oh yeah, bring a set of needle nose pliers too.

I love the crankbait because it offers a presentation for the aggressively feeding bass or the neutral or even non-aggressive feeding mode fish. A tantalizing slow retrieve or a stop and go and even some times a steady retrieve are all at sometimes rewarded with hits.

I hate the crankbait because they can be confusing. Dozens of colors, square bill for shallow water fish, oval bill for deeper residents, lipless—I carry all three but have a preconceived idea what they will strike.

I love the crankbait because at times I've caught all three species of bass, also crappie, catfish, walleye, bluegill, and more on the cranking variety of lures. A mini model is a fish catcher for panfish and small waters, the upsized version can bring bites from trophy musky.

I hate the crankbait because improperly stored they seem to become almost welded to each other. The cure for this is to pick up the pile and shake them until they release the grip on themselves. The same way they went together they will come apart.

I have a box dedicated specifically to crankbaits. I carry it all the time. Some days I love 'em, some days I hate 'em but I always have them with me.

Guide Tip: Another common practice is to change out the front hook on crankbaits to a same size red model. After the alteration you'll be surprised how many times the fish is caught on the red hook. To experiment, move the hook, replacing the rear treble instead on an identical bait with the red same size treble hook. Again, the bass are most often on the red hook.

6

The Misunderstood Strike Zone

Cast after cast and no fish, invariably anglers look at each other and say what they are thinking, "No fish here, let's move." One of the most misunderstood and exaggerated aspects of bass fishing is the size of the strike zone. Natural influences play a large part on the positioning of bass and their range of movement to eat and strike artificial or live bait. There exists a popular misconception that bass will move a great distance to *attack* a moving target. Bass are naturally curious creatures. Consider the lifestyle of bass and other gamefish. There is a high infant mortality rate due to predation and even in some cases cannibalization. Out of every thousand bass that hatch out as fry only two make it to two pounds. As we venture out onto the water we go into recreation mode. Bass, on the other hand, are always in survival mode. To borrow an economic industry phrase ROI—return on investment—is critical to all wild things. The point being that if a bass or any other predator has to chase something a great distance to catch it and ingest it, potentially it could be a losing proposition. Simply stated, if a fish gains less energy than it expended to catch the food source, the fish actually losses weight and energy—not a good scenario.

What creates the size of the strike zone? Essentially there are two determining factors that lead to the size or lack of size of the bass' strike zone; water color and water temperature. Because bass and many other species feed predominately by sight, water color plays a role in feeding frequency and efficiency. Whereas catfish depend largely on smell and minimally on sight, bass see, stalk, and catch forage by use of their eyesight. All species of bass possess a highly developed sense of sight, depth of field. Colors and even shades of colors favor the fish. Clear water makes it easier to see food and also detect flaws in angler presentation. Stained water; not so much. Muddy water; easy on the angler tougher on the bass.

Make no mistake bass are great predators but the odds for the angler increase under certain conditions using certain baits. Water temperature also plays a key role in the strike zone of bass. In weather / water extremes, hot or cold, bass slow down. The ranges between the mid-50 degree Fahrenheit mark and water in the high 80s are relatively comfortable for the fish. They also eat and digest a faster pace. Hence, eat, digest go back on the prowl and more than likely an expanded strike zone.

On the other side of the spectrum, cold or extreme heat, and they slow down; add muddy water and a high current flow and then the game changes. Bass will *hunker down*—a southern technical term—and the strike zone can be drastically reduced. Bass will avoid current and the work it takes to be smack in the middle of it. Muddy water is akin to being in a dark room to humans—they move slowly, find a comfortable spot, and stay put. Take heart—a change in baits, tactics, and retrieve will help you to boat a few bass.

In the expanded strike zone, not as common as what we would like, you can just open your tackle box and tie on the first thing you see and catch a fish. An example of this might be a spring day, surface water temperature 65 degrees, water level stable, a slight breeze from the west, and a full moon—optimum conditions for bass, crappie, bluegill, and others to go into a feeding frenzy. When it gets tough the lures that can be held in the zone for an extended period of time create the best chance of repeatable success. With assistance from the fisherman, there are baits that excel when the bass seem to have lockjaw. Suspending hard plastic jerkbaits, crankbaits, jigs, and spinners can all cure the smaller strike zone situation. Any other lures that can stay in the restricted area for a longer period of time could temp a bass to hit. When fishing gets tough, smaller lures and slower retrieves are highly desirable and will produce a few fish. The more drastic the conditions, the slower the bait should move and spend an extended period of the time in the strike zone. Additional criteria could include baits equipped with rattles, bright colors, and upsized artificial lures. Each offers increased appeal to the senses. Couple all these factors with casting accuracy to minimize the need for the fish to move to feed, and you're in business.

Sometimes the answer may be live bait. With no inherent flaws in live bait, it could increase your chances of a catch. It swims/moves naturally, exhibits predator fear factors like fast escape flight or darting motions, and with creatures like crawfish they take a defensive posture, back end tucked down, claws up and open. Catching your own live bait is fun and effective.

Check your local regulations for rules regarding catching and using live bait.

Learn to recognize the strike zone and what affects it, and you are well on your way to your limit of fish and fun.

Guide Tip: Another rule of thumb not necessarily specific to strike zone conversations is the unwritten rule that when using live bait use the largest you can find and the smallest (small being relative) artificial you lure you can get by with. The large live bait offers no negative clues; the smaller artificial lure makes it more difficult to pick up on the fake fish catcher.

7

Bass Feeding Factors

For those who consistently catch a bunch of bass, *big* fish, or always cash a check at the tournaments there are few commonalities—being prepared, having reasonable equipment, a little luck, and an intimate knowledge of the habits of their quarry. Knowing the habits and habitat favored by the fish are a giant advantage. At the top of the list is the understanding of the preferred food sources of three major, most well-distributed species—the largemouth, smallmouth and spotted Kentucky bass.

Most commonly consumed forage for bass are bait fish. In the category of most often digested food sources are minnows of all varieties, several of the sunfish family but most meals are the shad. Gizzard and threadfin shad comprise the majority of bass meals. The reason for this is that the shad are the most available forage food therefore the most frequently eaten.

The most preferred but not the most available are crawfish. Good populations of a large variety of crawfish exist in waters all over. Simply stated, bass love crawfish because of the nutritional value of the clawed creatures. Scientifically proven, for every five pounds of crawfish a bass eats it gains a pound in weight. This is most important for trophy fish, because in order to maintain or gain weight they must eat the best fish food and a lot of it.

For bass chasing shad (or other baitfish) there is a critical concept understood by live bait fishermen that everyone should understand.

When a solitary bass or a bunch of fish are after a concentrated school of shad they opportunistically chase, engulf as many or the closest they can catch, often hitting the forage from the back, moving off, and literally turning the shad to swallow it from the front. The reason for this, if the finny bait fish flares its fins—many have at least five fins—potentially the bass would choke on the extended multiple appendages. This is the reason bass shy away from eating the crappie equipped with very large fins. This is not to say bass will not eat crappie. Bass are opportunistic and will, especially in early spring and fall, feed on anything they can catch and will fit in their mouths.

Trophy Tip: Match the color and erratic swimming motion of the bait fish to draw more strikes. The best shad imitating baits are swim baits, crankbaits, and spinnerbaits. Consider upsizing your offering to give the bass a big bite. Poor presentation will be troublesome for larger lures—concentrate on retrieve speed and bumping cover to hook more bass.

The crawfish, (aka mudbug, crawdads, freshwater lobsters, crayfish) known in scientific circles as crustaceans share almost all waters where bass reside. Found in clean waters, especially in rocky areas, crawfish come in multiple colors, go through stages of being soft-shelled and various seasonal color shades, are recognized as having more than 300 species, and are capable of regeneration of lost claws. Another interesting fact, they walk forward but escape in backward bursts utilizing their skeletal muscles and segmented tail. When threatened craws take on a defensive posture, backing away, claws extended, open and upraised, hardly striking fear in a bass of any size. Once again slurping up the craw and eventually turning the hard-shelled creature to more easily facilitate the swallowing process. The early spring emergence brings pre-spawn bass in search mode. Once surface water temperatures reach the low 50-degree mark, bass and other fish are on the prowl ready to eat

Bass Feeding Factors

before going into the exhausting spawn. At this point everything is fair game, but the crawfish provide the most return for the *seek out and find* food process used by the bass affected by the winter layoff in cool water environments. Adding weight to their frame now and in the fall triggers fish to gorge themselves on every forage food available to carry them through the spawn or winter depending on the geographical location. Bass are in competition with most other gamefish for consuming the crawfish. Everything including catfish, crappie, musky, and other fish prize the crawfish as a normal part of their diet.

Trophy Tip: The two baits that best mimic the look and motion of the *real* thing are a rubber-legged jig and the soft plastic craw imitator. In most instances the jig is trailed by a soft plastic craw, but the craw can be rigged in many ways to be fished solo. Texas rigged with a slip sinker and an appropriately sized worm hook (I prefer a 4/0 Daiichi copperhead hook) Carolina rigged, added to a leadhead or even locked onto a shakey head, the soft plastic craws are available in several sizes and a veritable rainbow of colors. My jigs are Strike King models including, but not limited to, casting, swimming, flipping, and finesse, a few different weights ranging from the tiny finesse 1/8th or ¼ ounce to ¾ ounce flipping versions for *punching* matted or heavy vegetation, but standard is 3/8th ounce casting jig. Colors are chosen mostly to match the current color of the crawfish. Roll a few rocks in shallow water, and you will conform the presence of the crawfish and the color stage they are in. My preference and the bass' is the Strike King Rage Tail craws as trailers or primary bait. The trick to imitating real crawfish is a varied cadence working either bait in short intermittent hops /swim motions which matches the escape action of the fleeing craw. Keeping the medium heavy action rod between the 10 o'clock and 12 o'clock position, keep constant contact with your craw lure of choice, concentrating on any change in the feeling of the swimming bait.

While bass will eat anything that can't get away and fits in their oversized mouth the shad and the crawfish comprise a majority of what they ingest. Most available or prized matching the normal activities of either is almost a guarantee to more bass at the end of your line.

8

Crappie Class—Lessons Learned

Late one fall day while I was fishing for crappie, the wind changed direction, and the crappie that were actively chasing small soft plastic curly tail grubs stopped cold. The north wind shut down the bite, or so it seemed. Confident that crappie were still holding in the same vicinity and on the same structure—large submerged trees—I tossed out a small tube jig on a lightweight leadhead and was rewarded with a bite from a 14-inch crappie.

Aha, the cold wind and weather change moved the fish closer to cover and apparently decreased the size of the strike zone. To test the theory I went back with the horizontal presentation, and the fish seemed again to be resistant to the cast, twitch retrieve. Back again to the vertical retrieve with the more subtle bait, and again the bite resumed. That revelation not only repeated itself but proved to be also applicable to bass. A weather change such as wind direction, cooler temperature, or cloud cover often times moves or changes the mood of the fish, regardless of species. I've seen it work with bass, crappie, bluegill, catfish, and more.

Understanding each species:
Lure categories / Water columns—The most consistent categories of artificial lures are those that can be worked in all three water columns. Surface, mid-level, and bottom bumping would be a breakdown of the three levels. I have managed to catch a

few crappie on topwater, but it's more the exception that the rule. I've never seen a distinct surface pattern emerge for crappie. A list of lures to catch crappie at mid-level and deep presentations would include running-crankbaits, spinners, and soft plastics in the form of grubs and tubes. Each of these can be fished in a few inches of water to down deep. The same list of lures can also dive to depths that could harbor deep spots in weather extremes, like the dead of winter or summer. A technique called pulling has become popular on crappie factories like Kentucky Lake, Reelfoot Lake, and many of the reservoirs in the states of Mississippi and Alabama. Bass size crankbaits trolled at multiple depths adjusting the boat speed to catch offshore schooling fish in the summer is extremely effective (*my recommendation Strike King series #3 and #5 diving to 8 and 10 feet respectively*). A GPS mounted in the boat to register the speed down to mile per hour fractions is vital for this presentation. With several rods out in holders it's not uncommon to have several fish on at the same time. *Be sure to check your local regulations for the number of rods you can use while drifting, trolling, or pulling.*

Another excellent choice, and popular with panfish including crappie, are the traditional small tube baits and curlytail grubs fished on leadheads. A wide range of colors can be helpful or confusing. Consideration of water color is the deciding factors for me. Ask a dozen dedicated crappie chasers their favorite color, and you'll most likely get a dozen different answers. Here's what you'll find in my species-specific crappie tackle box.

Leadheads ranging in sizes from 1/16 to 1/4 ounce, which I use based solely off the wind velocity. To make casting easier and more accurate while also maintaining contact with the bait is best accomplished when the weight matches the conditions. In no wind and clear water I opt for the lightest leadhead to deliver a slow fall. As the wind increases the leadhead weight goes up. I usually start with a 1/8 ounce round head tied to four-pound test line. My *go to* colors are a special color I helped develop 0095 Monteleone silver by MidSouth tackle, chartreuse with red glitter, pearl white, red /chartreuse and black / chartreuse.

Vertical versus Horizontal—Almost all the dominant natural food sources crappie, bass, and other gamefish eat have the ability to move both vertically and horizontally. Being able to match these escape and lifestyle swimming motions positions you to catch crappie and other species. A hot topic for anglers is color. Typical favorites come in many shades and patterns. There has been an explosion of custom painting of cranking baits and a rainbow of soft plastics in natural and unnatural colors, shades, and combination offerings. To avoid confusion on and off the water my preference is to go to basics. Light or natural / neutral colors, next mid-level shades, and finally bright colors are essentially all that is necessary. A case can be made for any color, but with an accurate cast and the correct retrieve speed, color becomes secondary. These two factors, casting accuracy and retrieve speed, are worth the most consideration.

Retrieve speed is the least understood aspect of fishing!
To best explain this, almost everyone has experienced the frustration of fishing with someone who's using the same rod, same reel, same line, *and* the same bait—and they're catching fish, and you aren't. That can only be the difference in presentation and most certainly retrieve speed. Adjust and know that slower in most cases is almost always better. A stop and go retrieve is also more likely to draw a hit because it simulates the flight instinct of natural food sources or gives the appearance of being injured—either one rings the dinner bell for crappie, bass, and most game fish.

To achieve the most lure action and the greatest depths, line size is a critical factor. New lines offer maximum strength and smaller diameters. My preference for crappie is monofilament line—it has some stretch, great knot strength, and performs well. I have experimented with braided line and like the sensitivity, but when you get snagged—as you often will fishing submerged wood for crappie—it is difficult and must be cut.

Finally most worthy of noting is *the orientation of the mouth and eyes of any of the crappie species*. With a mouth that opens wide and faces dramatically upward, it makes it much easier for crappies to take prey from above. The eyes of crappie are large and set to the side and up giving them a wide range of vision. Both of these factors make keeping the bait above the assumed position of the fish a huge plus. No sight, no bite.

Predictable Criteria—In the search for fish, certain places seem to consistently hold numbers and varieties of fish. Shade in summer is a key spot. Overhead cover creating shade makes for a good ambush spot, cooler water temperatures, and consistent hideouts for all types of fish. Weeds can fall into this category, surface vegetation can provide a canopy and comfort. A plus for any green vegetation is additional available oxygen produced naturally by the weeds. Submerged wood is also a potential *hot spot* for fish. Crappie and catfish enthusiast have known this for decades. Why wood? Algae grows on most wood after it's been submerged for a while. Quite simply the food chain is fueled by small baitfish moving in to feed on the algae, and game fish feed on the baitfish. The wood serves as cover for a feeling of safety and a top ambush location.

Follow the moon to fish. *A quick check of the list of world record fresh and salt water fish shows a majority of the records were set on or close to the new and full moon phases.* The feeding, natural phenomenon of mating, and the eventual hatching activities are all closely related to the moon. Crappie move shallow to spawn when the water temperatures are near 55-58 degrees. Pre-spawn and spawning crappie are easily the easiest to catch. Late March and April are prime months in many states. Also hatches of bugs, minnows, frogs, and the fish all have correlations to these phases. I'm a fan of the full moon. This is just the short list of natural criteria that can be the key to locating and catching fish of all sizes.

Locations and Why—Common denominators for many creatures including fish are dictated by lifestyle and the survival of the species involved. For most fish, the list is distilled down to these:

Crappie Class—Lessons Learned

1. Oxygen—If fish (or any other living thing) can't breathe, nothing else matters. Aquatic weeds, current, wind, springs, and incoming creeks all increase the capability of additional oxygen. Extremely hot water has minimized oxygen levels and at times to dangerously low levels. Cold water decreases the need for oxygen in fish and also slows down their metabolism.

2. Food—Next to breathing, eating is high on the list to survive and thrive. The list of food sources for bass are only limited by what will fit in that cavernous mouth. Most of their diet is dominated by minnows and shad because of their abundant populations, but crappie—like bass—love crawfish because of their high energy nutritional value. But anything near or in the water is a potential meal.

3. Cover—Safety and security is the top reason fish hold around, near, or in cover. Another plus is the possibility of an ambush point for many types of fish. Cover manifests itself in many forms, and almost anything can qualify for cover. Most common are natural components, wood (stumps, fallen trees) aquatic weeds (lily pads, coontail moss, bull rushes aka cattails, pencil grass, hydrilla), shoreline willow trees (famous for bug hatches), rock, and more. Man-made cover includes but is not limited to, boat docks, rip rap dams, and brush piles.

4. Deep Water Access—Deep water close by is an escape route for fish. Knowing they can quickly seek the safety of deeper water is important to bass of all types. If all these components exist in a compact area you can bet fish will frequent that location consistently. These are the spots we all recognize as *honey holes*.

Commit these lessons to memory, cast, catch, and repeat.

9

Finding Fish 101

With an abundance of high-tech equipment used by today's anglers there exist the possibility of people separating themselves from their senses. What that means is reliance on electronics to give you the exact location of fish. Used as tools to assist you in seeking out your prospective catch your electronic gadgetry is fine, but don't allow yourself to drift into staring at a screen or listening for a fish alarm to begin casting for your favorite species. A common sense approach will serve you well, and in the event that your batteries go out or your bottom-scanning, temperature-taking, speed-monitoring, GPS navigating equipment goes haywire, you can still find and catch fish using your visual and cognitive skills.

Knock on wood
Fishing wood is a great start. Submerged trees, wooded stake beds, or underwater log jams are gold mines for bass, crappie, and catfish to mention a few. A basic need of bass is cover. Wood serves as cover. Another aspect in the hierarchy of bass is food. Wood grows algae, algae draws minnows and baitfish, minnows and baitfish draw gamefish of all sizes and descriptions. Wood also presents a spawning place for crappie and a current break for river or stream inhabitants like catfish, trout, bass, and more.

Shade is another benefit afforded by waterlogged trees. There are lots of reasons for fish to hover in and around wood, and it makes it a great place to start your search for fish. Make sure you don't pass fallen trees and submerged wood with making a cast or two into and around this critical cover.

Rock and roll
Most waters have places where rock in different sizes and amount are found. In man-made lakes a rip rap bank is very common. Rip rap is chunk rock plied around an earthen dam to keep it from eroding and washing away. Boulders, scattered rock, large expanses of limestone and pea gravel are more examples of rock found in and around waterways.

The big pluses to rocky banks, shores, and bottoms are the natural retention of heat in the spring and winter by hard surfaces. When the water is warming in the spring, a few degrees difference will draw and hold bait and fish. The comfort of warmer waters is important to a creature whose lifestyle is in part predicated by temperature. Keep in mind the spawn send fish by the hundreds into areas with rock bottom structure.

Another advantage to rock is the eventual emergence of crawfish from their hiding places in where there is free standing rock or rock piles. Gamefish will cruise rock strewn banks and bottoms enjoying the warmth radiating from the rock and the presence of food sources. Keep rock of any size and amount on your list of places to work for fishing early season, at night, during the spawn, during cold fronts, and for that matter year round.

Bass in the grass
Cutting the grass is admittedly a little low on my list. Fishing the grass is a whole other thing. Aquatic vegetation in the form of cattails, hydrilla, lily pads, coontail moss, pencil grass, cabbage leaf, and others has at one time or another paid off for me. Keeping with the theory of bass being object oriented and preferring cover, working the weeds is a great strategy.

Other fish also migrate to vegetation. The presence of green aquatic plants signifies healthy bottom composition, oxygen essential to the breathing function, and an ambush point for several of the freshwater fishes. Green weeds are at times magnets for fish in search of comfort, food, and higher levels of oxygen.

In the spring the first greenery to emerge draws and holds fish. Conversely in the fall the last of the vegetation becomes a hangout for fish. Even the use of plant life like lily pads as overhead cover is common from Florida to the natural lakes of Minnesota. Flat out fish love green, weeds, moss, and plants that grow in and around the shorelines and the depths of lakes, rivers, and streams. Many types of life forms will be in close proximity of the watery garden spots. Forage for fish, shady relief from the heat, a hiding spot or just a curiosity, aquatic vegetation in all shapes and sizes should not be ignored by anglers.

10

Jig Tips: Turn the Beginner into a Bragger

Not a glamour bass bait, jigs don't get the attention swim baits, custom color crankbaits, and other new age lures do. Versatility comes in the form of colors, sizes, weights, and styles. Casting, flipping, finesse, and swim are categories of jigs. Grass heads, football heads and more, conventional casting, pitching or flipping, equipped with rattles or no rattles—all this create fish catching potential and maybe some confusion.

The beauty of jig fishing for bass and other species is it produces year round and in almost any type of water conditions. The most important aspect of jigging for bass is it's a *big* bass technique that will never be outdated. Why? Every angler will fish it differently. I refer to this as random action. Fish the jig with a sweeping motion, a series of short hops, ripping it at lightning speed or dragging it painfully slowly across the bottom, this all creates multiple combinations of these factors which add up to an infinite possibility of presentations. Everyone will work it differently which mean that bass rarely will see the same jig look.

A white swim jig with a swimbait body simulates a shad. A bottom-bumping brown/orange skirt jig with a soft plastic trailer mimics the movement of the escaping crawfish. Vertical jigging in grass mats, the branches of submerged trees, or employing the underhand pitch cast to the farthest recesses of boat docks are just a few techniques used by bass anglers during tournaments or fun fishing.

Weighing In—The weight of the jig is important for casting and presentation. The weights range from diminutive ⅛ ounce heads to massive leadheads exceeding a full ounce for punching through mats of aquatic vegetation. A good starting spot is about ⅜ ounce jigs—easy to cast, allows for full time contact and falls at a reasonable rate, all which matter over the course of a day.

The bass seems to react well to crawfish soft plastic trailers. My preference, and the bass seem to agree, is the Strike King Rage Tail Craw. Vary the colors to make the jig more visible in low light or dirty water, or match colors of the jig skirt to make a more subtle looking lure for clear water, pressured, or spooky fish.

As a rule the lighter weight the jig and the larger the trailer, the slower the fall—and vice versa, a heavy jig and small trailer produces a faster descent to the bottom.

Color Choices—Matching the seasonal or local color of the crawfish is my plan. Blacks, browns, subtle shades like pumpkin, and an accent color like orange, red, or chartreuse makes for good contrast and additional visibility. Can't miss colors—black/blue, brown/orange and pumpkin/pepper—are good for most water colors and conditions. Contrasting colors of trailers adds visual attracting qualities.

Again in the Strike King Rage Tail line #50 Okeechobee craw, #229 Roadkill, and #38 Black neon are effective crawfish imitating trailers. Texas rigged flipping tubes work in the same colors and under similar conditions.

On The Line—For years I used monofilament. When big bass broke me off, I just moved up to heavier mono. With the quality of lines, you have three viable options. I dislike fluorocarbon because of the lack of reliable known strength. A heavy action rod adds to the hook-setting ability of a reel spooled with monofilament. My recommendation would be minimally 20-pound test mono, and ram up to 30 around heavy cover. Check your line often for abrasions and nicks. Retie as often as needed.

Most of my jig and worm rods are spooled with braided line.

Jig Tips: Turn the Beginner into a Bragger

Braid ranging from 15 to 30 pound test is best. Because fishing *feel baits* are my technique of choice, I use the best rods I can find. My jigging rods range from heavy action to medium heavy and are 7 foot to 7 ½ foot long. I choose rods designed and constructed to my specific needs, taking into account my height, the weight of lures I plan to throw, and the line type and size I intend to try. I use Lew's baitcasting reels because of the power and control I can exercise over the fish. The majority of the time the reel is a 6.3:1 gear retrieve ratio on all my jig and worm outfits.

Occasionally I will opt for open faced spinning combos for finesse jigging. Jigs in the ¼ ounce range with a smaller soft plastic craw trailer are the norm. The rod is a 6 ½ foot model, the reel is spooled with braided line and a fluorocarbon leader for sensitivity, no stretch, and minimal visibility for the bass.

Jig Targets—Shoreline cover, aquatic weeds beds, creek channels, boat docks, and submerged wood all deserve some jig time. Seek out shallow water and heavy cover—3–5 five feet of depth is ideal from spring throughout fall. Keep constant contact with the bait, and be prepared for strikes ranging from subtle and the line just swimming off to a sharp, rod-rattling thump. Meet each with a quick snapping over the shoulder hook set.

If the jig rod isn't in my hand, it's not far away. My records show most of the bass over five pounds (and a half dozen over ten pound mark) came on jigs and soft plastics. You don't have to abandon your other baits, but as soon as you make a big bass do the jig, you'll be hooked!

Guide Tip: If the jig skirt is falling apart rather than tie on a new jig just change the skirt. The addition of the perfect skirt from Strike King adds bulk to the bait and creates a larger profile and a slower drop keeping the bait in the strike zone longer. This saves time and requires no retie of the knot too.

11

Simply Smallmouth

Built for speed, equipped with a natural camouflage pattern, thriving in lakes, stream, and rivers all across North America—ladies and gentlemen I give you the smallmouth bass. Loved by many devoted anglers and cursed by those who struggle to consistently find and fool them, the *brown bass* has a dedicated following of fishermen. The biggest problem for most is looking for smallmouth and using largemouth logic. While there are some similarities, they are very different creatures.

One item of intersection of the two species that is most notable—what they eat on the regular. A steady diet of shad and crawfish is normal for largemouth and its cousin the smallmouth. Even though they are not equipped with the cavernous mouth of their bigger rival, the brown bass will still seek big meals. Surprisingly all but two states in the continental United States boast of smallmouth bass inhabiting their waters (Florida and Louisiana do not). Many states have been successfully stocked, but typically the smallies don't do well in warm water. Another fact about the smallmouth bass is that they a good barometer of water quality. They thrive in clean, cold water environments.

A five-pound smallmouth is regarded by most as a true trophy, viewed much like a largemouth bass exceeding the magic ten-pound mark. One of the oldest existing freshwater records remains the giant smallmouth—an 11 lb. 15 oz. monster caught by David

Hayes came from Dale Hollow Reservoir on the Kentucky/Tennessee border on July 9, 1955, trolling a pearl-colored Bomber bait. As a side note, the three largest smallmouth bass ever weighed and certified all came from Dale Hollow Lake.

A recently conducted social media poll quizzing anglers from all over about what their favorite smallmouth baits were showed these results—most often mentioned were baits that imitated natural smallmouth forage in the form of minnows, crawfish, and hellgrammites. The specific results were 31% preferred soft plastics, actual live bait itself was selected by 25%, jigs an equal amount, with 12% using crawfish colored crankbaits, and 6% were slinging spinnerbaits.

A crossover characteristic from the largemouth is the variety of artificial lures a smallmouth will readily strike. Everything from the *vanilla* example of simplicity, the curlytail grub fished on a leadhead is extremely effective, to jigs, soft plastics, spinnerbaits, and crankbaits which all deserve a place in your tackle box when chasing the original *frequent flyer*. For incomparable visual fun toss 'em a topwater. Dog walking baits, cup-faced poppers, minnow imitators, and buzzbaits will draw hits that rival the surface strike of any fish for pure old plain excitement.

My own experience includes drifting big creek minnows, throwing spinnerbaits, catching them on jigs, cranking lures, and simple soft plastic rigs of every description. For live bait enthusiasts a freshly caught hellgrammite or a lively creek minnow on a circle hook is hard for these fish to resist.

Personal destination adventures for me include tiny Tennessee streams, larger rivers, highland impoundments, and the wilderness area of Canada known as the Quetico, aka the Boundary Waters on the United States side. In clear water once they've locked onto your lure, they appear to be bronze bullets as they zoom toward their prey. The strike, the screaming drag, and the fight likely punctuated by several surface clearing jumps is almost always epic.

In the search for the highly regarded brown bass, moving

waters can be a challenge. The most important aspect of finding smallmouth is understanding that they relate to deep water like a largemouth relates to objects. Deep being relative, in a stream setting deep might be five feet in a lake it could be 25 feet. A great starting point in waters in motion—creeks, streams and rivers of all sizes—is to look for riffles and rocks. Just downstream from the objects redirecting the flow, smallmouth are notorious for resting and lying in wait for the free food that is caught in the current.

Try casting above the current break and work the bait across the calmer waters. The rocks, ranging in size from gravel to boulders are hiding spots and habitat for crawfish, a favorite forage of every type of bass including the smallies. In lakes it's likely, depending on the season plus weather and water conditions, that these feisty fish will be located on ledges, points, creek channels, and steep banks to name a few potential hot spots.

As is the case with any gamefish, while oxygen is a necessity, if you find the food, the fish won't be far away. The bronze bass can be pursued with equal effectiveness in a high-powered bass boat or a kayak. Spinning rods, burly baitcasting equipment, or even fly rods are all part of the equation—just another reason this fish is such a popular target. I once asked good friend, Bill Dance, if he could only fish for one species what would it be. With no hesitation his one word reply was, "Smallmouth."

Good enough for me!

Sample smallmouth fishing, but be warned—it's likely to create that love/hate relationship!

12

Beyond Bass

While bass fishing dominates the world of anglers, there are enthusiast for many other species. People want to read about bass, see bass focused TV shows, hear about bass fishing at outdoor shows, and fish bass tournaments. There are so many other types of fish to chase maybe it's time we give the bass a break.

Overheard over and over, "Whatever is biting is my favorite for that day." I must admit I love the challenge, the hit, and fight of the bass, especially the trophy-size fish, although there are times and past trips that make me want to focus on other fish. Oh sure, there are places, boats, and baits dedicated to bass, but many more stories to unfold, and let's face it—there are time when the largemouth have *lockjaw*. Sometimes just a trip to a creek, pond, or small lake with the emphasis on what I call *junk* fishing—just catching anything willing to bite—is fun. Any rod works—a cane pole, push button spin casting, spinning or light baitcasting outfits can all be used. No pressure, just playtime.

Since I first started fishing one of my favorite techniques was to rig with a simple #8 light wire hook, a couple of tiny pinch-on split-shot weights, and a float. Baiting with a small section of freshly dug nightcrawlers and a random cast to a likely looking spot—now wait and watch. Soon the float starts a dimple-dimple-dance and disappears, and you set the hook. Generally a bluegill, sometimes a bass, or an unintended target like a little bullhead catfish would emerge. Bait up again and repeat and many times this scene is repeated dozens of times. When the action slows, a simple move to another area or start casting an artificial lure with the same fish in mind will usually produce.

A few rod and reel rigs are a plus. For beginners the push button reels and a five-foot rod are easily mastered and allow for the independence of casting and catching. Open face spinning combinations are also ideal for this style of fishing. There is still a place for the old fashioned cane pole and a pendulum cast. There might be some need to help unhook the catch, but in many cases the angler can take care of every aspect of this kind of fishing.

When you are looking for bluegills, you can use some of the same logic that you apply for bass. Aquatic weeds, submerged wood, gravel, rocks, boat docks, and they also relate to bottom contours like their larger cousins. Live bait in the form of worms, crickets, minnows, and meal worms all will lure bluegill to your line. Artificial lures look like bass baits only downsized. In-line spinners, small crankbaits, tiny tubes, and even flies delicately presented on a fly fishing equipment.

The ever popular, widely distributed crappie is of primary interest to lots of fishermen. They dismiss the idea of searching for bass. Crappie, because they school up, can be caught in great numbers once they're found. Therein lies the problem, finding them. Crappies love wood. Submerged trees, stake beds, and thick weed beds and bottom contours will hold white, black, and blacknose crappie in the same places. Crappie are fish that can be patterned. Water depth, temperature, and types of cover can all be replicated to catch these high desirable fish. Trolling in the dead of summer, vertical presentations in tree tops with long rods, live bait being tight lined or fished under a float, casting small tubes or curly tail grubs, all will at times, produce. The 0095 Monteleone silver tube manufactured by Midsouth tackle has been a huge crappie catching success. Contact them and don't be surprised when you catch everything that swims on this unique color.

Catfishermen are a different group. They are dedicated to certain types of odd-ball baits, fishing techniques, places, times of day, and even the boat they fish from. Catfish are found everywhere, and there are literally hundreds of species all over the world. From a country creek to the Great Lakes, catfish are swimming everywhere. In the spring they will aggressively hit baits cast for bass. Crankbaits, spinners, jigs, and more will be engulfed by catfish when they are spawning. Traditionally most folks just cast something that stinks. The short list of what has been suggested to me includes commercial baits, hot dogs, chicken livers, bubble gum, a gob of nightcrawlers, catalpa worms, and homemade concoctions with secret ingredients all have their own fans. Stouter tackle for fish that can top the hundred pound mark is a serious consideration. Strong line anywhere from 20-pound to 80-pound test lines, a good knot—I trust the Palomar knot, this is a great application for the circle hooks where once the fish swims off with the bait you merely start to reel and the hook slides securely into the side of the fishes mouth. If you are in a *big* cat spot use larger, stronger hooks.

There are others who specialize in stripers, walleye, white bass, red-eye, trout, musky, and just about anything that swims the underwater world. Each angler has a reason, whether it's an early childhood memory, a huge local population, or just whatever is biting. I'm not giving up bass fishing or selling all my bass tackle. I'll probably still talk, write, and film a lot of bass stuff, but I do truly enjoy catching fish—all kinds of fish. Whatever is willing to bite, healthy in population and size makes for a good target. So join me, grab a friend or family member, a couple of fishing poles, go dig or catch some bait, and let's go beyond the bass.

13

Why You Don't Catch Good Fish on Bad Casts

Let's be honest, while sitting or standing and fishing in our boats we've all made casts which we wish no one would witness. Awkward attempts that land in the trees, way short of the target, loud splashes, and more are what we mean. There is a reason why you seldom catch good fish on bad casts. Spooky fish, clear water, places that receive heavy pressure, shallow water patterns, and use of heavier lures, all require the need to be accurate and quiet in your presentations. Admittedly there are occasions when regardless of what you do the fish are all over the bait. Those days are few and far between. You don't have to be a world champion caster or the regions accu-caster, but let's try to keep it in the same zip code. Just a few casting tips.

1. Start with the same amount of line out each time. Reeling the line up to the rod tip or having a foot of line out before the cast makes it tough to be accurate. Generally a small amount—two or three inches of any type of line—is best for accuracy. If you are trying to launch a crankbait 200 feet, a little additional line may help load the rod tip to lengthen the cast. As a side benefit reeling any lure all the way back and slamming it into your top rod guide damages it and eventually it breaks.
2. Spooky fish are a bit more of a challenge. Clear, shallow water with no wind to ripple the surface makes it tough

Why You Don't Catch Good Fish on Bad Casts

to fool fish. Try making longer casts with lighter weight lures and a low trajectory cast which should create less of a splash upon entry. Camouflage or smaller diameter line is also a plus under these circumstances. This might be a spot for a side arm cast or even an underhand pitching motion.

3. When you are casting to a specific structure, for example a submerged tree, try to cast past the target in an effort to not make an *in your face* presentation to the fish. It's also advisable to have the sun in your face as to not cast a shadow on the fish you are trying to catch. With eyesight of most gamefish being good and allowing for nearly 270 degrees (almost a full circle view), casting past the targeted holding area doesn't give your fish as much time to study the bait. It has to react based off a quick look.

4. A key to being consistently on target is using the same casting mechanics each time. For me that is using rods that are close to the same length and action, and more importantly using lures that are very close in weight as to develop a feel for the presentation of each bait regardless of type. My preferred weight is ⅜ ounce for jigs, Texas rig slip sinkers, spinnerbaits, and more. That similar hand feel goes a long way when you are fish for extended periods of time and want to drop that lure in a tight spot.

5. As a rule shorter rods allow for more accuracy, longer rods help get more distance—somewhere in between is best but that depends on the each angler. Use rods that fit you physically. A five-foot rod for someone six and a half feet tall or a seven and a half foot rod for someone just over five feet tall makes casting a bit more of challenge. Let the equipment do the work and have rods that fit you and your fishing style.

6. Learn to use every style of reel. For open face spinning you control the line feed by pressuring the line using your pointer finger while the line rests on the extended digit. As the line exits the spool, and you visually recognize the flight

of the lure you can allow it to travel freely by doing nothing or cut it short by applying pressure to the line. Baitcasting can be tougher to master, but with practice you can become a pinpoint caster. Learn similarly to the spinning *feathering* technique to allow the line to control the distance of the cast, and use that *educated* thumb to adjust. Remember, in baitcasting the rod and the tip give the bait direction; your thumb gives it distance. You can become more accurate by using the side of your thumb resting gently on the spool instead of your entire thumb in controlling the cast. It's (the side of your thumb) less surface area makes for a more sensitive casts and lighter landings.

7. There is a gigantic advantage to learning the pitching technique. Many times incorrectly referred to as *flipping*, pitch is the use of an underhand pendulum motion used to send the lure out inches above and actually skimming just above the surface thereby making a much less intrusive, no splash, subtle entrance to the water. I pitch almost every artificial lure with the exception of crankbaits and certainly all single hook baits. If you want more distance on your pitch casts, merely lift the rod higher and faster. Pitching, in my opinion is for presentations of 50 feet or less. It is well worth the time and effort to learn this casting technique. Flipping is an up-close presentation generally in heavy cover (wood, weeds) or around boat docks. If you're right handed a length of line is looped in your left hand, and with a forward swing of the rod, a bait is dropped into the cover while the line is released. As the lure descends often it never makes it to the bottom. If it does come to rest begin a slow, up and down jigging motion and hang on.

8. Stand up and fight! I'm much more accurate when standing, and it is my belief that you can generate better hook set when standing. I choose boats that make this easier and safer for me. I have good balance, and with the exception

of a canoe, in Jon boats, bass-type boats, or even kayaks I stand. Regardless of the boat I'm in, I have a life jacket on all year long, in any type of water.

Guide Tip: A big bass from public waters more than likely has been caught or at least hooked several times before. Bass, like other species, can become conditioned to the sights and sounds that artificial baits send out. Tilt the odds in your favor by honing your casting skills. Making a good cast positions you to be more likely to catch a good fish.

14

Love at First Bite

Artificial lures, I have them all, I throw them all, and I catch fish on all of 'em. My tackleboxes are filled with spinnerbaits, crankbaits, topwaters, *and* jigs. Under the right conditions you can almost close your eyes and tie anyone of them on and catch bass. You know, water temperature 65-70 degrees, slightly stained, a gentle breeze creates a ripple on the surface, full moon, and bass are hitting everything in sight. Whoa, just a minute, that doesn't happen very often, but it does occur.

When conditions are less than ideal, essentially opposite of what was previously stated, extreme water temperatures, windy or dead calm, clear, muddy, or any other number of variables can all make for a tough bite. Options, smaller lures, slower retrieves, live bait all can be the answer. I have put all those adjustments into practice, and each at the correct time produces. With all those lure choices, decisions can be difficult.

Early in my fishing life I sought and found something, anything that worked and beat the water to death with it. As memory serves it was a small minnow plug, silver black back and cast out on a 5 ½ foot light open faced spinning rod. Cast it out, twitch back, catch fish, and repeat. The TV guys were tossing these plastic worms and showing stringers of huge bass. Hmmm. Enter the new rod described by the old timers as a "pool cue" because of its thick base and very little give. They further explained when the fish hits the "rubber" worm you "cross their eyes" with the "pool cue." All very descriptive. Rod change, bigger reel, still a spincaster, and heavier line and I started casting the bogus baits like the big guys. While working, and believe me it was work, a six inch Mister Twister Texas rigged centipede (purple with a fire tail) the line swam off to my left, and moments later I sunk my thumb in the jaw of a four pound bass. Yippee.

Time to do a Jig
In their infancy, jigs were popular in certain regions. At that time (the early 80s) most were made of bear hair, fox or rabbit fur, or some other wild creature's hair, and they were generally tipped with a piece of pork that came from a jar filled with a salt brine. Described simply as an eel or a frog and available in a couple of colors, these combination seemed to work pretty well.

I was relegated to a lot of night fishing because society demanded I have a real job and *after hours* fishing had a certain appeal anyway. There was no competition for fishing spots and ample doses of solitude on cooler summer nights. I began to fish points, ledges, and secondary structures. Previous luck by beating the bank made me like most other fishermen—I'd go to my security blanket, shorelines and shallow water. The deep water experiment was uncomfortable. In karate we say, "When you're uncomfortable, you're learning."

Points produced fish after fish, and I learned by fishing in the dark to depend on my sense of feel. New jigs appeared with bunches of rubber legs. Bigger baits can be made to look even bigger by adding a larger soft plastic trailing bait attached.

I've always enjoyed fall and October/November. It was dusk on a November night while jigging a drop-off when a strong tug followed by a swimming motion resulted in a furious fight. A six pound eleven ounce bass weighed on grocery scales was the result of dedication to learning the jig. I've never looked back.

My constant companion, at latest two rods dedicated jigs and not far behind, a rod set up to Texas rig soft plastics. My preferred method for fishing and most productive way to fool *big* bass.

1. Size Matters—Visual appeal is huge. A bulky bait when searching for trophy size bass is a plus. A little trick I use is to take a Strike King Perfect skirt viewed as being a spinnerbait replacement skirt and using it on a jig. Add a full size Rage Tail Craw as your trailer, and you've supersized the bass version of a happy meal. Pull up to the next window please!
2. Color Choices—In keeping with the franchise food theme, I view colors of all baits just like going to a chicken restaurant. "Do you want light or dark?" We, I believe, are drawn to colors only because we catch fish on them. We develop confidence, thus we tie that color on consistently. So what color works best? The one we throw all the time. Matching natural crawfish patterns is highly desirable. In clear water colors matter a bit more.
3. Weighing In—Lure weight facilitates casting, fall, and feel. Accurate casting is important from the standpoint that the strike zone of a bass is greatly exaggerated and at times shrinks. Cold weather, muddy water, falling water, extreme heat are a few examples. A lighter lure falls at a slower pace; add a bulky trailer and the descent is even slower. Keeping contact with any bait is important but even more so with jigs. Sensing the hit comes from the feel transmitted through the line and rod, difficult bordering on impossible, certainly hard to accomplish on slack line. Start with a ⅜ ounce model and adjust up or down as dictated by successful fishing activity.
4. Right Rod—Having the correct rod is essential. The length dictates casting distance, makes for a better hook set, and ultimately playing the fish. The rod should match you. For me being five foot and ten inches tall, I go for a seven foot rod for the above stated reasons. A little shorter than that try a six and a half foot version, taller go a bit longer. I personally am a fan of a medium heavy action rod for jigs. A reel with a high speed retrieve, minimally 6:3 to 1 is a good

choice. Spool the reel with braided line 15-30 pound test and now you're ready.
5. If I had to guarantee bass catches, any time, any place, under almost any conditions I would suggest tying on a jig and keeping it wet.

15

The Bountiful Bluegill

Found almost everywhere in huge numbers, bluegill, bream, warmouth, pumpkinseeds, and other sub-species swim the waters of lakes, river, ponds, creeks, and anywhere there is a foot of water and food. Feisty and always seemingly hungry, bluegills are fun, willing to bite, and a mess of 'em makes a great fish fry. Easy to find when they come in to the shoreline for spring spawn and cooler water temperatures, they will, like many species, scatter and go deep. Deep is a relative term—in a creek that might be four feet, in a farm pond, six feet or more, and in lakes we've caught them in 30 feet of water. Not just n*ursery* fish but *big* bluegills up to 12 inches!

There is just about as many ways to catch them as there are to find them. As anglers we can test skinny waters, small lakes, farm ponds, and larger impoundments. If you do happen to be bank bound, don't dismay. You can find them all over. As with bass, they don't all do the same thing at the same time. While filming a segment for *Wild Side TV*, I caught several bluegills on a bass size crankbait, the #504 Strike King model in a color known as "bad to the bone." These feisty fish will hit a number of upsized bass-type baits. When you're fishing a soft plastic bait for bass and you get a "machinegun hit, *rat-a-tat-tat*, it's almost always an aggressive bluegill bite.

Another appeal to catching bluegill and other panfish is the size of your tackle box. A tiny box with a dozen compartments is ample space for all you need to catch them on a regular basis. Stock the box with small plastic tubes, curly tail grubs, small spinners, mini-crankbaits and other undersized offerings, in-line spinners, and small surface lures all should be in the tiny trays of your tackle box. And if that's not enough you can catch a stringer full on almost any live bait. Crickets, live worms, and tiny minnows will catch their share and can be collected on the shoreline or by seining in the shallows of your favorite creek.

A small float—I use natural cork—about 6-8 inches up the line, a small pinch-on split shot four inches further down, and a small light wire hook, a #8 or #10 is a solid choice. Drift fishing is highly effective and casting near cover in the form of aquatic weeds and wood also yields fish. Creek channels and underwater contours hold large schools of bluegill in the weather extremes. Ultra-light spinning rods, spincaster combinations, and the fly rod are all likely choices for bluegill and others. A few sponge spiders (white and green), subsurface streamers that imitate minnows, and tiny poppers all deserve a shot. Kids all the way to seasoned anglers, we all enjoy the tug of these mighty mites! Plan a trip or just pack an extra rod for the bountiful bluegills.

16

Bass Techniques That Really Work

Initially when you start to fish you are limited to either what you are being taught or what you might already know. With time comes the TV, magazine, or seminar presentation that educates you to something new or minimally new to you. Whether you specifically plan to try something new or are frustrated and resort to a different twist out of frustration, there are adjustments necessary to make bass bite. The best anglers make adjustments. New bait, techniques, or rigs are not easily accepted by traditional fishermen. "This has worked for years, there's no need to change now," is the mind set. Technology and fishing pressure go hand in hand with developing new ways to catch bass. Here are a few examples of fun and effective ways to catch fish when more conventional techniques fail.

Flippin'
- Flippin'—often confused with pitching—is the up close and personal presentation to bass in and around cover. The cover could be above the surface and or submerged wood, weed beds, boat docks, irregular bank features, or more. Quiet approach is vital to the success of this technique. Try to drift into the spot with the wind or minimally use the trolling motor as slow as possible to keep from alerting bass to your presence. This technique utilizes a pendulum motion to place a bait gently into a short strike zone. While normally viewed

as using a jig, soft plastics of many kinds and other lures (I've used spinnerbaits) can be flipped. A stout rod, at least medium/heavy if not heavy actions are best to winch fish away from their hideout. This generally also requires baitcasting reels spooled with 16 to 50 pound test line depending on the type of cover you are fishing.
- Why flip? Fish during sharp cold fronts, hot water, bright skies, and heavy fishing pressure will retreat to tight quarters. Conventional casting makes it hard to reach them, plus their strike zone decreases in extreme weather or confined surroundings.
- Why does it work? You can make repeated casts to a fish that is known to be an opportunistic feeder. Essentially you put something in front of them and make it look like something to eat, that's exactly what they will do. They also feel safe in heavy cover and in some cases migrate to the ambush mode if they are resident fish for that area.

Drop Shot
- Credited to west coast anglers, drop shot fishing looks much like an altered Kentucky Lake crappie rig to me. Not a method that is desirable for fishing dense cover, it doesn't evoke a big bass feel from anglers either. Situational at best, it can help find fish and also puts fish in the livewell for competition anglers in difficult weather and water conditions. This approach uses open faced spinning gear, generally a six or six and a half foot rod and light weight line, six to ten pound test. Many fishermen opt for fluorocarbon line for its invisible nature and low stretch. Rigged normally with a bell-shaped sinker at the bottom a small drop shot hook tied with the point facing upward and a swivel to eliminate line twist, this set-up keeps a finesse worm—my personal choice is the Strike King #46 green pumpkin 5 inch version—or grub in the strike zone for fish suspended just off

the bottom. Cast it out and do a slow drag back. The bite is a *tick* and slight but steady pull on the line.
- Why drop shot? In cold, clear water fish spook easily. Something less obtrusive doesn't send them scurrying for open water. The appearance of the bait which is stationary, looks very, very alive. It jumps and moves around the line. It also allows the fish to swim up to it, inspect it, and then decide whether to bite which they often feel compelled to do. Great way to find fish.
- Why does it work? Lure-shy fish can be caught on smaller baits and slower retrieves. This rig allows for and actually excels at both qualifications. Schooling bass are not scared off by the noise or large movement characteristic in other lures. It has a realistic live bait look.

Carolina Rig
- Simple, easy to learn, and effective defines the Carolina rig. Again not a technique that shines in water heavily laden with many underwater obstructions. A weight, normally a slip sinker or barrel sinker of ½ ounce or larger, is tied above a swivel with a bead sometimes separating the two, the hook is a 3/0 to 5/0 depending on the soft plastic bait used. The plastic is rigged Texas style with the hook buried in the bait to aid in keeping it snagless. Long rods, seven foot or more for launching the rig and heavy line, 16 to 30 pound test are the rule for the Carolina rig fans. Cast it out and use the reel to retrieve the bait at a steady pace, the strike is just a dull pull. An animated side sweep of the rod is needed to move the line, weight, and fish, and sink the hook into the bass' mouth.
- Why Carolina Rig? Lure-shy bass seems to still be drawn to this technique. For those who do not like *crank* deep, this is a great alternative. Bass on points, ledges, and in open water zero in on this presentation.

- Why does it work? Bass are susceptible to the subtle look of Carolina rig baits. It is also versatile in what can be fished. Lizards are popular, but French fry type plastics, tubes, craws, and soft jerk baits all work. Bass that have moved off shore will readily approach and engulf lures retrieved in this style.

Fish in conventional ways and always make sure the way you fish is fun for you. When fishing is slow or you feel the need to experiment, try one of these or another method. You might surprise yourself and add a technique to your mental tackle box that helps you at the weigh in or just gives you the satisfaction of doing something different.

17

Big Bass Secrets

For any angler that targets bass, very little evokes a higher adrenaline rush than the sight of a trophy bass at the end of their line. It's been said that, "10% of the fishermen catch 90% of the bass." While most folks just want to catch a limit or finish well in tournaments, there is a small legion of folks dedicated to fooling the superior of the species—trophy bass. While each angler has a certain system, many factors and facets of their approach intersect. The equipment, tactics, and search for bragging size bass amounts to the collective details that make catching monster bass predictable and apply almost anywhere they swim. Use your mental highlighter to follow the system that has produced several seasons of posing with bass that will make you the envy of all. Consider these suggestions, this collection of information and strategies, apply them in the hope that the next cast will, for you, fool that bass of a lifetime. And remember: the hard part is finding fish; it's easy to catch them.

Know the fish
Regardless of the quarry, for any type of trophy hunter, it is critical to position yourself for success by knowing as much about your intended target as possible. Open your mind, don't be distracted by *dock talk* or many of the theories presented in all forms of media. A combination of experience, the willingness to experiment, and common sense is a great start to developing your own system to

find and fool bigger bass. A quick look at the major species of bass—largemouth, smallmouth and Spotted (Kentucky) bass—clues you into the predatory nature of bass. A natural camouflage coloration specific to each helps them blend in when necessary—they are clearly ambush predators and eating machines. Bass are able to track down their food sources with underwater burst of speed up to 15 miles per hour, equipped with a massive mouth that makes them capable of swallowing anything that they find in their world, and highly developed senses that assist in feeding and surviving the underwater world they inhabit. An in-depth look also show rows of gripping, gristle like teeth and gill rakers that help bass retain their catch. They will follow bait fish, strike from behind, and instinctively turn the forage as to not become choked by the shad, bluegill, crappie or other gamefish that will flare their dorsal fin and consequently get lodged in the throat of the bass and thereby dooming it.

Take Their Temperature

Water temperature, generally communicated as surface temperature, will dictate predictable location and other lifestyle events of bass. Species specific ranges exist for each bass type. For example the spawning mode is determined by a few degrees for each type, smallmouths go first at the high 50 degree mark into the low 60s. Next is the spotted bass, when the water reaches around 60 degrees, and then the most widely distributed largemouth bass at the mid-60s. Similarly the amount of active feeding is stair-stepped at different temperatures.

An ideal scenario is water temperature of 70-80 degrees Fahrenheit. This temperature creates a direct correlation to the digestive rate of bass. Feeding frequency and metabolic rate are dramatically impacted by the ability of fish to find, eat, and completely digest any of their food sources.

A five pound bass, in 78 degree water can digest a five-inch shad in about six hours. The same bass and same size shad in 40 degree water takes five days to completely digest. The obvious conclusion is that bass should be easier to catch when they have to feed more often.

Bass, as all wild creatures, are slaves to their stomachs.

Making Sense of Senses

The eyes have it! Bass feed almost completely by sight. With eyes set at the side of their heads and field of vision at around 270 degrees, bass see extremely well. The eyes of all bass are great at discriminating color because of a multitude of rods and cones similar to, but more developed than, most other creatures including humans.

Keep in mind a fish closely visually scrutinizes something prior to deciding to *hit*. The sense of hearing is well developed in bass. Although many manufacturers and anglers choose lures heavily loaded with noise making devices, sound can have a negative influence on bass. Water is a great conductor of sound. Sound travels through water five times faster than through air. Spooky fish and older bass can be conditioned to retreat from certain sounds.

Another myth is that bass are highly intelligent. They have a brain about half the size of a hazelnut—tiny. Fish don't learn in the true sense of the word—they become conditioned.

A popular marketing tactic is to tout the appeal of scent in bass lures. Unfortunately bass have limited olfactory senses. Later in life, at five to eight years, a bass' the sense of smell does slightly increase, but not to the point that bass find their food using smell as a major factor. And the application of common sense quickly dispels the myth that bass hit a bait because of how it tastes, although they may in fact hold on longer because of taste, especially salt impregnated baits. *Blood has salt in it,* so it is not a foreign taste to bass.

Logically bass hit something because of how it looks (remember feeds by sight) and how it moves. Reality check: think about it, when it tastes something it already has the object in its mouth! Set the hook!

Lesson one, now you know what makes the bass tick, and the lifestyle of America's favorite gamefish.

Let's take a closer look at rods, reels, line and lures to help you fool that trophy fish.

Hot Rods

I was once asked how many fishing rods I owned. My tentative reply was, "over one hundred." I proceeded to defend a certain amount for different size and weight lures and for specific techniques. Having an extreme number of rods is not necessary for any angler—having the correct length and action is vital. If your target is a trophy bass, a five foot ultra-light rod should not be in your boat.

When choosing a fishing rod consider what I preached for years as the four functions of the fishing rod.

- First you should be able to cast reasonably accurately—come on, let's at least keep it in the correct zip code.
- Second, you should be able to feel everything that's happening at the end of your line.
- Next the rod should effectively help you set the hook.
- Finally the rod is critical to you playing/landing your catch.

Length, action, material, number of rod guides, handle material, and more all make for a sensitive, accurate, and strong *pole*. When deciding on the length, think about the areas you fish. Is there vast amounts of open water, heavy cover, do you stand and cast, how about setting the hook? The rod length affects each of these factors. In big waters or the ocean, a two handed cast is facilitated by a longer handle and rod. Long casts and stronger hook set and even playing the biggest bass is easier when there is additional length. The extra inches load and launch the lures, the longer rod *picks up line* faster for hook setting chores, and the fish works harder against the rod that bends toward the fish and recovers when the pressure is decreased.

Take a Q-tip and run it inside the rod guides—any cracks or rough spots are revealed by the presence of cotton strands. Repair or replace the guide before it costs you a monster bass. One other little trick when battling big, strong bass is to keep the rod tip and line down in the water. Now the bass is working against water pressure instead of air.

Keeping it Reel

Spinning or baitcasting? I prefer the power of baitcasting but when the wind howls or lighter lures are called for, open faced spinning gets the nod. In choosing a baitcaster, for comfort of all day angling, a low profile reel is best. A moderate retrieve ratio is best for all around casting and reeling in your bait and bass. 6:0:1 is a logical choice for all around bass activity. To slow down for crankbaiting a 5:3:1 retrieve ratio is good, and for burning lipless crankbaits or topwater buzzbaits 7:0:1 works well. Most of my reels are from the Lew's line—they are dependable, well built, and last a long time.

Consider weight of the reel—frequently a mere seven or eight ounce—and line capacity, 120 yards of 12-pound test is common. The drags in my opinion are superior on baitcasters. Spinning has it place, but for most big bass techniques, baitcasters are highly desirable.

A small amount of maintenance goes along way on reels. Some spray lubricant on all external moving parts and a Q-tip to apply in tight places keeps them operational. Become acquainted with the adjustment settings, any knobs in the sides of the reel for changing the spool tension, make small adjustments. When the thumb bar on a baitcaster is depressed your bait should drop slowly. The best insurance against the feared backlash is an educated thumb. Keep a small amount of thumb pressure on the pool at all times. Simply stated, a backlash occurs when the spool is turning faster than the bait is traveling outward. When instructing someone on the mechanics of baitcasting, I suggest that they keep as much pressure on the spool as they would a rotten egg.

Low Down on Lines

For most bass bait applications monofilament is the best all-around line. Rods in the past have been designed for mono. Monofilament has a high degree of stretch and aggravating coiling memory but also has great knot strength, often measured at up to 95% when the knot is tied correctly. The stretch makes hook setting more difficult and is the reason this line is less sensitive. For fans of low visibility and sensitivity, fluorocarbon is popular. Many anglers use fluorocarbon for leader because it's low stretch, sensitive, and virtually invisible. Because it is heavier and actually sinks it's not a good choice for topwater applications.

For the ultimate in strength and sensitivity, braided lines are used by serious bass anglers. For zero stretch and extreme sensitivity, braid is the logical choice. For those who prefer fishing the category of bass baits we refer to as *feel* baits braid is the ticket. Jigs, worms, and all soft plastic lures are ideal when coupled with a reel spooled with braided lines. The downside—braid line knots can slip easily because of the wax like coating used in the manufacture of these lines. To counter this I tie double knots. I opt for a Palomar backed up with an improved clinch knot snugged up behind the first knot. Problem solved.

The Lure of Lures

Entire books have been written on bass fishing lures—more detail on lures later. To fully understand why bass hit artificial baits it's important to present the premise for fooling bass of any size into striking pieces of metal, chunks of soft plastic, plugs of wood, and other materials. Fire up the mental highlighter.

All lures have two categories—sensory attracting and bite triggering qualities.

Sensory attracting qualities catch the attention of the fish, are larger sizes, brighter colors, possess noise-making capabilities, and have a mechanical swimming movement. A lipless, chartreuse, rattling one-ounce crankbait is a perfect sample of a bait full of sensory attracting qualities.

Bite triggering qualities are these—easily swallowed shapes, neutral colors, and natural swimming motions, maybe a seven-inch, green pumpkin plastic worm. These characteristics induce the bass to actually bite. Bass, being an inquisitive species, will look and even follow objects out of sheer curiosity. To seal the deal, baits heavily loaded with bite triggering qualities are the ticket to a trophy fish. This is the most vital consideration when buying or tying on bass baits.

Color choices can be overwhelming. Consider the crankbaits. It's easy to get caught up in having a hundred fish catching colors as touted in catalogs and infomercial videos. The best three colors match the weather and water conditions. The formula is simple. Clear water, light or no breeze, and bright skies—white, or lighter shades such as shad colors. With slightly stained water, some wind and cloudy sky, a crawfish pattern is ideal. For muddy water, windy weather and dark skies, firetiger is perfect.

Trophy Tip: When bass are hitting the "search" baits like spinnerbaits or crankbaits and stop hitting one of them, switch to the other bait that matches in size. The crankbait should be the same size as the blade on the spinner or vice versa, you have the size figured out now just change the look.

Finding Big Bass

After years of chasing bass I said, "Little fish are liars, big fish hold the secrets." Of primary concern is, does the body of water you fish have big bass? Word of mouth, pictures, and a history of producing trophy-size bass are all good indicators. Prior to the development of electronics, dedicated bass fishermen learned to *read* their waters by studying the shoreline and mostly common sense applications. The sun rises in the east and sets in the west; this makes the northwest side of your fishing hole get the longest exposure to the sun and makes it a few degrees warmer—a huge advantage in the late winter and early spring. The goal is to find fish quickly and efficiently and replicate results.

Eventually technology yielded tools for the ardent anglers anxious to apply new-fangled *sonar* devices to help determine the bottom contours, depth, and even little hump-like figures indicating fish. With the advent of crystal clear images and marking waypoints with GPS, fishermen can easily navigate to within mere feet of spots that have previously produced fish. Hopefully when choosing and using your electronics, you do not fall into the trap of separating yourself from your senses.

When a body of water gets an inordinate amount of boating and fishing pressure, the bass adjust by moving to the next offshore cover, finding a more remote area, or even change their feeding habits and possibly go nocturnal. It is generally believed that fish in more than eight feet of water are not affected by boat traffic. In conjunction with this theory my records indicate the majority of my trophy fish catches come from the magic depth of three to eight feet.

One flaw of the trophy hunting bass anglers is to establish what I refer to as a *milk run*. They return to the same spots, on the same body of water, throw the same baits, and wonder why they never catch any large fish. What convinces folks to use this approach is the almost accidental success of catching the occasional big bass. Sorry, but this is just a lucky cast, lucky catch. It doesn't diminish the achievement, but if you want to consistently catch lunker bass, adjustments are required.

Fish location is dictated by water temperature, food sources, and what I term the four bass factors. Bass need oxygen, food, cover, and deep water close by.

Oxygen speaks for itself, if you can't breathe very little else matters. Water within flowing creeks, aquatic vegetation, moving waters, springs, areas below dams, and the windy side of the specific body of water all are highly oxygenated.

It's also likely an abundant food supply will be there for the same reason. Largemouth bass are object-oriented creatures. Smallmouth relate to deep water like a largemouth relate to objects. Don't try to force largemouth tactics on smallmouth. Largemouths are ambush and chase predators.

Cover offers the opportunity for both, concealing themselves and darting out is how they catch the majority of their meals. Target weeds and wood—both types of cover are bass magnets. Besides being cover, wood grows algae and brings baitfish in, and weeds provide oxygen so necessary to the lifestyle of the largemouth.

A big bass will eat anything that fits in its cavernous mouth and comes within range. That's how they get and stay big. Another of my frequently used quotes is, "all creatures are slaves to their stomachs."

Find the food = find the fish.

The last factor, deep water, only matters because it gives the fish the comfort of an escape route—a common trait among many other wild creatures. Secondary cover—off shore objects—has the potential to produce that one huge bass.

Mental note: find a compact area that serves all these needs, and you can drop the anchor, just start saturating the water with lures, and begin your quest for Mr. Big. These types of places will consistently produce monster bass.

Your approach in the hopes of catching a big fish cannot be stressed enough. My term for this is *ninja stealth mode*. Fitting in and becoming part of the entire scenario is critical. Look for natural signs—herons and fishing eating birds are there for a reason. Minimize noise, fish with the sun in your face as to not cast a shadow on the fish you are trying to catch, let the wind drift you into the zone, pitch cast underhanded to make the least amount of splash, and create a silent entry of the bait. Consider even dressing to match the background of the place you are fishing.

Bass relate to any kind of an edge—this is the shoreline, the bottom, the surface. Bass can push bait and school of shad to edges and gorge themselves. Think edge! Don't discount that sixth sense, intuitive feeling that you are in the right place at the right time, the great anglers have this.

Techniques For Trophy Fish

- House calls—During weather extremes bass minimize their movement, it's time to go to them.
- Best Baits—Using lures that possess random action is essential to consistently catching big bass.
- Approach—Silent, least obtrusive techniques yield benefits in chasing trophy fish. Learn the underhand pitching cast for silent entry into the water and subtle presentations.
- Follow up baits—Often a fish that misses a topwater bait is fired up, and a quick return cast with a slow falling soft plastic lure is rewarded with a fish.
- Working with Mother Nature—Use the wind, the sun, cloud cover, and anything else that offers a tip off as to location or feeding activity.
- Water/sky color is a color clue—Clear sky, no wind, clear water; throw natural or neutral colors. Partly cloudy sky, wind that ripples the water, and slight water stain; try mid-level shades like crawfish colors. Dark sky, water choppy from higher winds, and murky color; break out the brighter colors, bigger sizes, and maybe baits equipped with rattles.
- Bass-stronomy—Know and follow the moon phases. There are natural activity levels directly attributed to the major moons, new and full.
- Boat control—Position your boat to thoroughly cover any type of structure or potential holding area.
- Retrieve speed—Vary your retrieve speed to find what the fish are reacting to at that time and change periodically. Make adjustments for weather and water changes.
- Seeing red—Red is a sensory triggering color. Bass seeing red believe that something is injured and easier prey.
- What they eat—Crawfish are Red Bull for bass. For every five pounds of crawfish a bass eats, it gains a pound of weight. They eat more shad and minnows only because they're more available.

- Bait performance—The fall of a bait and the tail action depends on the weight used. A slow fall is generally best. To get the best action from curly tail baits, rig the tail opposite the direction of the hook.
- Colorized—Add red or a false eye spot (the black spot on the shad body) to baits—both add a dimension of realism.

Trophy Tip: Start by using the quietest baits that you have the most confidence in first. Then move up each time you change lures in size and sound. For example, try the plastic worm, jig, spinnerbait, crankbait, and then topwater noisemaker. If the bass are spooky you increase the odds of hooking and catching the biggest fish in the area using this trick.

Ten Tips For A Trophy Bass

After fooling hundreds of trophy-size bass all across North America, we have never gotten tired of it. Your first good size bass will change you—years later you will recall every detail. Season after season we have honed our skills at finding and fooling heavyweight bass. Last year was another banner year for big fish with more than two dozen bass in the five to eight pound range coming to our boat. Here are ten tips to help you set the hook on your own monster fish.

1. Know the fish—Study everything you can possibly learn about bass or the fish that you are targeting. Food preferences, life style elements, tolerances, and physical characteristics are all important. Bass for example can swim in bursts of up to 15 miles per hour. Many fishing techniques are crossovers for taking superior size fish, so learning about several species can produce similar results. Anticipate where they will be and why they will be there. Where they were last week, what they were doing, and what they were hitting is last week's old information. It becomes a guessing game of what bass will do next, but seasonal migration, changing

weather, and water conditions can make bass predictable to the observant angler.

2. Match your tackle—Get tackle stout enough to handle the chores of trophy bass—they will tax your equipment to the limit. Along with a good rod to set the hook and play the fish are the ability to tie a good knot and set the drag properly. Strong, fresh line and a good knot are the keys to consistent success. Longer rods give you good hook-setting capabilities and help to play fish down more effectively. You can't make many mistakes and land a big fish. Sharp hooks and the correct action rod are critical. It's not enough to just get them to bite—you want to be able to control the fish and ultimately land them.

3. Learn to master the right lures—Bass will hit a variety of baits. Equip yourself with spinnerbaits, crankbaits, jigs, and plastic worms. These categories of lures catch bass appetites anywhere, anytime. The right bait in the hands of a good angler can fool a bass. In your search for a true trophy, your best bet almost always will be a *feel* bait, a jig or soft plastic lure. These baits have a random action intentionally, or not supplied by each angler, because everyone fishes them differently. Cast, swim, twitch, drop, lift hop, twitch, twitch—it looks different to the fish. Bass and other fish can become conditioned to the external stimulus present in artificial baits and will avoid them or become *lure shy*. This is especially true of lures with mechanical action, crankbaits, spinnerbaits, and others. Sound-making capabilities can also provide a negative influence on fish.

4. Fish often—As simple as this sounds, try to get out as often as you can. Fishing under all conditions teaches you how to make adjustments and what to do to counter certain situations, and sometimes it's just as important to know what not to do. Eliminate mistakes, and try to establish patterns that make *big* bass catches repeatable. Winds, bright sun,

discolored water, cold fronts, are all formidable, but more often than not fishermen are affected more than fish by harsh, natural influences. Be aware of everything that happens on your trip, and note how fish react to various weather and water conditions.

5. Details—Sharpen hooks, change line on your reels, set your drag, experiment with new lures and techniques. While I worked to figure out every type of lure, I centered my attention on being the very best I could be at fishing specific baits that positioned me to catch big bass. Learn to use lures new to you. Try flipping and mastering the underhanded *pitch* cast. Note all the variables about area and the experience; commit them to a journal or memory or both. If you journal, note details like water temperature, wind direction, cloud cover, and presence of baitfish. Chronicle the catches specific to structure, weeds, wood, and subsurface contours and cover.

6. Find a Fishing Friend—Find a fisherman that has the same level of interest you do. As you fish with them, pick their brain—ask questions and observe everything that they do. There's a distinct advantage to having someone with you willing to fish a different bait or style. You double your chances of finding out quickly what is working.

7. Bass-strology/Moon Phases—For years we have followed the moon phases as preferred times to fish. New and full moons are critical times in nature because many hatches of food sources are coordinated with the moon phases. Also the spawning of game fish occur then, but keep in mind they don't all do the same thing at the same time. Mayflies, crawfish, minnows, and more hatch in profusion to propagate their species—the same goes for fish. If they were born in smaller, staggered numbers they would likely all be eaten eventually. My catch records show a correlation between three days before the new and full moons and catching bragging-size bass. This is born out in checks of previous

world record catches on both fresh and salt water. The two long standing black bass records are George Perry's catch of a 22 pound 4 ounce largemouth bass on June 2, 1932—it was caught right on the new moon—and David L. Hayes caught a record which I believe will never be broken, a smallmouth bass weighed 11 pounds and 15 ounces. It was caught on July 9, 1955, within a day of the full moon. Moon phases matter.

8. Key to the Catch—Study motion and movement, observe the forage and food sources of bass. A clear water creek or even a pond is a great laboratory. A great example is knowing and watching as crawfish walk forward and swim backward in short bursts. Try to closely match that with the retrieve of a jig. Minnows are in the most danger of being devoured when they exhibit the flight instinct or appear to be injured. As the angler who learns to mimic the distressed minnow, or the bait in fear and flight mode, you will hook more fish.

9. Ninja Fishing—Use everything to your advantage. Fish with the wind at your back to minimize trolling motor noise. Fish with the sun in your face to not cast a shadow on the fish you are trying to catch. Use a low profile casting motion to make the least amount of commotion with the entry of your lure. Fitting in is important. Your target is in survival mode, while you're in recreational mode. Be stealthy!

10. Manage the Resource—Release all *big* bass. Use 3% peroxide in your livewell. The chemical sign for water H_2O. Peroxide is H_2O_2. You add many parts per million of oxygen with just a few capfuls. Never touch eyes or gills of any fish you plan to release. Removal of natural slime or touching the eyes creates the possibility of a bacterial infection much like that of a human being that has been burned—death is inevitable. Delayed mortality occurs when a fish has been mishandled, the gills injured, and often when blood flows from the gill area. After quickly snapping a few pictures release your fish as quickly as possible. If you don't have the capability to

photograph your catch, it's recommended to leave them in the water and immediately unhook them for release.

Trophy fish are rare, handle them carefully and allow another angler to experience the joy of landing one by your choice to preserve the resource by returning and recycling of your catch!

18

Family Fishing

Although summer is over, fishing—especially family fishing—is a year round activity. Too often fishing trips are tournament oriented—not to say there isn't a time to compete, but it is vital to get and keep kids and families together in the outdoors.

So often in the Monteleone household the activity level ran at a feverish pace. Soccer games, church, school functions, and social calendars all ran together. But I always made time to take my kids fishing. Some trips were just one of the kids. In my brave years I would take both. A change of mindset is important to minimize conflict and maximize fun. I stress during *Take a Kid Fishing* seminars that it is critical to not turn a fun trip into a fishing contest pitting one against the other or mom or dad competing against the kids, although I would occasionally *front end* the other occupants of the boat.

Here are a few pointers on how to get your family started and keep them fishing through the years:

Tackle the Issue of Tackle

Don't start family members out with cast off junk that isn't fit for you to use any more. The same frustration we feel using substandard *stuff* translates to someone else sitting and watching while you try to fix old reels, retie bad line, or untangle a mess of lures, line, and malfunctioning equipment. This equals *zero* fun for everyone.

Buy affordable rods and reel combinations for the beginners

and infrequent fisherpersons in your life. New is neat! With the proper instruction, young or novice anglers will appreciate their new equipment and take care of the same. A sense of responsibility is a good thing to teach with rods and tackle.

Let's talk tackle. A small tackle box should be loaded with the following items: Pliers—a good set of needle nose pliers to attach lead split shot weights and unhook fish is a necessity. It also keeps someone out of your box hunting your own pliers. Small clippers for removing excess line after tying a knot is also needed. Now the fun begins as you assemble artificial baits, hooks, line, and all the things that end up rattling around in your personal collection of the tackle box.

I like single hook lures for little folks and the inexperienced angler. Single hook baits like spinners, topwater buzzers, plastic worms, and curly tail grubs will catch fish but are also less likely to get hung up, snagged, or buried in the seat of someone's pants or flesh. In the event the hook is in an unlikely place, it is easier to free one hook then two sets of trebles. Unhooking your catch, too, is made much simpler rather than the multiple hook lures. That being said, smaller crankbaits are a good addition to any tackle box—they are easy to use and catch all kinds of fish. A few carefully chosen colors will serve you well.

Soft plastic baits, crawfish imitators, minnow-like lures, and worms are good producers but do require some additional instruction and possibly a little frustration with identifying a bite and getting a good hook set. Once mastered, the soft plastics are versatile and effective. Smaller lures like ¼ ounce spinners, jigs, and undersized plugs often catch more fish, and are easier to cast and retrieve. Load the box with the littler lures. Make sure everything your partners' need is in their box. This gives a sense of independence and ownership but also keeps them out of your stash.

Rods, Reels and Smiles
Fishing equipment has come a long way. There are rods and reels to

accommodate every fisherman and type of fishing. For beginners the ZEBCO type combos are a good fit. The classic Zebco 33 and 5½-foot rod are suitable for bass, bluegill, crappie, and medium size catfish. The easy casting reel spooled with 10-pound test line makes for simple casting and retrieve type activity. For those with a little more experience or with adequate coordination and a few more dollars, an open face-spinning reel attached to a six foot medium action rod is a good choice. Lighter lures and longer casts are the reward for the use of these outfits.

After a few seasons, a medium priced baitcasting reel attached to a 6 or 6 ½ foot medium heavy rod is a good option. Easier retrieve of heavier lures or the cumbersome cranking chores associated with crankbaits are less taxing with the baitcast equipment. The spincast combos should run in the $25 to $40 range. Open face spinning equipment might be $40 to $75, and baitcast outfits could be $50 to $100.

Planning the Trip
Set yourself up for success by planning your family outings carefully. Often a farm pond or a small lake is a good setting. A place where you walk the bank is desirable for a few reasons. Bank fishing means no boat is necessary. There is no launching or trailering involved. More one-on-one time can be spent with each family member, and casting, hooking, and fish handling is more easily facilitated with your position on the shoreline. Other activities, lunch, breaks from the action, and normal fishing related functions are less stressful when you don't have to worry about boating obligations.

Creek and stream fishing can be done from the bank, out of a small boat or while wading the shallower waters. A different view and new perspective is offered from the various methods. Lots of action and decent stringers of fish can also be the payoff in the small waters. A camera to record the day's events is a great way to relive each moment. Once casting and fishing skills are mastered, lake trips and the go-fast boat can be added to the options. In this case boat safety and handling becomes part of the lessons that every member of the family can join in and learn.

School is back in session, but some of the best lessons are learned in nature's classroom. Don't be surprised if you have more fun than anyone in planning and treating your family to that precious fishing trip and time on the water.

19

Simple System for Cool Water Crappie

Catching crappie in fall and winter can be really good or really great. It's always been my opinion that catching crappie isn't difficult—finding them is the challenge.

Search mode requires a quick study of water color, water temperature, available cover, and bottom contour. Each of these factors helps determine the location of the feisty crappies. As water cools in the fall, bait fish will *ball up* in giant schools. Find the bait, find the fish. Surface temperatures in the low 70s to the 50s are highly desirable. Clear to slightly stained water are also a good sign. Muddy water pushes the crappie tight to cover and makes them less likely to move far to strike a lure. Again we are describing ideal scenarios. If there is submerged wood in three to ten feet of water, get ready to launch into your happy face. Crappie strongly relate to wood and other types of submerged cover.

Crappie gear can vary by region and by the types of cover, water, and bait used. If you are a frequent fisher of panfish, you probably already have a few rods and an assortment of lures that will work for sporadic success. Before you *fire up the deep fryer*, assemble some crappie specific equipment. Because there are multiple methods to catch white, black, and blacknose crappie, this can call for a wide variety of rods, reels, and accessories. Let's rule out the hot water method of deep trolling and focus on drifting, vertical jigging, and casting. Spider rigs, the set-up for drifting with multiple rods and jigs, minnows, or jigs tipped with minnows employs long rods normally set in holders. When crappie are schooled tightly in shallower water this can produce several fish on many of the rigs at the same time. Sounds good, but it can be chaotic.

Vertical jigging in heavy cover requires a long pole—eight to 12 feet are commonly chosen—and lots of lead, line, and lures. Dropping the crappie bait in heavy cover is fun, but be prepared to lose a few fish and tackle. When it's right, this can produce a limit of fish from one spot. My preference is casting small tubes on five and a half foot ultra-light rods. I love the little thump you get when the crappies are active and hitting small soft plastic offerings.

Perfect Presentation

The dominant source of natural nutrition for crappies is minnows. With this knowledge making your lure look and move like a minnow is a plus. Color, size of lure, weight of jighead and line size all contribute to fooling these fish.

Color—Visibility is the key. In clear water natural colors dominate. Pearl, white, grey shades, or silver all catch clear water crappie. After years of hiding my own custom color, 0095 Monteleone Silver Midsouth tackle of Jonesboro, Arkansas, now offers them to the public. They are clear water killers. In slightly stained water, a staple in the crappie angler's box is chartreuse and the red/chartreuse combination. In muddy water, black or black/chartreuse combination works well. Changing colors often helps to coax lure-shy crappies.

Size—Crappie tubes are generally the same length. One and a half to one and three quarters inch is standard. I have caught crappie on four inch bass tubes! Bigger crappie-type tubes are available and work in stained water. Those seeking the bigger bite often upsize their plastics.

Jighead weights—Jigheads for crappie are available in microscopic $1/128$ ounce and also up to $1/2$ ounce; the rate of fall is dictated by the weight of the leadhead and the line diameter. The amount of wind, the water color, and the water temperature all help me decide where to start on lure weights. Light winds—light weight. In heavier wind, the heavier jigheads make casting, controlling the lure, and sensing the strikes easier.

Line—The lighter lines create a faster drop. The diameter of the line is proportionately larger on heavier pound test fishing lines. For a slower drop use heavier line. You can manipulate the descent of the bait by going with a heavy line and a light jighead for an agonizing slow drop, or lighter line and heavier jighead for fast fall. Light line is fun and effective. Sometimes as small as two pound test, rarely anything above six pound test line, is spooled on to open-faced spinning reels.

Catch and release or hook 'em and cook 'em crappie are abundant, willing, and once located easy to catch. I advocate the 50% rule regardless of the time of year. To keep my spots stocked I at most keep half of what I catch. It maybe a little painful in the fall, but it'll makes you smile again in the spring.

20

Ten of My Favorite Fishing Facts

In the ongoing quest for knowledge, fisherman are sometimes led astray or make incorrect assumptions. We've all heard something that sounds contradictory to a theory we've held. One sure way to dispel any doubt is to hit the water and work on either proving or disproving that theory. With many seasons under my belt it's my belief that there are no absolutes in outdoor activities. Whenever someone says "Always or Never," be on the alert. A favorite pet peeve of mine is the self-proclaimed expert who writes or presents his/her way is *the* way. My list of my favorite fishing facts contain things that I think are true based off of thousands of hours of water time, but they are my own opinion. Prove 'em or disprove 'em, here's a few of my favorites.

1. *Look for a spot with lots of cover and fish it hard.* **(NO)** My take on this is if you pull into a cover with 100 standing trees in it, look for another spot—maybe one with 10 trees in the entire area. When fishing the 100 trees you're probably fishing for 20 bass. In the place with ten trees, there are probably nine fish, and you'll find them a lot quicker. Big bass, with the exception of spawning season, are more solitary creatures, you putting yourself in position to be successful by fishing a spot with less cover but a higher probability of finding and catch fish quickly. Sometimes less is better!
2. *Big Fish/Big Bait.* **(YES)** My money on chances of landing

Basszilla increase when throwing a larger lure. The problem for many anglers is they don't realize the bigger the bait, the more likely the fish will detect a flaw in the appearance, shape, or movement. For truly big bass, everything must be right. On the plus side for larger lures, a bass sees that as a *one stop shop* for a major meal. Why expend more energy than you get from chasing down a mini-size morsel. Big jigs, a ½ ounce Strike King with a rage chunk offers a large profile and a big bite. Similarly the Premium ⅜ ounce Spinner attracts big bass. Elevated water temperatures means a high metabolism for the bass—high metabolic rate = faster digestion, hungrier sooner. This all means the upsized meal at the bass buffet is a good bet to get you bit. From a physical standpoint, the larger a bass grows the larger the space between its gills, they quickly learn smaller forage escapes through the bigger gill rakers and seek out something they can trap and swallow.

3. *My favorite rod works for every lure.* **(NO)** *Ding, ding, ding!* Wrong, but thanks for playing the game. The length and action of every rod is *best* suited to a certain situation. This is not to say you couldn't use just one, but under certain conditions a rod has the components to perform better. Case in point a really good jigging rod probably wouldn't make a very good spinnerbait rod—too stiff, possibly too long, more than likely would create a hook setting problem, lots of misses. The length of a rod in large part determines how accurately you can cast, the efficiency of the hook set, and how well you can control a bigger bass. Consider what you need to do with the rod. Is feel the highest on your list, hook setting, easy casting? You're the customer. Figure out what you want and match that in one of the hundreds of fishing sticks available.

4. *Line size matters little.* **(NO)** Afraid not. What lure you're fishing, where you're fishing, and even the weather can be a

factor in line size and type. Complicated by diameter, material, and strength, it can be a tough choice. For me, spinning reels call for 6 to 10-pound test line, bait casting reels, at least mine, are spooled with 12 to 16-pound lines. The nature of the bait, size, and shape will dictate which line size I use. Strength, casting distance, and lure performance are all impacted by line size. You can use about any size at night or when throwing a buzzbait, because the line is above the surface and almost unseen by the bass. All things considered, know this—the difference between 8 and 14-pound test is a 20% deeper dive on crankbaits and some increase in rate of fall on worms or jigs with smaller line sizes. Most of my reels are spooled with monofilament. Rarely do I use fluorocarbon and braided line for certain applications, just a matter of preference.

5. *The bait is moved by one factor.* **(Maybe)** Trick question. True, but with the need for a brief explanation. Think about it, the rod moves *feel* baits, jigs, grubs, and soft plastics; the reel does the work on spinnerbaits and crankbaits. This only matters because the effectiveness of the technique comes from correct application of this concept.

6. *Retrieve ratio doesn't matter; you can do the same thing with any reel.* **(NO)** Simply stated but seldom discussed are the mechanical differences and the outcomes of different ratios. Whether you're burning a buzzbait or pitchin' a jig, retrieve speed and the ability to reel in more line at a faster pace should at least be considered. In the every day typical situation, it's important to remember too slowly is much better than too fast. That's more in presentation than in retrieve. Just so you know the difference in a 5:2 to 1 and a 6.3 to 1 reel amounts to 5 more inches of line every time the reel handle revolves one full turn. Just keep in mind a bass can catch about anything it wants with that 15 mile per hour short burst of speed, but it won't chase anything any farther

than it has to and will sometimes snub anything moving too quickly.

7. *The best time to fish is at dawn and dusk.* **(MAYBE)** While fish seem to bite better in low light periods, consider why that might be. First and most important a bass has incredible vision. As a predator, it is armed with keen sight, and bass use it as a primary survival tool. Bass also are equipped with a unique vision quality; their eyes adapt faster to light change than almost everything in and around the water. Largemouth and smallmouth can approach schools of bait early and late in the day without being as easily detected in bright daytime conditions, hence the fishing tale about the magic of dawn and dusk.

8. *Bass move to deep water in winter and summer months.* **(NO)** It's been my experience that all bass rarely do the same thing at the same time. Another key for the fish is comfort and food supply. In conversations with some of the best fishermen in the world, there is a great belief that bass inhabit shallow water much of the time regardless of season. Exception would be smallmouth which relate to deep water like a largemouth relates to structure and objects. Clear water, like that found in the western Unites States, would also be viewed differently. Bass move shallow to feed and occasionally gravitate to secondary cover during cold fronts, dropping water levels, and other weather-related phenomena. By and large, bass like and spend most of their lives in three to eight feet of water.

9. *Crankbaits all run the same.* **(NO)** Most serious fishermen know you can look at the plastic bill of a crankbait and gauge if it's a shallow runner or deep diver. Now we're talking about the physical properties of these lures so popular with fish and fishermen. Forget for a moment the lip, and think about what material the lure is made of. Most baits are plastic or wood. Do they run the same? No. Even the same bait will run

Ten of My Favorite Fishing Facts

differently at different times of the year. It's true! Wood is fairly consistent; water is at its highest density at 39 degrees. Baits will react by running shallower in the *thick* water, but the plastic lures are really the story. Plastic crankers have an air chamber due to the manufacturing process. Consider this, when air is heated it rises, the hollow chamber in the middle of the lure contains air and will not dive as deep in warm water and air temperatures. Working a depth of three to eight feet, 80% of the time I have a Strike King #3 or #4 in colors Oyster, Sexy Shad, or orange belly craw tied to the end of my line. Remember when you're trying to coax a bite from a suspended stubborn bass, keep the bait in the strike zone for as long as you can. Long pauses allow the bait to ascend slowly.

10. *A tackle boxed crammed with baits will lead to success in bass fishing.* **(NO)** Been there, bought that! Hundreds of lures and thousands of dollars later, I figured it out. Simply stated, the more you have in your head, the less you need in your tackle box.

Guide Tip: Crankbaits constructed of wood run consistently. Plastic crankbaits are hollow, and the air chamber will cause them to run differently in warmer weather. Both work but be aware of the differences, especially in deep water applications.

21

More Big Bass Secrets

There are specific techniques, lures, approaches, and elements that consistently catch big bass. Surprisingly some of the same fishing factors crossover to multiple species but remain unrecognized. Trolling, fishing crankbaits or soft plastics, the needs of several different species all are but a few examples of proven aspects that intersect. When you develop your own system, the more of these techniques you incorporate and consistently apply, the more likely it becomes that you will experience multiple catches of trophy size bass. Here a are a few of my favorites.

- **Make a house call**—The easier you make it for fish to eat, the less energy they expend, the larger they get. Doing close quarters battle with bass requires stout equipment. If you wait for bass to come to you it's a less likely situation. Going to the fish (pitching and flipping) requires more of you and less of the fish. This does increase the odds of presenting your lures to monster fish. They do not get bigger chasing their food sources long distances.
- **Ninja stealth mode**—The silent approach. For years I have been a martial arts practitioner. One of the basic tenants of many physical activities is the ability to blend in and incorporate a silent approach. Bass are both predator and potentially prey. Loud noises, shadows cast over their position, anything that sends a negative sensory message all put

fish on high alert. When bass become wary they will move to heavy cover, secondary offshore objects, move off shore, go nocturnal, or shutdown. Small paddle adjustments and slow drifts into the prospective area are super effective. Couple this with the silent entry of your lure form the pitching/flipping techniques, and you are building your own personal *big* bass system. Bridgett Howard has her own take on approach. "When working a bait, I try to visualize that predator bass watching and inspecting my lure as it swims by. I stay alert and on point so I don't miss the strike—it may be one of a handful that I get that day."

- **Random action**—To consistently catch heavyweight bass with artificial baits consider this, any lure that has random action is the most likely to be effective. Bass never catch on to the quiet, random motion baits. Most large fish have more than likely seen a multitude of baits and been caught many times. Bass will snub baits overloaded with extreme attracting qualities. Not to say bass won't ever strike large, loud, brightly colored, mechanical motion lures. The most likely scenario would be defending the nest or at night. Day in, day out lures that achieve random action *and* speed imparted by each individual angler will catch the behemoth bass. This explains why two anglers fishing the same bait in the same area on the same equipment experience different results. Retrieve speed is, in my opinion, the least considered and the most important aspect of catching a trophy.
- **Object of our attention**—Largemouth bass are object oriented creatures. I, because of my experiences and past success, gravitate to submerged weeds and wood. Eric Jackson elaborates: "A good example is throwing to a big fallen tree with a nice drop off nearby four or five times and trying different lures on it. Then, finding a very small fallen tree, I might skip that and move to the next really promising looking spot. Finally, I don't trust the advice of others to find the

big fish so much that I don't try a variety of depths, lures, and locations." The best cover serves at least three of the bass four basic needs—maybe all four if located near deep water. My opinion matches Jacksons'. While many anglers like inordinate amounts of cover (more is better), I prefer to find an area where the same type of cover exists in smaller numbers. For example, in a cove where there are 100 flooded trees, I would seek out a similar size cove with a dozen trees. The hundred tress probably have 20 bass on them; the ten trees would likely have eight bass on them. You cut your search time and can cover water faster.

- **Bass-tronomy**—Simply stated, the moon matters. If you don't buy into the moon/big bass theory, do a little research. World record catches in fresh and salt water many times reflect the catches occurring in close proximity to a major moon phase, new or full. In one year I religiously logged my fishing trips and big bass catches. My logbook shows out of 26 bass topping the five pound mark (up to a nine pounder) 25 of the fish were caught three days before or after a new or full moon. The one fish that wasn't was one day off. Think those were isolated incidents? Study your own results. Fish as often as you can, but when given the chance center your trips around major moon phases. Many hatches take place on the moons. Hatches in profusion create feeding binges throughout nature.
- **Seeing red**—Red is a triggering color for predatory fish like bass and others. If your bait doesn't have any red on it, add it with a marker or red nail polish or paint. The addition of a red hook to the front of your crankbaits will surprise you with the number of fish caught on the red hook. For years the color purple for plastic worms was easily the most popular. What colors combine to make purple? Blue and *red*.
- **Match the hatch**—Trout anglers promote the *match the hatch* concept. This is why they tie their own flies. They can walk

the shoreline of the stream they fish, roll over rocks, and wade to see what natural forage is available. As bass chasers we *should not* match the hatch. Common sense and logic will tell you why. If a bass of any size has to chase a meal the same distance why would it choose the smaller food source? The other factor is that in a school of three-inch shad, any fish expending the same amount of energy will see and choose the six-inch version. Make your offering stand out and look real, and the fish will do the rest. Bass love crawfish and gain a pound for every five pounds of crawfish they eat. They eat more shad and baitfish because they are more available and are their primary source of food.

Trophy hunting bass anglers have a different mindset. You'll begin to look at your tackle boxes, rods, reels, line, and other accessories with a changed perspective. In many cases you are fishing for a few bites. The payoff is a braggin' size bass. Tournament anglers are notorious for saying that they are *fishing for a five*. Now you're fishing for a *five*. Once you catch that bass of a lifetime, consider releasing it to thrill another angler.

22

Game of Throws

Bass anglers try flipping, pitching, the wrist roll. Fly fishermen employ the double haul—there's even a bow and arrow cast for shooting under docks. All of these and more are used to describe casting techniques. In the *Game Of Throws*, it determines how many presentations you can make during your fishing trip. If you are the average angler, you make at least two casts a minute. If between paddling and pitching you spend five hours on the water actually fishing, the calculation would be you made 600 casts. In my case I keep the bait moving and cast at least four times a minute—same amount of time yields 1,200 casts to the bass.

As a dedicated kayak angler, I prefer short-range pitching for almost every technique I use in the pursuit of any fish. I do on occasion back off and launch crankbaits to deep water fish, but I like to make a *house call* and get up close and personal. My pitches are most likely from a distance of 20-40 feet. I put a premium on accuracy because of the true strike zone of most fish species. It just makes sense that the shorter the distance a fish has to move the more likely it is to hit your bait. The closer you get it to them the better your chance to set the hook on one.

When faced with a tight target area the underhand pitching technique allows for a pinpoint presentation and minimal splash and noise, it's a pendulum motion that allows the line to stay just above the surface and merely *dimple* the water as it enters.

For even closer encounters the flipping technique used with a small section of line and a pendulum motion to the fish staged in and around heavy cover works well. Try quick repeated presentations to the stubborn fish hugging submerged wood, weeds, docks, and any other potential hideout.

After years of doing casting demonstrations at outdoor shows, I have realized there are a few factors that make anyone good at casting. Like any other endeavor practice is important. If you've mastered the baitcasting reel, the next thing is to work on your mechanics. Do the same thing the same way each time, and you will find that your results are repeatable. You don't have to sacrifice distance for accuracy. For any type of casting equipment know that if your goal is longer casts you can leave extra line with the bait dangling off six to ten inches of line at the rod tip. This allows you to *load* the rod with energy that sends the bait a greater distance. For short range accuracy, reel the lure up to within an inch or two of the tip. This gives you a bit more control.

For the pitching and flipping techniques, you have a longer length of line, a rod's length for pitching and flipping. Generally you have a longer length of line in your hand that you allow to flow out as the bait heads to you target. The efficiency of both these short range techniques logically allows for several more casts/presentations per minute. Longer rods (7-7 ½ feet) allow for distance, some additional control, and a degree of accuracy. For a consistent feel and uninterrupted accuracy, I try to use the same length rod and the same weight lure when at all possible.

Side arm casts create less splash than overhead casts and can be used to work under docks and overhanging tree branches. Skipping soft plastics under overhanging trees into the shade is a summer tactic that pays off. In ultra-clear water longer casts will help you to catch a few more of the wary fish already spooky because of the water clarity. Lightweight artificial lures including smaller soft plastic craw imitators, finesse worms, and minnow plugs are all good choices. In dirty water bass retreat to shallow water. Sloppy casting and presentations are less likely to shut bass down. In murky to muddy water, I use the same baits I would use at night. Dark colors, larger lures, and sound making capabilities all might help the fish in low-visibility conditions.

Wind is the bane of the bass angler and even more so when working from a kayak. Casting large profile or light baits in the wind can be disastrous for those handing baitcasting equipment. An educated thumb and a little common sense rule in breezy conditions.

I pride myself on my ability to cover a lot of water and make hundreds of casts. It starts with accuracy and the ability to gauge the retrieve speed necessary to fool the fish. I've even worked to improve my casting from my off hand—in my case my left hand—so I can work cover from every angle, and if fatigue sets in I can go to the alternate side.

Does all this seem extreme? Not when you're trying to win at the *Game Of Throws*.

23

Spinnerbaits—Spinner Bites

Probably the most versatile artificial bass bait there is—the spinnerbait. A little confusing to some because of the *vibration theory*—the blades *do not* vibrate, the spinnerbait upper arms do—and the multitude if sizes, styles, colors, and blade configurations, day in day out spinners are more likely to boat a bass than just about any artificial lure. Attached to the rods of beginners and seasoned anglers, spinners should be in the box of every serious fisherman.

My own love of spinnerbaits comes from personal success stories. Easily my favorite form of bass fishing is working jigs and soft plastics around cover. But spinners have accounted for some of my best catches. One December day after launching, the boat trolled to the first point, with cold temperatures and slightly stained water. I launched a ⅜ ounce, willow/Colorado spinnerbait, and as it slowly descended, a solid, steady pull was transmitted through the line. One cast, one fish—oh yeah, it just happened to weigh ten and a quarter pounds.

The spinner has been instrumental in smallmouth catches on my Canadian trips for over 25 years. One spinnerbait smallie was a legitimate seven-pounder. Season after season, year after year spinnerbaits have produced bass for me.

Bait Break Down
Why they work—Spinnerbaits work because they imitate bass'

most frequent meal, bait fish in the form of minnows, bluegill, the occasional crappie, and shad. Providing flash and water displacement for the blades and vibration in the arm, spinners can be configured to look and produce various amounts of water push and vibration. With the ability to be worked shallow—in one foot of water—or deep—20-30 feet—spinnerbaits will catch almost everything that swims.

Components
- The skirt—The skirt, in my opinion, is more for the angler than the fish. The blades, the motion, and the amount of flash are the selling points for the fish. Skirt color might matter in very extreme water conditions. Very clear, white or neutral colors; muddy water, black, black chartreuse and combo colors could be more of a visual draw. You can also pull the skirt and add a swimbait or soft plastic minnow to create a new look. This works well on waters with a high degree of fishing pressure.
- *The weight*—Coming in tiny 1/16 ounce versions and heavy duty sizes weighing in at well over an ounce, it's all about casting and retrieving and where you want the bait to meet the bass. Size, profile, and overall action can be dictated by weight. Certainly casting is more effective for minimally a mid-weight spinner. My choice is generally, at least to begin with, is 3/8 ounce models. I do this because my other artificial baits are often the same size. This gives me a consistent feel when casting and promotes accuracy. When bass are deep, to get the bait down to them quickly, pick the overweight bait.
- **Blades**—Here's your chance to customize or go from package to directly tied to the line. A good starting point is a 3/8 ounce, willow/Colorado spinner. Mine has a nickel Colorado blade first followed by a # 4 1/2 gold willow. This accomplishes two things; first, you have different flash colors, and second, different water displacement because of the shape

of the blades. The possibilities are endless; double Colorado, single Colorado, Colorado/willow combination, single willow (excels in cold, clear water), double willow (great for muddy water), colored blades, red, chartreuse, white is a killer in the late fall or winter when bass are chasing shad or the shad are dying off from cold water. Black bladed spinners are a great night time choice, coupled with a slow steady retrieve they flat catch after hour's bass.

Where To Fish Them
Pick a place. Everywhere that bass hideout has the potential to produce with a spinnerbait. Classic areas include, boat docks, weed beds, submerged wood, drop offs, rocky shorelines, creek channels, distinct bottom contours, and isolated cover. Bass in cover are in ambush mode. As the sun rises, especially in clear water they seek overhead cover. Throw past the cover and work the bait through with an occasional twitch or drop simulating an injured minnow brings out the predatory instinct in all game fish.

How to fish them
Slow rolling deep for summer/winter fish is popular. Casting to bass chasing bait on the top is deadly, retrieving to the edge of any cover and then *killing* the short arm spinner and letting it free fall is a great way to draw a hit. Waking, the retrieve of the spinner just below the surface, will bring bass from a distance or out of thick cover. There are many ways to work the spinnerbait and sometimes multiple patterns emerge.

The Best Rod, Reel, And Line
A little tricky is what might be viewed as the best set up for casting, cranking, hook setting, and landing fish. My personal favorite is a seven foot medium action rod with a 6.3:1 retrieve gear ratio baitcasting reel attached to it. You can make a case for a faster retrieve ratio reels available now up to 9.0:1, but the mistake most anglers

Spinnerbaits—Spinner Bites

make is reeling baits back to quickly and causing fish to doubt the wisdom of chasing down the fast moving intruder. Line discussion always creates a debate. Fans of fluorocarbon will tout the *no stretch* capabilities while the braid folks talk about the sensitivity and feel of braided string. Monofilament has a fair amount of stretch. This can be desirable in crankbait and spinnerbait fishing. Mono allows the fish to actually take the bait and the rod plus a sweeping hookset provides pretty sure penetration and good playing capabilities.

Most serious fishermen head to the water with a few rods. I take five, and one is always a spinnerbait rod. I've caught many species of fish of every description and size on spinners. I love my soft plastics and jigs, but spinners will day-in, day-out, draw strikes under a wide variety of weather and water conditions.

24

Ten Essential Kayak Bass Fishing Tips

1. **Research**—In this age of information, almost any topic is readily available. New to bass fishing from a kayak? Thousands of articles, opinions, and facts can assist you in lessening your learning curve. Seek out videos, podcasts, and online or print information. With tons of tournaments and fun fishermen, there's bound to be someone local who is willing to mentor you. Don't allow yourself to be overwhelmed. Choose a style of fishing that most suits your interest. Bass are object-oriented, smallmouth a bit less than largemouth. Largemouth relate to submerged wood, weeds, rock in all sizes, man-made structure in the form of docks, bridge pilings, and rip-rap banks. Bass will eat anything that fits in their cavernous mouths but prefer crawfish first and minnows, shad, frogs, and anything they can track down and catch. They need oxygen, food, cover, and deep water as an escape route, and they're happy. Found almost everywhere they are a most worthy opponent.
2. **Kayak Choice**—As important as anything is the choice of a kayak that fits you, is affordable, high in quality, and critical is fishing friendly. Consider models that have options that suit your fishing spots. A little research will go a long way. Most of us wouldn't buy a vehicle without test driving it—same here. Climb in a kayak, and go for a ride. Handling, casting room, paddle or pedal all matter. What about hauling and

Ten Essential Kayak Bass Fishing Tips

handling? Options include car topping, trailering, or the bed of a pick-up truck. Make sure you're comfortable with loading/unloading your kayak. Consider carts like the C-tug and others to lighten your load.

3. **Safety**—Regardless of age or experience, safety is a top priority. Would you put your child in the set-up you have? The most important piece of gear is the life jacket. There are several models that make paddling, casting, and fishing comfortable. Invest wisely, and consider highly visible colors if you're sharing the water with larger water craft. Light poles and flags add a degree of visibility. Have a whistle attached in a handy spot as an audible signal to other boaters. Try to make sure everything you carry is tethered or floats—including you.

4. **Simplify**—Bass fishing offers simplicity or a high degree of complexity. Simple is basic tools, minimal electronics, and functional equipment. Clutter and confusion go hand in hand. A dry box for keys, wallet, and phone is securely attached to the kayak. A dry bag to hold other items you wish to keep dry is another option that can be stowed below the deck of many boat models. Strategically, carabiners are your friend—they allow security for other accessories—and a rubberized short handled net can be carried to assist in landing your catch, equipped with a lanyard and secured in a spot behind your seat is more than adequate. While you might own tons of tackle, a minimalist approach is possible. Consider storage space, necessity, and cost. A couple of Plano #3600 plastic tackle boxes will hold literally dozens of bass baits.

5. **Knowing Nature**—Another aspect of safety and bass fishing success is knowing and understanding nature. You're in hot pursuit of a wild creature. Every type of weather is an indicator of activity of the all species of bass. Arm yourself with as much information regarding wind, weather, and

water conditions to assist you with safety concerns and to land more bass. Air, and more importantly surface water temperatures, are valuable clues. Bass will be in pre-spawn from 50—62 degrees—they are eating machines in preparation for the spawning rituals. Smallmouth go first, then the spots aka Kentucky bass, and finally the legendary largemouth hit the beds. At about 70 degrees and a couple of weeks they finalized the function (post-spawn) and move off to deeper water haunts. Wind direction gives you an idea of the prevailing future weather patterns. A north wind brings cooler changes, south warmer, east possibly some unstable patterns, and west seems to bring the bite with it. High winds and lightning are the bane of the bass anglers. *Get off the water.*

6. **Bait/rod choices**—There are hundreds of colors of crankbaits, thousands of blade configurations of spinnerbaits, a never ending rainbow of colors of soft plastics—*attention, attention*—You don't have to have them all. A cross section of bass baits will prove dependable, even deadly, for bass. When slinging lures, single hook lures do offer a lesser chance of being embedded in anything. Highly effective models of spinners, jigs, topwater buzzbaits, and soft plastic rigs work just fine. On the plastics, learn to rig worms, craws, and creature baits utilizing the Texas rig—popular and highly productive, yet simple. It starts with a conical slip sinker, usually lead with a hole drilled through it, and ranging in weight from ⅛ ounce to a hefty one ounce version—⅜ is standard for me. Slide it onto the line small side first. Next attach you hook varying in size from 2/0 to 6/0 dependent on the overall size of your bait. Learn the Palomar knot, the Clinch knot and the Blood knot to use in attaching two lines. Stock a few crankbaits in you bass boxes, three necessary patterns/colors 1.shad 2. crawfish 3. chartreuse black back. Done! Add a few rubber-legged jigs in a couple of weights and colors. During the warmer months a few topwater *plugs*

and minnow imitating baits are solid choices. I developed a *one-year rule*, if you carry baits that haven't been tied on, gotten wet, or caught a fish after one year, they come out. Soon you have your own selection of favorite bass baits for you and, more important, the fish. As for fishing rods, length ranging from the 5 ½ foot ultralight spinning models to the 7 ½ foot medium heavy baitcasters have earned a place in my kayak. Longer casts, lightweight lures, and light line beg for the spinning combos. Lures down to an ⅛ ounce, launched on four to six-pound test calls for open faced spinning reels. To cast and retrieve the bulky bass baits, I opt for a more muscular rod and reel with some guts, baitcasters. These reels are spooled with heavier monofilament 12 to16-pound test and another option is the super strong and sensitive, no stretch braid in 20 to 30-pound test range. Go armed to battle bruiser bass. Generally two baitcasting outfits and a spinning set up are staged at my feet. Depending on the available structure—rocks, docks, submerged wood—I might add another rod.

7. **Go Silent**—Bass can be spooky, wary, and downright finicky at times. The kayak by its nature offers a silent, stealthy approach. A time-proven tip, throw the quietest baits first. Subtle, smaller silent lures will catch *big* bass consistently. If you climb the scale of sound going to next level in decibel graduations, you'll find you get more first cast bass bites. Save the loudest for last. Always exceptions, but generally this tactic pays off. In murky or muddy water, try brighter colors and bigger sizes. No bites? Go to louder lures. Sound travels through water five times faster than through air. Water is a great conductor of sound unintentional *or* intentional. Paddle quietly, and pedal using some drift.

8. **Small Water Advantages**—Big water = Big bass. *No!* Several state records for largemouth bass come from smaller lakes, rivers, and even ponds. The kayak makes the smallest

and larger bodies of water accessible—another advantage kayak! Smaller waters can be worked thoroughly and are often underutilized. Even urban, close to home spots can be great testing grounds for new baits and for developing your fishing skills. Covering water quickly gives you more opportunities in your busy world to fish. Tiny spots can hold *big* bass.

9. **Comfortable Kayak Clothes**—Comfortable footwear is a plus. Nonslip soles for standing, entering, and exiting your kayak are recommended. The Astral Lowyak is my personal choice almost year round. For the ultimate comfort, wicking, water-shedding material is functional if not fashionable. With water all around, mist, rain, and hopefully some dripping fish, water resistant and waterproof is desirable. For warmth you can't beat wool. Fingerless gloves, hats, socks, and more keep you warm as you work the water in search of bass.

10. **Journal**—A bit of a chore, but the bass fisherman's bible is a journal. Notate surface water temperature—easily determined with a swimming pool thermometer—moon phase—major moons, full and new are great—wind direction, the most productive baits, depth that you find the fish, and any distinct cover or pattern that is producing.

Bass fishing is a never ending game of hide and seek that takes place in some beautiful places. Experience and the fish are the best teachers.

25

The One(s) That Got Away

You're on the prowl for a big bass, catfish, crappie, or any other species. The water conditions are great, you're on a major moon phase, and the water your kayak is gliding over is known for trophy fish. A likely spot to cast the bait, you start the retrieve, and you are literally holding your breath in anticipation of *the hit*. Sensing the strike, a quick snap of the wrists and you feel the power of a massive fish and then—then the line goes limp.

What happened?

Everyone who ever wet a line experiences *the one that got away*. While I've boated lot of *big* bass, I've lost fish of every type in every conceivable way. Figuring out what happened and taking measures to correct each gets you closer to that flawless set of factors to help you consistently grip instead of gripe. The proper equipment, correct techniques, attention to details, and perfect execution all add up to more fish and less frustration.

- **Line**—In many instances a particular very specific part of the entire rod and reel set up is the culprit. The fishing line spooled on the reel itself can be suspect. On top of the list of problems with the line—too old. Monofilament should be changed for the active angler minimally every six months. When asked, it is not unusual to hear from the infrequent fisherman, that the line is just a couple of years old. *Arrrgh!* Normal use and heat are the enemies of mono. Sunlight, stretch and heat from being on the deck or during storage all causes the eventual breakdown of monofilament. Add to that, nicks or abrasions from being run in, around, and through wood, rocks, concrete, or other objects and you have a formula for fishing disaster. Too light a line, mini-mono in the two to six-pound test range also requires caution. Lightweight line when battling heavyweight fish calls for a loose drag set. Fluorocarbon is invisible but breakable while braid it is pretty much indestructible.

- **Bad Knot**—Knot tying skills are paramount to getting any fish all the way to the kayak. A poorly tied knot on monofilament breaks or is evidenced by the curly end that comes back after the epic fail. Wetting your knot before pulling it snuggly down avoids the destruction of heat on the dry pull. With braid the danger is more likely that the knot slips rather than breaks. The cure for braid is a double knot—the first knot for me is a Palomar knot, followed by a clinch knot. This means even if there is slight slip you have a knot against a knot. Problem solved. For a quick snip, I keep clippers handy. I recommend learning just a few knots. The Palomar is relatively simple and gives 95% strength when tied properly on monofilament. Learn a clinch knot and maybe a blood knot for connecting leaders. Fluorocarbon is problematic because of its poor break strength, while with braid a good knot makes it golden.

- **Hook Set**—The statement, "I'm not sure if it's a bite" followed by a halfhearted hook set almost assures you will see a bass waving bye-bye. Sometimes after repeated casting with no action, anglers slip into a casting coma where they lose focus. When the hit happens they're caught napping. Perfecting the hook set techniques is highly recommended. Feel the bite, drop a small amount of slack in the line, slam the rod back to firmly push the hook point into the fish. Of course there's a little more to it. Consider a GoPro video of

your hook set where you can video the entire process and break it down for effectiveness. Any doubt, set the hook.
- **Object Escape**—Most fish that attain trophy size have been hooked or even caught a few times before. Big fish, once stung by the hook, will head to deep water or deep cover. Open water presents very little in terms of the possibility of ultimately getting your prize. Bass or others bolting for cover is a much bigger dilemma. Fighting for survival and attempting escape sends a largemouth launching itself toward boat docks, weed beds, submerged wood, or any heavy cover it can bury up in. The line strength, the good knot, and the correct rod gives you more control and can reduce the possibility of a heavyweight hanging you up.
- **The Rod**—The action of the rod that matches the lure, its weight, the location, and the technique are the fighting factors that come into play. For jigs, plastic worms, a medium heavy action rod in the seven to seven a half foot range facilitates the hook set and playing any fish. For crankbait casting and catching, a medium action rod has the proper amount of *give* to sink the treble hooks into the jaw of any fish and holds as the fish darts around pulls and pushes trying to dislodge the lure. There are many manufacturers that produce specialized *cranking rods*, a good investment for the dedicated *crankensteins*.
- **Dull Hooks**—The sharper the hook is, the more fragile the point because there is actually less material making them easier to dull, damage, or break. Check the point for that *sticky* sharp feel. Ideally the super sharp point drags and catches on a fingernail, a sign that it qualifies as stick sharp. As hooks dull because of normal use or being run across foreign objects, take time off the water to replace inferior hooks or minimally sharpen the point. A diamond file is the best tool for the task.
- **Drag Set**—My drags are set using three pounds of weight

to test the slip of the drag—any tighter you may break a fish off, any more loose than that and your fish can go where it wants to. I've lost fish both ways. Because monofilament has more stretch, I go a bit tighter on the drag set. Because braid and fluorocarbon are low/no stretch, I can go just a little more loosely.

- **It Just Came Unbuttoned**—A combination of these foul up factors, or not enough tension when playing the fish, or the unexplained phenomenon is generally referred to as *it just came unbuttoned*. Hey, it happens. It's not always an obvious set of circumstances. Tilt the odds in your favor by controlling the variables. Then you can CPR (catch, photo, release) as evidence of the one that didn't get away!

26

Bass Without Borders

Bass, of all species, are now swimming waters internationally and worldwide. Stocking programs and interest in fishing and more specifically for bass crosses language and other barriers and borders. Billions of dollars, media attention, and the clever promotion of our sport sends the message to all corners of the world. Travel of any kind is enlightening, and the observation of other cultures interesting. What drives many anglers is the promise of bigger bass and incredible catch numbers. Doing what I've done for six decades has given me the privilege of traveling to some very unique places and mostly on someone else's dime, all in the name of catching fish and communicating the same. Not a bad gig.

A Bass is a bass is a bass. While the surroundings change, as might well the species you target, there are numerous commonalities. I have been lucky enough to catch bass in 30 of the continental United States, in the freshwater lakes in Hawaii, and the wilderness areas north of the border in Canada. I have cast lures into waters of different sizes, depths, colors, and under all conditions. There exist a few special circumstances but many more similarities. Because of their range and the populations in foreign countries, the diet of the indigenous fish may vary. There is no denying bass behavior in searching out and chasing down food sources by the fish is likely the same regardless of location.

Bass have four basic and specific needs—Largemouth bass need oxygen, they want abundant food supplies, cover, and deep water in close proximity. Breathing, eating, and hiding out with an escape route to the security of deep water. Find these types of areas, and you are sure to find bass. The more compacted the area, the more dynamic the factor, the more likely those bass will become resident fish, and even when one moves out, is caught, or dies another moves in. While the discussion centers on bass, every gamefish will respond the same way. Smallmouth differ in that they relate to deep water like largemouth does to objects. The other *bass-pects*, oxygen, food, deep water escape routes are the same.

Water depth in many scenarios is very predictable. Just because you're not catching bass doesn't mean they aren't there. While largemouth will migrate seasonally, they are home bodies when the conditions are right. My records indicate that the majority of big bass that have come to my grip have come from three to eight feet of water. One doubter responded to this statement with the comment, "That's because you just fish shallow waters." My line has been cast into highland reservoirs with water depths exceeding 100 feet and into glacier lakes of equal or greater depths, and I can assure you I go where the odds favor the fish being present and willing to bite.

Water temperature and water color are key indicators to the daily lifestyle activities of bass anywhere. They eat, digest, spawn, and seek the comfort of specific waters. Smallmouth bass north of the border still spawn in the high 50 to middle 60 degree ranges. Largemouth make bass babies appear later, surface temps around 62-65 Fahrenheit, spotted Kentucky bass land somewhere in the middle. The other bass subspecies also are close to the same spawning temperatures. Water colors are critical because bass feed by sight—discolored waters limit the distance of all sight feeders. If vision is impeded, bass they will react in like fashion. Muddy water limits their strike zone; clear water will draw them from greater depths. I choose casting proximity by these variables. Muddy water flipping, clear water long distance casting.

Bass Without Borders

Largemouth bass in Mexico were very obliging to seeing and immediately engulfing plastic worms. We were there filming a video. The lake was part of a natural river system. I found a cove that was 12 feet deep at its deepest. While we were seeking out fish for TV footage, in less than five hours I boated 99 bass. My triceps ached into the next morning. That *wad* of fish was in six to eight feet of slightly stained water. Twenty-five years later I am doing some promotional filming for a development property called Long Branch Lakes in Spencer, Tennessee. Not having ever been there, I paddled my Jackson Big Rig kayak to a channel lined with standing timber. With rods rigged with Strike King 4.5 flipping tubes and a ⅜ ounce jig, I picked up a strike almost immediately. Two hours and 62 bass later I invited two fishing team partners to join me for the incredible action. The bass were, no surprise to me, located in five to eight feet of water. The school of fish was huge and hungry. The three of us lost track but I'm sure in about three hours we caught and released over 150 bass in a spot that was no more than five acres!

In Canada, for me many legendary smallmouth bass catches came from fishing windblown banks and points. Over and over again, for over 25 years, we could pull up to these spots and find fish that would crush spinnerbaits and topwater oversized buzzbaits. Usually in August, the water was tannic acid stained and about 63 degrees. These fish were predictably feeding up for fall. The exact same scene could have been taking place hundreds of miles away place on a Tennessee lake in October.

Don't let geographic borders or distant locations frighten you. Bass in similar circumstances will predictably respond the same way. I look for areas identical to places that produce on local waters with which I'm familiar. Travel adventures, vacations, fishing tournaments—whatever the reason that takes you to a different locale, fish the same baits and the same type of areas in the same way you do your favorite fishin' hole. Bass fishing has no borders.

27

Natural Clues to Stream Health

When concern arises about the health of the body of water you fish, there are, especially in flowing waters like rivers and streams, some specific clues as to the evidence that graphically demonstrate the current health of that place. Many factors exist that make a place average to outstanding. In several places the local government agencies can help with information about water quality. Moving water has the potential to be extremely healthy and yield large sustainable populations of multiple species of fish. Because the support system in particular, aquatic vegetation can very effectively filter water, rivers, creeks and streams in many parts of the world. Fabulous fisheries exist in these places. Along with nature's filtrations, the other forms of life that can create a *blue ribbon* river or stream are crawfish as a high energy food source. The presence of crawfish is also an indicator of good water quality. They thrive and are responsible for fast growth of bass and other types of fish. Crawfish are Red Bull for bass.

Other forms of underwater health evidence are hellgrammites and freshwater mussels. Each of these creatures exists only in waters that are clean, devoid of contaminants, and of superior overall quality. In the search for clues of the water quality, wading into the water and flipping a few rocks over will quickly confirm what you might suspect. The hellgrammites in particular are top notch confirmation as to the cleanliness of that body of water. Often found clinging

Natural Clues to Stream Health

to the bottom of rocks, the hellgrammites are almost irresistible to smallmouth bass and other members of the bass and sunfish family.

Baitfish and other moving water inhabitants on my list of positive residents include the ones I call *creek minnows*, shad, chubs, *hornyheads*, and tiny other minnow-type baitfish are all evidence that the water quality is at the minimum, decent. If there are bottom feeding fish like carp, suckers, and catfish that also sends the message that any body of water is in reasonable shape. Checking with government agencies on the mercury and PCB levels found in creek samples is also valuable information, because this group of fish eat and scavenge mostly off the bottom they will show the effects of contaminated water. Tissue samples are studied and the results available to the public.

Check your local regulations and get a seine or net that meets local regulations. If you can get a partner to help and sweep pools of the water you will be amazed at what shows up. The same seine is useful for gathering bait for your live bait fishing adventures. For this purpose it is also beneficial to learn how to throw a cast net. Sightings of water birds, herons, and shoreline inhabitants in the form of frogs, snakes, and other creatures is a good indication that the immediate waters are fertile and of good quality.

What does all this mean? It means that properly managed, these stretches of water can provide super fishing for many different species. Catch and release of large fish is important, as is the selective harvest of a few fish. I always add the disclaimer that once you land a fish, using legal means it becomes a matter of personal preference as to what you do with that fish. From an ethical standpoint it's important to understand more than likely the fish you are holding has been caught before by someone who chose to return it to the water. The gene pool and the future of your fishing hole will be forever changed by the decision you make.

A little time monitoring potential pollutants in and around your favorite fishing spot is also high recommended. It's not necessary to become a local nuisance, but periodic checks with local officials and watching industrial business or new close-by construction is a good idea. Many problems are correctable, but it's always better to prevent the entry of pollutants and contaminants. As sportsmen we also need to be responsible for not littering, leaking oil and gas, or leaving anything behind that has the potential to harm the water and it inhabitants above and below the surface. Plastics especially and glass as well as metal take years to break down.

Water quality, an abundant food supply, cover, and water deep enough to protect the fish in extreme weather along with oxygen will produce good populations of fish and good fishing. Other factors including protected spawning areas. Ethical anglers and good conservation practices will normally also provide trophy size fish.

Another plus to studying the types of creatures in and around the waters is also a good tip off as to what to use for bait—be that live or artificial. Live bait application speaks for itself. In choosing and using artificial lures, consider the size, color, and natural motion of each type, and stock you tackle box with those lures. Jigs and soft plastic craws are the most likely to imitate the look, size, color, and natural backward burst movement of crawfish. Minnow plugs a bit larger than the current population position you catch more and bigger fish. The common sense explanation of this is a fish having to move the same distance and choosing between a small or large version of a food source has no reason to hit other than the bigger offering. Spinnerbaits are very versatile, and they come in sizes to suit bass, bluegill, and crappie. Experiment with blades, sizes, and even skirt color, and cast them all over and around cover and bottom contour changes.

Clean water is a key to great catches. Maintain clean water, coupled with good outdoor habits and maintaining healthy populations almost always ensures great fishing for years to come.

Trophy Tip: Selective harvest begins with knowing size and number limits. Taking the smallest legal fish helps recovery of the resource. By their nature the smallest legal fish are the most renewable resource.

28

Making a Hard Case for Soft Plastics

Ask the most seasoned bass anglers, "What's the best bait to position you for a trophy fish," and the answer will produce a variety of their personal favorite fish foolers. Spinnerbaits, crankbaits, the exciting set of topwater lures, jigs, and eventually soft plastics will receive mention. While almost every lure cast at the right time in the right place will get bit, there are others that produce anywhere, anytime. It's the large family of soft plastics baits.

If any bait changed the future of fishing, the introduction of soft plastic worms in the 1950s was surely it. It immediately began with the use of the newfangled bait that could probe the bottom and was visually enticing to largemouth bass that made fans of fishermen everywhere. Along came new rods, reels, hooks, and other items geared toward the worm crowd. Heavy rods likened to pool cues, baitcasting reels with guts and rigging possibilities that produced different looks, action, and fish!

Fast forward to the new millennium, and there now exists endless aisles of colors, shapes, and sizes. Pick an aquatic creature, and there is a plastic bait to match it. Worms, lizards, frogs, crawfish, minnows, shad, and creature baits that really do not match any natural forage food. Pick a color, and you can be guaranteed that it has been poured into a plastic form. Micro sizes to maximum offerings, tiny finesse models to super snakes a foot long can all be found and fished to match any conditions. But the magic is contained in the presentation possibilities. My own introduction was a feeble attempt to imitate the success TV icon Bill Dance displayed on his long running show. He thumbed bass after bass for 30minutes, and I was *hooked*.

A small Missouri lake was the scene of my initial plastic pitching trip. At the end of my worm rod was a purple plastic creation dubbed the centipede, a slip sinker, and a hook touted as a worm hook. After a few tries at getting the bait to hang straight on the most popular Texas rig, I was ready to launch my lure. Peck, peck, peck, and a hook set. Nothing on the business end. Bumping branches and the bottom several more sets and an empty hook. This wasn't as easy as it looked on TV.

Why Soft Plastics? For fisherman looking to land a trophy largemouth, there are several advantages of the lineup of soft lures. Because of the looks, size, shapes, and colors there is a bait to match just about any weather and water condition. A simple rule of thumb would, be in ultra-clear water smaller finesse type baits are a good bet to get a bite. Neutral colors, straight tails, and slow retrieve will generally draw a hit or two. For slightly stained water, going with a bulkier bait, a little longer and mid-range craw colors is pretty surely the ticket. For dirty water, muddy from recent rains or natural stain, bigger, combo colors dark with brighter accent tails, and more appendages or a ribbon tail will be more visible, displace more water, and make the bait easier to locate in the dark waters. To really seal the deal are the plastic presentation factors. Triggering qualities in bass include, easily swallowed shapes, natural colors, realistic swimming motions, and most of all random action and retrieve speed.

Bass will closely scrutinize any potential food source. Most big fish or fish that receive a fair amount of pressure can become *lure shy*. The plus with worms, craws, grubs, lizards, swim baits, and others is the various retrieves employed by the individual angler. Cast... settle... hop... twitch... swim... drop... and start again. Everyone has their own cadence, rod sweep, twitch distance, and amount of time the bait is allowed to swim, drift, or descend. This personal preference essentially makes it difficult for bass to become accustom to the look of this category of lures. The mechanical action of spinners, crankbaits, and others only offers the ability to control retrieve speed which must match the mood of the fish. You can bump cover and go rattle or silent on cranks, or change blades on spinners, but nothing matches the random action and subtle retrieve speed available to the caster, flipper, or pitcher of plastics.

Another couple of facets of plastics is the infusion of salt in many models. When bass get a taste of the salt they are in fact more likely to hold onto their freshly *found* meal. The taste of salt is not foreign to fish. Blood has a certain percentage of salt in it, and bass are used to the taste from various forms of forage. In early years the pork rind baits were bottled in salt brine to preserve the baits, but in fact as a byproduct, it also served to help get fish to hold on longer also. Another point in the favor of plastics is the mouth feel from the initial pick up. Bass are notorious for spitting out anything that feels unnatural. They don't get the chance to do that with the moving category of baits like spinners and crankbaits.

With the development of non-stretch braided line, super sharp hooks, rods designed specifically for worming and jigging, the advantage is in the hands of the modern soft bait fisherman. A longer rod facilitates the cast allowing for more distance, the space age materials add sensitivity, picks up slack line faster, controls the fish after the set, and also supplies a surer hook set. Couple all these pluses with use of braided line, and you have a more sensitive, no stretch, and less likely to break capabilities.

The pressure on the point of a single strong hook increases the possibility of driving the hook home on plastics and or jigs and makes it tougher for the fish to throw if the set is executed properly.

As for the most common question, "How do I know when I have a bite?" As soon as you feel anything different set the hook. Another explanation, when your bait feels it's been cut off, is moving sideways, or the ½ ounce rig feels like it now weighs two ounces, set the hook. When in doubt set the hook.

Jigs fall into a very similar category of presentation as do the family of soft plastics. Most often trailed by a chunk or craw, jigs are maneuvered very much the same as most plastic lures. Multiple rigging possibilities add to the charm and versatility of plastics.

The always popular Texas rig consists of a slip sinker—lead or tungsten—and a hook that balances the size of the worm or other soft bait. Suggestions: 3/0 hook for a seven-inch worm, a 5/0 hook to penetrate the bulk of a flipping tube. Worms, tubes, craws, creature baits, and lizards are among the lures that are fair game for being tossed in the Texas rig. The weight also controls the cast and the speed of fall on your lure. Carry ¼ ounce up to ¾ ounce sinkers in graduated weights to give you options. It's a good idea to have a small box dedicated to the soft plastic lures with various hook sizes and weights.

The Carolina rig for open water and finding fish, rigged wacky style for a slow drop and pressured bass, shakey head for stubborn, spooky fish, or the swimming worm for use around shallow cover—each have their fans and their place. Cast in and around cover in the form of boat docks, weed beds, downed trees, underwater stumps, bottom contours, points, creek channels, and just about anywhere there's enough water to hold a bass from six inches to 60 feet, the fantastic plastics produce. Because bass are object oriented there's hardly a place you can't cast plastic and expect to get a bass bite. Largemouth, spotted Kentucky bass, and smallmouth bass are all susceptible to a properly presented plastic. All of these components undeniably make a hard case for soft plastics.

29

Advanced Topwater Tips

The tap-tap signal of a bite on a plastic worm, the dead stop to a crankbait hit, the slam of a fast moving spinnerbait—yep, each one holds a special place in the heart of fishermen regardless of the region or water craft they drift in. But if you want to see excitement go from zero to crazy in a millisecond, watch and feel the explosion of a surface strike from almost any species of fish. I imagine a ten pound trophy bass busting a topwater bait. How about a 40 inch northern pike, or a giant tarpon spraying salt water everywhere? Any surface hit, even that of a trout or maybe a spawning hand sized bluegill makes for an instant memory and a fish tale. While there are an enormous amount of ways to fool a fish, there's no denying, topwater action has no parallel.

Most game fish relate to and use edges to migrate, but more important to seek out, chase, and catch food sources. While most people describe edges as the shoreline, a concrete sea wall, a creek channel, or a rip rap dam, seldom does anyone mention the surface as an edge category. The water's surface is the premier edge! When bass, as well as other species gang up and use the *wolf pack* method of following and then busting schools of baitfish, they are utilizing the edge in a way like no other. Pinning the bait to the surface produces what is popularly known as the *jumps*, schools of fish annihilating wads of shad and minnows. After being *herded* to the surface, the bait sources have nowhere to go. Similarly bass will push bait towards the shoreline creating the natural trap of a distinct edge. Make no mistake, edges—especially the surface—are crucial to fish behavior and their lifestyle.

Topwater fishing is effective for a number of reasons. At the top of topwater teasing is the fact that bass feed primarily by sight. Equipped with eyes that are superior to our own, bass have the advantage of discerning colors and light much better than their human predators. Sensing vibration and movement through the use of their lateral line—many fish have the same set up, the salty snook, etc.—you can add that to the list of appeal.

Bass also are blessed with exceptional hearing. From a physical perspective look at the natural tools of a largemouth bass. A camo color pattern, side set eyes, and a 270 degree field of vision, capable of a 15 mile per hour underwater burst of speed, and a mouth oriented to easily feed on things above them, and you have a topwater feeding machine.

Understanding the bass and its behavior positions you to take 'em from the top. Regardless of the food source, a fish inspects the potential meal. The longer it has to look, the more likely it is to snub an artificial because of the negative clues or the presentation errors by the angler. This is why live bait can be so deadly. Live, natural forage food gives no indication to being phony. They look, smell, taste, and swim like a normal meal.

To excel at topwater success, consider a few factors. The color in most instances makes more difference to the fish than the fisherman. In topwater most of the time the fish sees only the bottom of the bait and maybe a bit of the sides. The profile, actual shape of the bait can be important especially in low light, dawn, and dusk, or in muddy water. With a ton of baits to pick from, the most important factor, once you tie the bait to the end of the line and cast it out, is retrieve speed. The most overlooked and underappreciated factor in fishing success—retrieve speed. The ultimate in sealing the deal is making the lure look alive and easy to tack down and catch. In surface bassin' there are several ways to work a bait.

Advanced Topwater Tips

Here's a few: I love the take on a buzzbait. It ranges from a silent vortex and the buzzer disappearing, to a huge, aggressive bone jarring attack sending spray in every direction. My personal preference and what in my experience appears to be most effective is the slowest, steady retrieve that keeps the bait on the surface. Try casting past the fish, holding target, and bumping the buzzer into any cover to get a deflection strike. Edges of weed beds, submerged wood, around boat docks, and secondary cover all deserve a cast or two.

Cup-faced poppers—my favorite is the Strike King Spit-N-King in a color known as Oyster #584. Fished on 12-pound test monofilament with a Palomar knot pulled tight toward the bottom of the line tie—makes it spit more water—you cast it out, let all the ripples disappear, and begin with a downward snap of the rod, the bait will create a *bloop* sound and send water spitting around the area. Pause and repeat. Pre-spawn bass, summer schoolers, and fall feeding fish all can't resist this lure and presentation.

Dog Walkers are in a whole different category. The side-to-side action imparted strictly by the angler is accomplished with the use of a slack line downward snap. With a little work and some timing you can make the bait *walk* which brings bass from a distance to bust the two steppin' intruder. This bait is work and takes time to master but catches monster bass of all species.

An oldie but goodie from generations back is the Arbogast Jitterbug. A floater at rest, the shape of the lip creates a natural wobble and gurgling sound that bass have blasted for decades. A number one night time bait for any serious *after hours* angler is the black Jitterbug.

A minnow plug twitched across the top has been a lone forgotten tool of many bass fisherman. Considered antiquated and not sexy enough for today's bass caster, minnow imitating bait have caught—and given the chance—will continue to catch bass for as long as there are some swimming.

Open faced spinning outfits are an advantage for the twitch, pause, retrieve for plugs ranging from a diminutive two and a half inch model to the giant versions.

Not to be left out the fly flickers. With the introduction of the Jackson Kayak MayFly, bass should beware. Surface flies resembling mice, dragonflies, cicadas, frogs, and more are often fashioned from deer hair because it's hollow and is an exceptional floater and bass fooler.

Popping bugs and other cork-bodied flies are fun and hard to beat for fooling bass under many conditions.

You could easily argue the merits of many other surface skimming baits, colors, sizes, rods, reels, retrieves. With so many methods to fish and catch bass, everyone could make a case for their favorite, but for sheer fun and the visual excitement of a bragging size bass, topwater is tough to beat.

30

Big Bass Secrets

For the kayak angler that targets bass, very little evokes a higher adrenaline rush than the sight of a trophy bass at the end of their line. It's been said that, "10% of the fishermen catch 90% of the bass." While most folks just want to catch a limit or finish well in tournaments, there is a small legion of folks dedicated to fooling the superior of the species, trophy bass. While each angler has a certain system, many factors and facets of their approach intersect. The equipment, tactics, and search for bragging-size bass amounts to the collective details that make catching monster bass predictable and apply almost anywhere they swim.

Use your mental highlighter to follow the system that has produced several seasons of posing with bass that will make you the envy of all. Consider these suggestions, this collection of information and strategies, apply them in the hope that the next cast will, for you, fool that bass of a lifetime. And remember—the hard part is finding fish; it's easy to catch them. Eric Jackson, who has several largemouth bass over ten pounds to his credit, offers this insight, "I either find fish on my Ray Marine Dragonfly, to get the depth they are at, or simply go for the best looking spots and skip the others."

Know The Fish
Regardless of the quarry for any type of trophy hunter, it is critical

to position yourself for success by knowing as much about their intended target as possible. Open your mind—don't be distracted by *dock talk* or many of the theories presented in all forms of media. A combination of experience, the willingness to experiment, and common sense is a great start to developing your own system to find and fool bigger bass.

A quick look at the major species of bass—largemouth, smallmouth and Spotted (Kentucky) bass—clues you into the predatory nature of bass. A natural camouflage coloration specific to each helps them blend in when necessary. They are clearly ambush predators and eating machines, able to track down their food sources with underwater burst of speed up to 15 miles per hour, equipped with a massive mouth that will swallow anything that they find in their world, and senses that assist in feeding and surviving the underwater world they inhabit. An in-depth look also shows rows of gripping, gristle like teeth and gill rakers that help bass retain their catch. They will follow bait fish, strike from behind, and instinctively turn the forage as to not become choked by the shad, bluegill, crappie, or other gamefish that will flares its dorsal fin and consequently possibly get lodged in the thorax (throat) of the bass and thereby dooming it.

Take Their Temperature

Water temperature, generally communicated as surface temperature, will dictate predictable location and other lifestyle events of bass. Species specific ranges exist for each bass type. For example the spawning mode is determined by a few degrees for each type. Smallmouths go first at the high 50 degree mark into the low 60s, next the spots when the water reaches around 60 degrees, and then the most widely distributed largemouth bass at the mid 60s.

Similarly the amount of active feeding is stair-stepped at different temperatures. More importantly at the ideal rate, 70-80 degrees Fahrenheit, the temperature creates a direct correlation to the digestive rate of bass. Feeding frequency and metabolic rate is dramatically impacted by the ability of fish to find, eat, and completely digest any of their food sources. For example, a five-pound bass in 78 degree water can digest a five-inch shad in about six hours. The same bass and same size shad in 40 degree water takes five days to completely digest. The obvious conclusion is that bass should be easier to catch when they have to feed more often. Bass, as all wild creatures, are slaves to their stomachs.

Making Sense of Senses
The eyes have it! Bass feed almost completely by sight. With eyes set at the side of their heads and field of vision at around 270 degrees, bass see extremely well. The eyes of all bass are great at discriminating color because of a multitude of rods and cones, similar but more developed than most other creatures including humans. Keep in mind a fish closely visually scrutinizes something prior to deciding to *hit*.

The sense of hearing is well developed in bass. Although many manufacturers and anglers choose lures heavily loaded with noise making devices, sound can be a negative influence on bass. Water is a great conductor of sound. Sound travels through water five times faster than through air. Spooky fish and older bass can be conditioned to retreat from certain sounds.

Another myth is that bass are highly intelligent, they have a brain about half the size of a hazel nut—tiny. They don't *learn* in the true sense of the word—they become conditioned.

A popular marketing tactic is to tout the appeal of scent in bass lures. Unfortunately bass have limited olfactory senses. Later in life, at five to eight years, sense of smell does slightly increase but not to the point that bass find their food using smell as a huge factor.

When it comes to taste the application of common sense quickly dispels the myth that bass hit a bait because of how it tastes. They may in fact hold on longer because of taste especially salt impregnated baits. Blood has salt in it, so it is not a foreign taste to bass. Logically bass hit something because of how it looks—remember, feeds by sight—and how it moves. Reality check: think about it, when it tastes something, it already has the object in its mouth! Set the hook!

Lesson one, now you know what makes the bass tick and the lifestyle of America's favorite gamefish.

Trophy Tip: To avoid spooking bass, go into *ninja stealth mode*. Fish with the sun in your face as to not cast a shadow on the fish you are trying to catch, use the wind and current to position your kayak, learn the underhand pitch cast to increase your accuracy and minimize lure splash upon entry, wear clothes that blend in with the sky and shoreline cover.

31

Between and a Dock and a Hard Place

There are numerous variables in the world—the outdoor world included. Water color, temperature, sky color, wind velocity and direction, water levels, and more all create a complex puzzle for the fish and fisherman. Conscious decisions can lead you to more fish of various species and maybe a trophy. One of the keys to a successful day on the water is a pre-trip game plan and making adjustments. Experience, experimentation, and a large dose of common sense can lead you to a tournament win, a trophy bass, or a couple of fish for the skillet.

Yes, selective harvest is acceptable. The smallest legal fish and no more than you can consume in a meal are my recommendations.

Three likely areas are boat docks, rock, or submerged wood. All offer cover and are potential hideouts for bass and bait. With the changes you are likely to face, a couple of minor changes could make a major difference in your day. In some bodies of water, boat docks have the potential to harbor seasonally resident fish. If there are baitfish, insect, frogs, crawfish, and small gamefish available ,bass have no reason to leave. Food, cover, and possibly a deep water escape route pretty much ensures a fish or two. As for rock, multiple factors make rocks a great target for casting your fishing lures. Rock radiates heat for comfort and fish egg incubation during spawning seasons. It is also a good home for crawfish. Wood offers potential food supply and superior hiding/ambush spots.

Work boat docks and fishing piers from all angles. Practice tossing baits under the piers and posts. Don't be surprised if you develop a mini-pattern such as three feet of water on the shady side. You might also find bass on docks with wooden piers. Wood grows algae, which in turn draws bait who eat the algae, and so the cycle begins. Fish of other sizes come in, and bass feast on both the smaller bait fish and the larger forage. In the winter, docks with concrete piers warm up faster, retain and radiate heat. This fact is important to the comfort of the bass and also pulls food sources to the immediate area. Rock is spread by people around lake sites to battle erosion. It is also found naturally in many places. Early spring warmer water temperatures around rock are bass and bait magnets. Couple places frequented by bass with the ever changing weather and water conditions, and you could be in for a memorable day.

A key comment to catching bass in neutral or even negative feeding moods is deflection. Armed with this knowledge consider the crankbait. Don't forget everything you knew previously about cranking lures. Do consider the performance of the bait. While they can be cast and retrieved with some sporadic success, they also are tools for certain situations. Square billed crankbaits are super successful for bass in and around cover. The shape of the bill will cause the bait to hit and deflect with infrequent hang ups. The collision with the cover, deflection, and start up draws many, many hits from fish of all sizes. Yes, you'll lose some baits, but the results will offset the cost of reloading your crankbait box. A 6 ½ to 7 foot rod with some *give* in the tip, a bait casting reel spooled with 12 to 16-pound test monofilament is my choice of set up. The softer tip lets the fish take the bait and sink the hook as they move off.

Another favorite deflection lure is the spinnerbait. Cast 'em to cover, bounce them off docks, rocks, and tree limbs to call bass from cover to strike the startled intruder. As wind picks up, sky darkens, or water muddies up, change style or size of blades. Adding a skirt that matches the conditions is another favorite trick. A small supply of different color skirts is beneficial for the angler willing to make adjustments. Short arm spinners are deadly. When you reel and *kill* the lure and let it drop, it causes the blade to helicopter down. This is a great imitation of an injured or dying shad. Try the docks, rocks, and downed trees and hang on.

You can also use your cranking outfit effectively to work your spinnerbaits. A few different blade configurations will position you to fish the different water and weather condition you may encounter.

Don't get stuck between a dock and a hard place.

32

Until Depth Do Us Part

Spring fishing is almost too easy. Just reach into your tackle box and throw it to the shoreline and reel 'em in. After the winter when fish of species slow down and feed less frequently, they move into the shallows and eat everything in sight. Add to that the preparation for spawning, commonly known as the pre-spawn, which occurs at 55 to 62 degrees. Now fish of all types eat at every opportunity. During the bass spawn, approximately 62 to 68 degrees, fish go into protection mode and guard their nests. They do not eat. Obviously after the completion of the spawn they are ravenously hungry, and because they are exhausted, they move off to deeper water and in many cases suspend, just feeding when they can. You might say to the previously successful shallow water kayak anglers, until *depth* do us part.

Where did they go? Casting to the spring spots might produce a fish or two but can be frustrating. Post-spawn fish, suspended fish, deep water inhabitants are some of the hardest to catch. When you do find them you can fire up a school and have a memorable fishing experience.

Time to use your electronics, visual scanning, common sense, and a little instinct. Bass are still object oriented and will migrate to specific objects and bottom contours or distinct changes. Some of the same baits used in early spring might still work, but a few different choices might add up to lots of kayak catches. Easily one of the most critical keys to catching deep water bass is putting the bait in—and keeping it in—the strike zone for as long as possible. Baits in this category include but are not limited to crankbaits—lipped and lipless, jerkbaits, spinnerbaits, drop shot rigs, and some soft plastic lures. My first choice is the crankbait. Previously I've had a love/hate relationship with the cranks. Hooking many bass while crankin' but not being able to land them was frustrating.

Going deep. Retrieving the bait in a controlled level even with or above the suspended bass is important—it creates a normal attack position for the fish to *rise to the occasion*. There are multiple ways to accomplish this. Once determined what depth the fish are found through the assistance of electronics or trial and error, you can use the rod position—tip up, shallower or tip down, deeper—to change the depth reached by a crankbait. Another potential depth determination is by changing the line. I prefer monofilament in the range of 12 to 14-pound test. You can easily change the diving capability of a crankbait by utilizing a simple change of line. Simply stated, a line change to a smaller diameter line ten-pound test will drive the bait deeper. A heavier, larger diameter line will make the bait ride higher.

Looking at the plastic bill of the bait gives you strong indication of how deep it will dive. Coupled with the information normally printed on the packaging, and you have a great start. Hard jerkbaits are made to suspend slowly or rise slowly. Bass have a hard time ignoring something that stays in front of them for an extended period of time. Jerkbaits excel in cold, clear water or when bass seem reluctant to bite. With soft plastics, worms, tubes, creature baits, grubs, and other bogus wigglers you can control the speed of the fall and the retrieve. The fall is determined by the amount of weight used with the bait. For Texas rigged plastics, a slip sinker varying from a tiny $1/16$ to a full ounce of lead will change the descent of the lure. Line size and lure size will also contribute to the fall rate. Drop shot rigs have the weight tied to the end of the line so it aids in casting and the rate of fall, but after that the weight stays close to or is just used to drag and make continuous contact with the bottom.

The weight of a spinnerbait will figure into the fall, but the anglers retrieve will definitely decide how deep in the water column the lure travels. In lieu of electronics, a good pair of polarized sunglasses are very helpful A pre-trip game plan can also minimize choices but maximize your casting time. Fill the tackle box compartments with lures that cover water quickly, search baits, crankbaits, and spinners. While bait colors matter, they take a distant second place to putting any bait in the zone and retrieving the lure to make it look injured, easy to catch, or like the real deal.

Likely hideouts are objects like submerged wood or setups which are a great for the *deflection* bite, that is intentionally bouncing the bait off of cover. Bass find it hard to turn down a bait that hits and deflects off any type of hard cover. Creek channels are great when fish are in transition for any reason. Essentially a bass highway, creek channels serve as travel areas for bass and bait. To pattern deep water bass, you must be alert to minute details. They can be like the famous Kentucky Lake ledge fish where a solid pattern emerges, or they could just as probably be on the channel break. Inside bends or outside bends could also be in play.

Other potential honey holes are points. Very much a possible pattern, points can go from a long, minimal dropping grade to a steep drop into the specific body of water. Highland reservoirs are notorious for this fast falling topographical phenomenon. Isolated cover in the form of aquatic weeds is a gold mine when early season bass relocate to beds of coontail moss, hydrilla, cabbage weed, or other greenery. The oxygen, ambush point, and cover created are made to order for bass and the informed angler.

While cruising the shoreline in search of fish is more comfortable to the infrequent angler, abandon the bank and look for the first type of secondary cover that might hold fish. Deep fish being schoolers means you can catch several fish from one spot much like the offshore bonanza you can find in the fall. Fewer *thin* water bass requires moving to deeper areas because very predictably fish take on the attitude, *if you want to find me it is in accepting the commitment we are now at a relationship status defined with the statement, "until depth do us part."*

33

Master Muddy Water

You can be sure, regardless of where you live or cast your favorite bait, at some time you will be faced with fishing muddy water. To soften the description of muddy water, it is termed discolored or murky, but the truth is it's flat out muddy. I call it just too wet to plow. It can be intimidating when you prepare to launch and spot water that delivers inches of visibility. I've learned to love muddy water.

Stop and think about it. If I had to choose between gin clear and *off* color, I'll take the stained water every time. Because I frequent moving waters, I also realize that strong current often accompanies those dark waters. I do not compromise safety when deciding where to paddle and pitch my baits at fish. But the current does give strong clues as to where the fish will stage. Almost any type of gamefish will avoid current.

Finding fish in *dirty* water can be accomplished in a few ways. First—setting up behind natural or man-made elements that redirect or deflect current. Bridge pilings, docks, rocks, fallen trees, points ,and aquatic weeds all fall into the category of structure that fish will gravitate to in stronger current. Fish may also go to deeper haunts where the flow is minimized and wait for the flow to calm down before returning to regular spots. In lakes of almost any size, murky water will bring lots of bass to the shallows. Once in *thin* water, they will still set up around objects—stumps, weeds, wood, and any cover are likely hideouts. The discolored waters allow for a close up encounter with fish. With limited sense of sight you can get close to present your best bait choices.

To prepare to battle bass in the low visibility conditions, I look at baits that appeal to the dirty water sense of gamefish, in my case mostly bass. Because bass primarily feed by sight, I use lures that are heavily loaded with visual capabilities and will also occasionally employ sound chambers on jigs or cranking baits. I remain a fan of subtlety and know that bass sense the presence of life in the water with sight, sound, and the use of the lateral line which telegraphs vibration.

Unless you are targeting catfish, forget about that overrated sense of smell in the black bass species. Limited sight also means the strike zone of fish is diminished in muddy water conditions. Now is not the time for tiny finesse jigs and scaled down lures. First for me, because I'm a jig addict, is the large profile of a full size jig, probably ⅜ to a ½ ounce model depending on the current and a regular crawfish trailer. My first choice is the Strike King Denny Brauer Structure Jig in watermelon red flake. I trail the jig with the Rage Tail Craw in 229 Roadkill color. In the dirtiest of water I will opt for the Ratlin Pro-Model Jig for the sound making capabilities. Texas Craw # 8 has a little shot of chartreuse that adds to the visibility. Another color that has produced over the decades is black/blue.

Don't discount soft plastics. I have had great success with a 4.5 Flip-N-Tube black neon #38 Texas rigged and worked around heavy cover. I use the same rod I would for jig fishing, and standard set up is a ⅜ ounce slip sinker and the bait rigged on a 5/0 Daiichi copperhead hook. For multiple fish sense appeal, a spinnerbait is a great choice. The most obvious pick on the spinner is the willow leaf versions. In the dirtiest water, a double willow is your friend. The willow blades produce the maximum amount of flash and the most fish for me. I prefer to toss the gold/nickel combination so the fish can pick the color they are most attracted to. The bluegill skirt color #234 or straight black #210 offers the most contrast making it the most visible in the dark water conditions. To be flat out evil, throw a single Colorado black-skirted spinnerbait that's normally reserved for night fishing. You throw it for exactly the same reason as you would after daylight hours. The heavy vibration, noise making capabilities of rattles, and bright colors bring you to the lipless crankbait. The Red Eye shad, again from Strike King, in color #419 fire tiger is good, as is the #451 Rayburn Red Craw.

I like the weight of any good size boat for stability, and they're less effected by moving water. It stays in place a little better for me. Another plus is the ability to stand and fish when working the highly colored waters.

Casting accuracy is at a premium in muddy water because of the smaller strike zone. I rarely use open face spinning in muddy water situations. My choice for baitcasting equipment is Lew's. The Lew's line of reels are dependable, and there is a model and a gear retrieve ratio that fits all my styles of fishing. I've also found that a slower steady makes more sense and consistently produces more fish that are relying on their ability to find the bait under adverse conditions. Working cover from all angles especially on the jigs and soft plastics is advisable.

Don't be intimidated by water color. You can master muddy water!

34

A Big Fishing Challenge—New Spots

Many outdoorsmen are creatures of habit like the quarry they seek. Hunting deer, turkey, casting for bass, crappie, or other gamefish, they go to the same spots and do the same things. Why? Because it's worked in the past, it's comfortable, and it doesn't require a lot of risk or exploration, and in some cases it reproduces results. What happens when you are challenged by new water or woods? *Uh oh, my playground has changed, I'm outside of my comfort zone.* Relax, there's a cure for your anxiety.

After several seasons on the water and trudging through forest and fields, I can assure you new spots do not spell disaster. When fishing and faced with an unfamiliar body of water, I immediately start looking for similar circumstances from fishin' holes of the past. I try to maintain my same mindset—look at the depth, cover, and any condition that might produce a few fish and help establish a pattern for repeatable results. Regardless of your outdoor pursuit, take a deep breath, look around, tap into your memory bank, and start making applications using the similarities that you recognize.

Gazing at the water, is there any visible submerged wood, any aquatic vegetation, boat docks, rock structure, or points? Each type of cover is a potential fish holding habitat regardless of geographic location. I've found the same results, using the same criteria all across North America. Spending more than 25 summers guiding in Canada, making the transition to smallmouth and walleye water

A Big Fishing Challenge—New Spots

was a bit of a daunting task. Solution—fish the flow or current, go to the points, irregular shoreline features, and offshore structure. All this was done without the aid of electronics. Water color, water temperature, moon phase, and wind direction all play a part in determining fish location and feeding mode.

Fish are not hard to catch—they're harder to find.

Look shallow first. Shallow fish are there to spawn—for a limited time—or to feed. Faced with fishing massive waters? If you find yourself on a 10,000-acre lake, treat it like 10,000 one-acre farm ponds. Most everybody has fished a small farm pond. Don't be intimidated by the size of the water. If you're casting for bass, arm yourself with two or three rods, a baitcaster or two, a spinning rod, and a few tackle boxes—the Plano #3600 is ideal—containing baits that fit the location. If you're in a shallow impoundment, think minnow-imitating hard baits in shad patterns, ⅜ ounce willow/Colorado and single bladed spinnerbaits, medium diving crankbaits (something that can get you down to 4-10 feet), a few jigs, ⅜ to ¾ ounce and accessories to Texas rig soft plastics. Each of these categories of baits allows you to effectively work the water columns—shallow, mid-level, and deep. In cold clear water, a few jerkbaits; waters loaded with cover, a buzzbait and some popper type lures. Carry a few light and dark color lure selections, a spool of 12-pound test line which is pretty universal in its use, pliers, and the standard equipment you use on your normal outings.

Be prepared to do a little *junk* fishing. Go with rods rigged with a few different lures and try a few casts with each in search mode. Watch for natural signs including shoreline activities, shorebirds looking for minnows, bug hatches, fish feeding from the surface, and anything that gives a specific clue as to what the fish are doing and feeding on creating a natural transition to bait choice and retrieve speeds. Be acutely aware of the first fish. Note what depth and kind of water did it came from, the cover type, or man-made structures. What bait did it hit? Was there any clue that would lead to a pattern? All these add up to all day action. Be prepared as in any case for condition changes that might also change the bite, including but not limited to wind direction, cloud cover, rain, or anything else which may call for a tactical switch. Experiment, vary your presentations, look for similar conditions and rely on your memory and natural instincts. With any outdoor activity, under tough circumstances including unfamiliar territory, reduce variables to their lowest common denominator.

Use the wind to position your boat into the most desirable locations. Sitting or standing make small paddle adjustments to compensate for current, wind, or drift. In short, do the same things that play to your strength and have created success in the past. Vacation, stay-cation, or exploring in search of new water and unpressured fish, lean on essentially doing the same things, in the same type of areas, just in new spots.

Guide Tip: When rigging soft plastics with curly tails, turn the tail opposite to the bend in the hook or leadhead. Otherwise the hook acts as a keel, breaks the water flow, and minimizes the motion and action of the tail.

35

Smallmouth Bass—Why and How to Catch 'em

Bass fishermen talk a great game. Each can make a case for why they love to catch the black bass. For the most part there exists three popular species of bass—largemouth, spotted, and smallmouth. The lion's share of the publicity and interest goes to the largemouth bass. Primarily because of the availability of largemouth, they are wide spread, and geographically you don't have to far to find a body of water in which they swim. Spotted or Kentucky bass are found in many of the same waters. The last major species is the smallmouth, their range is a little more limited, but in the areas they are found, they are highly regarded and sought after. The ferocity with which they hit and fight is unbelievable. The smallmouth is reclusive, revered, and sometimes repulsive for their elusiveness and their reluctance to hit an artificial bait

Fun and Frustrating
Smallmouth bass are found in highland lakes, generally deep and clear. They are also in several impoundments all around the Mason-Dixon line. The northern states as well as Canada also maintain a decent population of *brown bass*. Native to rivers and streams, the *smallies* found in moving water are muscular and tricky. While a five-pound largemouth is the object of attention, a five-pound smallmouth is the envy of every other devoted angler. Tie a five-pound smallmouth to the tail of a five-pound largemouth, and

it would drag it backwards for two miles! Smallmouths are built for speed and power. With an aerodynamic profile, broad across the back, and a tail that resembles a boat paddle they are built to be strong, lightening quick, and have the ability to chase down any food source.

Largemouth, spots, and smallmouth all have diverse lifestyles. In some cases inhabiting the same lakes and rivers, they eat some of the same things but spawn at different times, prefer different locations as well as temperatures, and relate to objects and depths in various ways. Largemouth will spawn at water temperatures in the middle 60s, at that point most smallmouth are done with reproduction for the season. They go on bed as water reaches the high 50s, and spots are somewhere in between. It is also appropriate to point out that none of the fish all do the same thing at the same time regardless of species and size.

As far as food sources, all bass have a size mouth made to accommodate just about anything that they encounter. Primarily feeding on the most abundant forage, shad or indigenous minnows, they will still eat from the wide menu available that includes frogs, snakes, all sorts of bugs, and at the top of their list, the bass' candy is crawfish. Whereas a largemouth bass relates to shallower water and cover, smallmouth love deeper water hangouts. Suffice to say a 15-foot ledge or a hump in 20 feet of water is the same as a stump in six foot to a largemouth.

The single biggest mistake most anglers make is trying to force largemouth tactics on smallmouth bass. Abandon the bank, as uncomfortable as it is, and move to deeper water structure to find and catch smallmouth consistently. The one exception to this rule would be small stream and river fish. They relate to moving water and will position themselves predictably in eddies and current breaks to wait for the flow of water *and* food to be delivered to them. High, muddy water makes things tough—gin clear water isn't much better. Are you starting to get the picture? Ideal conditions are some color in the water, a slight breeze to make a chop on the surface, and being on a major moon phase doesn't hurt either. Because smallmouth can be spooky, a stealthy approach is very desirable.

Tackle and Techniques for Smallmouth
First and foremost get over the idea the smallmouth bass are anything like a largemouth. They do some things that are remotely similar, but they are two very different creatures. Not recognizing the difference is why most people struggle with the transition between catching these two bass species. The same way largemouth relate to objects, smallmouth relate to deep water. The diets of both are similar but different in what is available. Given the choice, crawfish is the preferred forage, but shad are more available and hence become a large part of their diet.

Outfitting yourself for tangling with smallmouth bass is a bit of a different proposition. The most effective rig is a six foot spinning rod, spooled with 6 to 8-pound test line, and a small assortment of leadhead jigs and curly tail grubs. A sure way to catch these fish is to cast out a grub and swim it back. Most people over work an artificial bait. Allow the bait to do the work, and it's almost magic how it produces strikes. My choices for sizes and colors are simple, leadheads in 1/8, 1/4, and 3/8 ounce and grubs in pearl, smoke/glitter, pumpkin, pepper, and chartreuse. The size of the jig head and the color of the lure are predicated by the amount of wind and the water color respectively. No breeze—lightweight jig and neutral color grub. More wind—heavier head and brighter curly tail bait.

Conventional bass baits will catch smallmouth also. Crankbaits lipped and lipless both catch their share of deep water fish, as will spinnerbaits in all configurations as well as topwater lures including poppers, buzzbaits, dog walking plugs, and minnow imitators. Rods and reels will be much like the gear used for largemouth. I prefer a 6 ½ foot medium action rod with a quality baitcasting reel and line in the 12 to 16-pound test range. Lighter line in some cases produces more hits, but smallmouth will test your drag, the line, the knot, and your ability to properly play fish. Drop shot rigs are also an excellent way to coax *smallies*.

Big smallmouths are tough to fool and get into the boat. Don't be lulled into thinking that bigger baits are not good for trophy smallmouth. My best fish have come on large spinnerbaits, the afore mentioned buzzbaits, and magnum size crankbaits. Keep in mind the soft plastic grubs will, day in—day out, produce numbers of these heavy hitting bass, but if your sight are set on a wall hanger, try large lures and be prepared to fish all day for three or four bites.

36

Get Right to the Point

You've been waiting for this—you launch your boat and head out. You have your favorite baits tied on, and you head straight to the bank because that's what you always do. I refer to it as a *milk run*. But today nobody is home—no bites, no activity. It could be a weather extreme; too hot, too cold, but no fish. Now what?

Quit messing around. Let's get right to the point.

- **Depth Change**—It could be in a two-acre pond or a sprawling 20,000-acre lake. Points hold fish. Depth changes allow the fish to stage in an area that could be holding a food supply and offer relief from the heat or boat/fishing pressure and give them access to an escape route. One of the four basic tenets of the lifestyle of largemouth bass is deep water close by points are perfect for this element of bass behavior. By the nature of a point, it puts its inhabitants in close proximity deep water. To bass deep water means a safety security blanket. Smallmouth bass are even more drawn to points because they relate to deep water as largemouth does to objects. Smallmouth love points as do the sub-species, spotted Kentucky bass. A point can go from a foot of water to 22 feet of water in a blink and under the best of conditions will hold a giant school of fish.
- **Which is the Best**—Because of the wide variety of places you can find a point, there can be certain ones that are the

most desirable. A compass reading gives you a clue as to why. You can choose a reason and a season to pick which points. In a south wind, bait will be pushed to the point. In a north wind and cold front, bass will shield themselves on one a side of the point. When barometric pressure changes, another advantage bass can abandon a spot quickly when staged on points. This is much more difficult on a long flat. Bass like to minimize the amount of time and water they have to cover to fulfill the other three factors of their lifestyle—oxygen, food, and cover. The correct points have each of these criteria. Points with weeds, submerged wood, or rock are potential honey holes. Depth and cover can create a very repeatable pattern on points.

- **On Point Baits**—Points are a perfect set up for the three major pattern type baits—crankbaits, spinners, and my personal favorite, *feel type* soft plastic baits—jigs, grubs, tubes, worms, and craws. Whether gently sloping points or dramatic drop-offs, certain baits excel at this kind of very specific bass fishing. Crankbaits can be used, but a slow retrieve to a moderate return is important to follow the contour of the specific point. This also allows for the bottom-bumping, deep-diving bait that draws the attention of crawfish hungry bass. Long casts and smaller diameter line are crucial to keep the bait in the zone. Spinnerbaits can be used similarly knowing you are trying to keep the bait in the vicinity of the feeding fish, but slow rolling the spinner of the deep water fish is effective too. Many anglers camp out on points in the dead of winter because the shad stage there. This is where a jigging spoon and a vertical presentation is deadly. Swimming a curly tail grub, pearl or smoke silver glitter, is another popular choice. My personal favorite is the jig. Scraping the bottom or swimming the bait back, jigs are the most likely scenario to fooling an off-shore monster residing on the point. The pick-up may be so subtle, especially during extremely hot or cold water conditions, it's almost undetectable, or they may bash it like a piñata at a kid's birthday party. On any points from depths of one to 12 feet, don't be afraid to toss a topwater, a dog walking lure, or a buzzbait. These have produced big bites for me in the dead of summer and in the middle of the day.

- **Don't Just Parallel Points**—Most bass anglers do the same thing when they're fishing points. They paddle or troll up and start casting from the shallow shore portion to the deepest part of the point, this might work, but you have options. Think and fish differently than others, and you may also connect with a heavyweight bass by casting across the point as opposed to paralleling points. You can pattern a specific depth and move to similar depths on other points and catch several fish on the same body of water. A big plus is structure on a point. Largemouth bass will relate to this almost any time of the year. Rock, submerged wood, bottom contours, even composition can make a great spot.

Some of the biggest bass I've caught have been pulled off points in lakes and rivers. Look for these places not in times of desperation but as you scout new water. They are found everywhere. You can find them in any size lake, river, or highland impoundments. Points are overlooked and underutilized hot spots for bass. Get the point?

37

Spring Statistical Strategy

In some areas of life it's all about the numbers. In some aspects of life, numbers are our friends. In the world of computers, there exists a data crunching factor that drives people to make decisions. By my own nature, I think there are details that lead to success in the form of predictability and repeatability. Interpreting data and knowing how and when to use it is also critical. I formulate game plans on data and then allow my senses to take over and guide me. Placement of a tree stand, when to fish (no—seriously), and other outdoor adventures are sometimes statistical driven. For example, historically my best month for sheer numbers of fish is April. I don't fish more often, but bass and crappie are preparing for the spawn in my area, and they are feeding ravenously. Often and predictably big bass come to the boat in the fall. October, November, and weather conditions cooperating, the first part of December produces trophy size fish also. I believe at least in the southeast, "everything has to eat in October." There is a diary affectionately known as *Joey's Journal* where I scribble notes about each trip, and this document has become the bass bible for me. Numbers, sizes, and types of fish caught, weather and water conditions, and what they hit all are memorialized on the pages of this small tablet.

In nationwide studies, statistically it shows that 60% of trophy size bass—in my view over five pounds—come from lakes, ponds account for 35%, and rivers 5%. The dangers of statistical studies are the lack of assumptions that may not accompany them. Do most anglers fish lakes? What about the river system lakes? Are they *really* lakes, or dammed up river system waters? What constitutes a pond? Would it be less than 25 acres? Are there studies that show the hours of time dedicated to chasing bass on each type of water? What about the best of the *big* bass foolers? What magic baits are most likely to coax a bass to say, *Ah*?

Another study generated these results; an equal amount of big bass ate soft plastic lures and crankbaits—33%. Which shape and description of plastics, worms, craws, tubes, swimbaits, etc.? Twenty percent were caught on live bait—which itself is a wide range of choices. Could that be minnows, nightcrawlers, crickets, frogs, grasshoppers, leeches? Finally lures described as spinners accounted for 12%. So is that in-line, safety pin, double willow leaf?

Now to that sixth sense that separates the outdoorsmen from the average person. A quick look, a feel for the conditions, even tapping into historical achievement might come into play now. In my won experience, it's rare for me not to have a jig rod in my hand regardless of water color, temperature, or time of year. The majority of my braggin' size bass fell for a jig worked in and around cover. As far as my fishing destinations, I've done it all. I love rivers because for me, "there's magic in moving waters."

When visiting a major lake, especially a new body of water, I go to what looks familiar. Creeks, boat docks, rip-rap dams, aquatic weed beds, submerged wood, shoreline cover, and more all draw me in for a close-up jig pitch. Tied onto other rods are a minnow plug, a ⅜ ounce willow/Colorado spinnerbait, in water over 50 degrees a buzzbait, and probably a Texas rigged tube or plastic worm. It's my belief I can go anywhere and catch bass on these lures. It's all about making adjustments to the current conditions and doing what you know best.

A key to any good day is *first fish*. You can tell more about what might lead you to a predictable pattern. Your personal style of fishing is also critical. Never having been a numbers guy, I target

Spring Statistical Strategy

Big bass waters, Big bass tackle, and Big bass tactics. When the question is posed to me by someone, "Why don't I ever catch any big bass? "My immediate question is, "Do big bass live there?"

Water quality, food supply, and genetics all play a part in developing and maintaining a *big* bass fishery. Another facet of spring fishing success is the moon phase. Often overlooked or minimized by nonbelievers, the moon matters. Lots of state, world, fresh, and saltwater fishing catch records can be researched and verified as being within the three days before or after the new or full moon phases.

Let common sense guide you in your search for fish. Where would they be, and why would they be there? Most fish are in specific places for very specific reasons. Oxygen, food, and cover are bass magnets. The effect of these is dramatically increased during warming or warm weather months. When you find two kinds of cover in close proximity, you you've hit the jackpot. Aquatic weeds and wood for example pull and hold bass. Casting to these spots doesn't ensure catching fish, but once you find the correct depth for your the lure and presentation, you can go to similar spots and test out the theory of repeatable results.

The statistics are interesting and make good reading as well as research, but I never advocate separating yourself from your senses. Stats are a good starting point, and there certainly is some truth in the information. Trust your judgment, past experience, and your intuition. When you do realize success, consider releasing your big bass to continue the gene pool. Also in a handy personal reference book, consider keeping a fishing diary to allow you to create your own statistical data.

38

Night Stalkers—The Night Bite

During daylight hours on public waters the scene is hectic to say the least. Watercraft of all sizes and descriptions are powered with big engines. Jet skis roar around, wakes, water activity, and the sounds of summer are all evident. To avoid the lake or river traffic and the heat, consider an after-hours adventure. Everything that bites during the day will hit at night. Catfish, crappie, bass, trout, walleye, and others are all susceptible to the night bite.

There is a certain amount of mystery and apprehension for fishing folks to venture out after dark. For years my only opportunity to fish was mostly at night. I enjoyed the solitude after sunset and having the waters mostly to myself. Generally my only company were bats, owls, and a bunch of bass. From a safety standpoint, the list includes wearing a life jacket, carrying a cell in a dry box or even a freezer bag, a reliable light source, extra clothes to accommodate current and possible weather conditions, plus a detailed plan of fishing location and departure time communicated to someone. Being able to see is important, more important is being seen. I have a visi-pole that has a battery-powered light to make my presence known to other boaters.

Now let's hit the water. I assemble smaller tackle boxes like the Plano #3600 for seasonal trips, various techniques, and species specific tackle kits. But I also have a tackle box dedicated to night time treks for bass. Understanding the difference in day and night plus factoring in the natural sensory capabilities of the bass goes a long way to getting your *string stretched*. Built for battle and feeding machines, largemouth bass inherently come with apex predator skills including eyesight, detecting vibration, and hearing. Don't underestimate the senses of the bass. While there is a place for the noisy baits making a ruckus, subtle baits and approaches are a great idea for hanging into a heavyweight.

While I'm a fan of working the shallow water in the evening, don't discount the fact that in deep, clear highland reservoirs bass can be found in deeper water. The shallow fish seems to be more in attack mode, but because of the cover of darkness, fish move freely in almost any type of water. Bumping the bottom, working mid-level areas, or taking from the top are all options.

Rods, Rigs and Baits—Choosing the appropriate tackle is relatively simple for night time fishing forays. Color selection… black. Oh you can throw the old dark grape-colored worm you grew up with, but the goal is to create a silhouette that can be seen by the fish. Because the fish is looking up it is easier to lock in on the darker shades of lures, black being the best. A little research will reveal the eyes of a bass collect light five times better than that of its greatest natural predator, man—or woman. Playing to this, consider the subtle approach for the underwater hunter. A seven inch straight tail or curly tail worm Texas rigged works everywhere a bass swims in the evening. Looking for a giant, you can upsize to a foot long plastic worm and increase your chances of catching a midnight monster.

My worm rig starts with a slip sinker, most likely $3/8$ ounce, followed by a red plastic bead then, attached with a Palomar knot, a 4/0 Daiichi copperhead hook. The sinker weight makes casting pretty easy and allows for a slow descent into the darkness. The beads primary job is to protect the knot from the sliding sinker and make a clicking noise when struck between the lead sinker and the hook. The 4/0 hook works well with soft plastics ranging from the worms, crawfish imitators, lizards, and tubes, all of which earn a spot in your night tackle totes. I prefer to cast my soft plastics on a seven and a half foot medium/heavy action rod with a Lews' baitcasting reel geared at 6.3:1 spooled with 30-pound braided line.

If you arrive prior to dusk, it's easier for your eyes to adjust to the change in light. Another advantage is tossing one of my favorite lures, the buzzbait. I go big on the buzzer, largest blade I've got and even the black bladed models to draw bass from a distance. The strike on this bait will be heart stopping. It's a big bass technique.

Another baitcaster, seven feet long, medium action, same reel and retrieve speed, and 16-pound test monofilament is my choice. The same rod and reel works well for slinging spinnerbaits. I modify my nighttime spinners. I like the ⅜ ounce version, mainly because you develop a hand feel for the same weight bait, and during the dark part of the trip it makes it more comfortable and accurate to use the same weight. I change the blade if necessary, but the Strike King Lure Company does offer the black blade on a few of their models such as Tour Grade Night Spinnerbait and Midnight Specials, and I prefer the short arm spinners for more solid hook ups.

A.C. Shiners, a small company out of Ohio, offers a black minnow plug that works well—with this I would suggest a 6 ½ foot spinning combo, and traditionally everyone that ventures out at night carries a black Arbogast Jitterbug. As you can tell, night fishing for bass requires more nerve than tackle. A small tackle box, three or four rods, and a few accessories will do nicely.

Hooked on after hour's bass fishing, I once pushed a canoe out on the Canadian wilderness area known as the Quetico. Upon my return I relived my trip with the outfitters and friends at Canoe Canada. He looked at me and said, "We've never had anybody go out at night, weren't you scared?"

My response, "Just another page in *Joey's Journal of Fishing Adventures.*"

Give a try. Be a night stalker.

39

Fishing Apps—Common Sense Clues For Big Bass

Too often people seek technology for a common sense problem. I describe it as, "separating yourself from your senses." There's an app for that, it's called *real world common sense solutions*. Shut off your iPhone, iPad, and other electronic devices. When used in conjunction with electronic aids, your natural cognitive abilities will have you hooking big bass before you can reboot. Here are a few tips so you can thumb a few more bass.

Do you feel me?
Keep three-point contact with your feel type baits at all times. This includes plastic worms, curly tail grubs, lizards, soft plastic craws, tubes, and jigs. Use the rod tip, the handle, and add a place to help detect even the most subtle strike by resting your line over the back of your thumb or between your fingers for a third reference point to sense a bite. When working your bait, lowering with each motion, the rod should be returned to the 10 o'clock position. Raised at the twelve o'clock spot you can't set the hook without dropping the rod tip and risk the fish sensing your presence. Watch the line, but trust your sense of feel. Braided line can help you sense more of what is happening at the other end of the line.

Loosen up
When fishing feel type baits, it's always better to hold the rod

loosely in your hands. A death grip on the rod makes it harder to feel the subtle strikes. Relax your hands and fingers, and you'll feel more of what the bait and the bass are doing. Your tight grip reduces sensitivity and puts a gap in the time you sense a fish and set the hook.

Go long or go home
When choosing the fishing rod, employ a longer rod for casting or pitching to get the desired distance. The increased length loads the rod for longer casts. A higher finish loads the tip and sends the bait out with a higher velocity, which translates into increased distance of your cast. Another major advantage of the taller rod is you can pick up the line faster on the hook set. But there is a limit to the length advantage. It's important to match the rod to the angler. If you can handle a seven foot stick, by all means use it. Go up or down in length by your height, the room you have to cast, and also room to store the rod in your water craft when not in use. A quality collapsible rod is a big advantage in both cases.

Go swimming
Swim soft plastics. Regardless of what some folks claim to be the best technique, I believe the presentation for plastic should be to just cast the bait and then after entry simply lift the rod to create a natural swimming motion. This is easy, it looks realistic, provides an arc, full contact with the bait, and a falling motion which triggers lots of strikes. Other retrieves work, but this, day in and day out, produces hits. Swim the bait and take the rod to the ten o'clock position, then lower the tip and make up line by reeling for full contact fishing. This is an overlooked method for catching open water bass, especially smallmouth.

Concentrate/Confidence
Learn to pay attention to exactly what the bait is doing, how it feels, and refuse to be distracted. Honing in on the feel of the lure

Fishing Apps—Common Sense Clues For Big Bass

will position you to identify a *pick up* and prepare you for the *big* bass battle. I trust my rod, bait, line, knot, knowledge, hook set, drag, and ability to hook and land any size fish.

I've never made a cast that I didn't believe I was going to catch a fish.

An Optical Conclusion

Depth finders aside, you can see many objects by just wearing quality sunglasses. If you spot a branch sticking up through the surface of the water, a little detective work tells you it's attached to a tree and maybe even the relative size of the tree below the surface. Aquatic vegetation is highly desirable bass cover and comes in the form of weed beds submergent (below) and emergent (above). No electronics required, pull up to the next window please. Boat docks equal overhead cover and potential food sources. Fish them from every direction and pitch or skip baits under these fish holding structures. Rock piles radiate the sun's heat in the winter, early spring, fall, and winter. A degree or two warmer of water temperature will draw and hold fish. Get the picture? Fish visible structure.

Keep Your Feel Bait Wet

It's easy to become disheartened when the bite is slow. It is, you remember, called *fishing*. Catching comes when you do everything correctly. Maintain a positive approach, try familiar techniques and areas first, and then go ahead and experiment with new techniques and seek out fresh waters. If you cast and retrieve your lure twice per minute, you'll make 120 casts per hour. If you fish for eight hours, you will make almost 1000 casts. You can expect, if you are the average fisherman, to catch one fish about every 90 minutes. Sorry, that's the average. Keep casting, stay focused, and be ready. If you're not casting, you can't be catching. Sometimes the biggest bass comes in the last hour of the trip.

Be an Accu-caster

Learn to cast accurately. You don't have to be able to put the bait on a dime, but try to keep it in the same zip code. The strike zone of a bass is greatly exaggerated, and in hot water, cold water, muddy water, and other scenarios their strike zone gets smaller. It's a simple fact that the farther they have move to catch their prey and eat, the more energy they expend. Therefore, if they move too far a distance to eat too small a meal, it's a losing proposition. They would actually get smaller. To gain weight, or minimally maintain their size, trophy sized bass feed opportunistically, they take advantage of close, easy to catch, and *upsized* propositions. The formula is simple—put the bait close to the bass, make it look real, and hang on.

Trophy Tip: Rarely do you make a mistake and catch a big bass. Make sure the variables are routinely considered and addressed. Fresh line, a good knot, drag set and mind set are all important to landing the largemouth of a lifetime.

40

The Shallow Bite in Deep Summer

They've all gone deep! That's the bass fisherman battle call when the water temperatures jump during the heat of the summer months. When it seems the bass are on simmer instead of summer, you certainly can make a case for deep cranking, throwing upsized plastic worms on the underwater ledges, and seeking out creek channels, humps, and distinct off-shore bottom contours. Bass behavior has taught us that they don't all do the same thing at the same time. The location of food sources has a great deal to do with the location of bass. Many fish are transitional even during the second half of the year. They will migrate to thin water and set up on secondary objects, and due to fishing or boating pressure go deep.

The trick is to be in the right place at the right time throwing the right bait. For bass that have been pounded from early spring, through the spawn and exposed to vacationers, you may have to employ a different approach. There are those who just change schedules, become night stalkers, and when most are hitting the sheets, they're hitting the water. But don't be fooled—daylight, dusk, and even mid-day can be very productive for hot weather heavyweights.

Where to go
Bass that receive boating or fishing pressure often seek deep water retreats, remote areas, or heavy cover. I don't like fishing in water

over 15 feet in depth for a couple of reasons—I don't use electronics, I'm generally in a kayak, and suspended deep fish are the hardest for me to fool. For many summer seasons I've taken trophy fish throughout the summer in water from two feet to eight feet in depth. The trick is to find an area close to deep water, which has lots of cover, a good supply of oxygen, and an abundance of food sources. In these magical spots, bass can seek shelter, wait in ambush, feed, and return to deep water with a few flips of their fins.

I look for submerged wood—the bigger the better. Large lumber offers a hideout, comfort from the sun, an ambush point, and draws in bait fish, bluegills, and other forage. I found this is a repeatable pattern during most of the year. An obvious summer secret—the shade. Overhanging trees, shoreline objects, and anything that casts a shadow gets my attention. Aquatic vegetation of any kind is high on my summer search list. Bass love the overhead cover of the summer bloom of lily pads, but submerged weeds in the form of hydrilla, coontail moss, cabbage weed, and more are all magnets for bass, crappie, bluegill, and just about any kind of gamefish.

You can add inflowing creeks to the hot weather targets. The moving water is cooler and adds oxygen so critical to the largemouth lifestyle. Rock, especially boulder type rock, harbors crawfish and bass. The crevices between the larger rocks provide shade and a logical place for the fish to dart out and devour freshwater crustaceans and also a break from current in moving waters.

I never pass up a chance to throw to a boat dock. While dock catches can become a pretty solid pattern, I generally view them as a *one-fish* spot. If you can find a combination of these elements you can pretty well figure fish should be around.

What to throw
Certainly traditional bass lures work, but there are a few odd ball baits they may surprise you *and* the fish. With the shad and bluegill spawn, I never venture out from late May until September without a buzzbait tied to the end of one of my rods. Buzzers have never

been a *numbers* bait for me, but historically a big bite comes on the buzzer. I carry at least two with skirt colors to match the shad and the bluegill. The secret is to match the blade with the wind effect. Dead still—I throw a small bladed bait. In heavy winds the biggest blade I've got is my choice. Don't be shy. Cast the buzzers all around the heaviest cover you can find. Since the line is off the water's surface, you can use heavy, large diameter line, 30-pound test or more. I stay away from the trailer hooks for fear of deeply hooking a big bass and killing it. If the strikes are short, trim the skirt and slow down the retrieve.

Floating plastic is often viewed as a spring thing, but it is not necessarily so. I like to rig a leader with 12-pound test monofilament or fluorocarbon—first a high quality ball swivel, the leader line, and then a #1 hook standard or circle hooks work well. The leader is attached to the main line of braided line spooled on open face spinning gear. My choices are a seven-inch straight tail worm in white or bubble gum (OK, pink) and a deadly piece of plastic, a Strike King 4.5 flipping tube! I use a 5/0 Daiichi copperhead hook on the identical leader and stuff the body of the bait with Styrofoam packing peanuts to ensure it'll float forever. The wild random action of this set up around weeds, wood, and boat docks is deadly.

Experiment with the cadence for the most effective retrieve. The deep summer can offer the shallow bite.

Guide Tip: A cup faced popper is a great shallow water summertime bait choice. I alter mine by replacing the front treble with a red treble hook for the injured eye appeal. I also shave the face of the bait with a pocketknife to change the shape and more important the sound. The bloop-bloop noise becomes more resonant and will call bass from cover.

41

Speed Trap

The slogan, *speed kills*, has been around for a long time. In sports speed is definitely an asset. In fishing it can be a liability. You see fish chasing schools of bait. Adrenaline flowing, you cast to the activity and crank your bait back as fast as your high speed reel can go. No bite. Insert sad face. You catch a big bass, and the next several casts you are busting it, *cast, crank, cast, crank*—but no hits. Your partner is boating fish, and you're not. Why? You got caught in the speed trap!

The world believes faster is better. In fishing it may leave you behind. In the underwater world, a bass can swim in bursts of 12-15 miles per hour. It's highly unlike you can take a bait away from them if they really want it. Other fish in fresh and salt water are built for speed. A look at their body structure, fins, and tail size is evidence that they're hydrodynamic, quick, and capable. Each species shares some similarity. Artificial baits should appear to be easy prey, injured, or in some cases trying to get away. Often bigger fish are looking for the easy meal and have become conditioned to expend less energy to catch the easy prey. That's how they get bigger—use the least amount of energy for the maximum pay off. When they are aggressive, they'll chase, but find them in a negative or neutral feeding mode and you have to make the adjustment.

Keeping It Reel
Most reel manufacturers have responded to the requests for reels

Speed Trap

that allow you to *burn* a buzzbait or a lipless crankbait. Gear retrieve ratios top out at a blistering 9.0:1 with average being about 6.3:1. To put that into perspective the 9.0:1 is taking in over three feet of line for every complete reel handle turn, the 6.2:1 a more tame 25 inches, almost a foot less. For presentation purposes there are limited applications where the *speedy* reel is an advantage. It' easy to unconsciously race the bait away from the fish. It's been my experience when fishing is really tough, slower retrieves produce. Late summer, most of winter, muddy water, cold front conditions—each warrant a try at decelerating the return of the bait.

Why So Slow

In studies and surveys done of people catching big bass consistently, the plastic worm and other creature type lures are found to be the most likely lures to fool a trophy fish. Rigging plastics such as the popular Texas rig, Carolina rig, shakey heads, and wacky rigs all incorporate slow motion, controlled fall rates, and creeping characteristics in their presentations.

Conclusion: easier to catch—more likely to be eaten by the fish.

Baits like spinnerbaits and crankbaits are often more effective with *stop and go* retrieves. Once you find the tempo that produces, you have to be aware of changes in the conditions. Cloud cover, wind, and water colors will cause fish of all kinds to change. They move to deep water, hug cover, stage on points, seek shelter under boat docks, or just shut down. Retrieve speed becomes a factor.

At times the initial cast draws a hit before you even turn the reel handle. Sometimes *dead sticking*, allowing the bait to rest motionless, brings the curiosity subtle strike. When fish, bass for instance, are aggressively feeding, they'll hit a faster moving bait with no hesitation. Examples of this phenomenon of seemingly perfect set up are on a full moon, surface water temperatures ranging from 65 to 75 degrees, with stable water levels, a slight breeze, and a falling barometer. Unfortunately this doesn't happen as often as we would like.

Fish set up at ambush points often require a hesitation in retrieve called *killing* the bait and letting it fall to bring on the strike. The momentary deflection of a square billed crankbait is another instance in the interruption of the lure retrieve that will draw a response from the fish. That defection hit can occur in the striking of a rock pile, a submerged stump or any object that is temporary housing the fish.

Topwater fishing can be tough. A cadence on hard *plugs* is an exercise in experimentation. An age old example is the cast, let the ringlets settle—yeah right, who has the patience for that?—*a twitch, rest, take up slack, twitch, rest, and repeat.*

For the froggin' fans, a steady hop, skating over lily pads, around various aquatic vegetation, downed trees, or along man-made structure is standard, but often a specific speed will bring the bass out of its hideout to slug the frog.

Not being a *numbers* bait, the buzzbait is one of my personal favorites. It excels in warm water, when fish are chasing baitfish, and around thick, heavy cover. I always use nothing but a steady retrieve, the velocity determined by the response of the fish. Start slow, ramp up, and be cognizant of the first fish, the one that hits the bait. Aggressive bite, halfhearted, short strike, or trying to destroy the noisy intruder? All those clues come from the speed and ultimately the strike.

The Low Down on the Slow Down
There are a few tactics to use in slowing down the descent of your baits. First go lightweight which will cause a pause in the fall. Try a small ¼ ounce spinner instead of the ¾ ounce model—once you stop reeling the bait goes into a slower fall. When jig fishing try the finesse version maybe a ¼ ounce, and then use the larger soft plastic trailer probably a crawfish imitator Ragetail from Strike King to make an enticing slow fall of the bait. In cold water a suspending jerkbait at rest will stay in the zone longer by the nature of a *suspending* lure. Texas rigged soft plastic worms can

Speed Trap

delay the drop using a smaller slip sinker, substituting a ¼ ounce instead of the ¾ ounce lead. Also using a larger diameter line, if you use monofilament, will by water natural resistance slow the fall of this set up. Avoid using fluorocarbon on any floating baits because it sinks.

Remember the Retrieve Speed

When guiding or doing any type of instructional media, I urged folks to learn to fish the *feel* baits. This category includes plastic worms, soft plastic craw, tubes, swimbaits, jigs, and creature style baits. Making the switch from moving baits, spinners, crankbaits of all kinds, and others almost always required the *slow it down* direction. Casting past the target area, maintaining contact at all times, feeling the swim of the lure, and being ready to set the hook at any sensing of a hit was always included in the lesson. This type of fishing is dependent on the ability of the angler to concentrate and a total awareness of the retrieve speed necessary to draw the strike. The speed control is literally in your hands. This is important in replicating the successful cast and catch. Think of it this way—two anglers using the same rod, reel, line, *and* bait. One is out fishing the other. The only logical conclusion is one has the speed dialed in.

On the toughest days, *Slooooww* down. When you feel like it's too slow, slow down more. The prize doesn't always go to the swiftest. Don't get caught in the speed trap!

42

How To FIND and FOOL Late Spring Bass.

Where are they?
All of the bass are never in the same spot at the same time. Many natural influences will dictate location. Weather conditions, water color, food availability, and other factors make finding fish a little more predictable. Bass are immensely easier to catch when they are shallow. They come and stay in the shallows for comfort, to spawn, and to feed. This means given the right set of conditions they could be there a lot and willing to bite.

Let's tackle water temperature first. In the early spring a degree or two difference will draw bass into an area. They recognize the warming trend and know food sources will migrate to the potential spots in hopes they will find food, comfortable temperatures, possible spawning grounds, and cover. The last two missing ingredients that make a bass *sweet spot* are ample oxygen and deep-water escape areas close by. Given a compact area that serves all its needs, most creatures, including a bass, will stay put. They have no reason to go. The appearance of aquatic vegetation also makes certain places more attractive.

As the weather becomes stable, all forage and food becomes more abundant. Naturally minnows and baitfish are year around meals, but frogs, bugs, snakes, crawfish, mayflies, and everything else emerges eventually as part of the largemouth bass buffet.

How To FIND and FOOL Late Spring Bass.

What's on the menu?
Bass of all species will eat almost anything they can catch and will fit in their mouth. Armed with this knowledge the prospective angler should be prepared to select either artificial bait that they can make move naturally or looks like the real thing. The look is predetermined by the size, shape, and color of the *bogus* bait. Bass have great eyesight, so things that appear to be easily swallowed, the right color, or provide a large meal in return for the chase are likely to appeal to the bass. A great edge goes to the fisherman who can mimic the movements of the local food supply. Natural swimming motions, the injured look, or the trying to frantically escape all will cause bass to open wide.

The feeding frequency of bass is determined by their digestive rate and the availability of food. Warm water means increased activity and the need to feed. Bass are slaves to heir stomachs. Given the chance bass will choose crawfish over any other food source—it's underwater ice cream to a fish. For every five pounds of crawfish a bass consumes, it gains a pound. Studies show that they eat more baitfish like shad, but that's just because they are more readily available. Know what lives in the waters you fish and match that in appearance and movement.

One other consideration is the use of live bait. It looks like, moves like, smells like, and tastes like the real deal—and bass love it.

Big or Little, Fast or Slow
The first rule for me when fishing under tough conditions is to use smaller lures and slower retrieves. Extremely clear water is a great example of how and why this works. On a recent wintertime trip, I went out with the intent of catching a mess of crappie. Because the water was both clear and cold, I opted for a 6-foot light spinning rig with four pound-test line and had a 1/16 ounce lead head and a smoke/glitter tube attached. After just a couple of minutes I had a sharp thump and reeled in a chunky 14-inch bass. As I continued on, one bass after the next hit the tiny tube. At the end of the day

the tally was 11 bass topped by a 3 ½ pound smallmouth. Little lures and slow retrieves will produce fish.

The big bait/big fish theory does also have some merit. As bass grow, their gill rakers expand, and the smaller baitfish escape, they learn that the bigger shad or minnows can't escape and seek the larger meal. Big baits are more likely to tip off the fish as to not being real, but when properly presented do yield trophy sized catches. As for fast retrieves, they work very well for aggressive fish, but a non-aggressive bass will not chase something and expend energy for something that moves like a rocket. It should be noted here that bass are in the non-aggressive mode about 90% of the time.

Zero in on Bass

Another tactic that puts you in a position to succeed is using search baits to locate bass. Bass will many times snub faster moving lures, but they do offer a limited time for the fish to inspect the bait and possibly draw more of a reaction type strike. It is vital to remember that you, the fisherman, give the lure its speed. Experiment with speed, cadence, and distance of movement. Certain groups of lures are primarily moved with the rod. Jigs, grubs, plastic worms, and Carolina rigged baits all fall into this category. It is important to understand the relationship between the distance the rod is moved and the motion this imparts to the bait. The lures moved with the reel include spinnerbaits, crankbaits, topwater lures like a buzzer, and other baits like a floating worm or a jigging spoon that are moved with consecutive activities such a twitch and reel, or raise, drop, and reel. Just be aware of what you do with the rod versus the reel and how it affects the movement of the bait.

Natures Challenges

No conversation about bass fishing would be complete without discussing the natural influences of rain, sun, wind, and moon phases. Rain can raise or lower water levels, change current, discolor the water ,and in general create some unique opportunities. Each possibility doesn't mean you can't or won't catch fish, but you may have to make some adjustments. Muddy water call for brighter colors and pinpoint casting, and makes approaching shallow fish easier because of their limited vision. The current increase that accompanies heavy rains makes boat handling a nightmare and even possibly dangerous.

The sun at high noon might send bass scurrying to cover or make lures more visible—meaning presentation might have to be perfect. Wind, while being a nuisance and making casting and boat control rough, does offer a bright side. The banks being pounded by the wind begin to churn, particles on the bottom are suspended in the water, and a natural feeding cycle begins, bait in the form of shad, minnows, crawfish, and other forage type residents stir, and bass zoom in to see what's available. Go to the windy side. While you don't have to be an astronomer to fish, the moon phases have over the years proven to be very solid predictors of increase activity. Bass are tuned in to the happenings associated with the moon. Insect hatches, bait hatches, as well as their own spawning activities are in large part tied into the moon phases. Suffice to say three days before or after a new or full moon is prime time to catch a limit of fish or maybe that trophy that has eluded you for several seasons.

Either way, you should be ready to set the hook on some of the best fishing of the year.

43

Seeing Red

When choosing artificial lures, most anglers struggle more over color than any other aspect. While color can be important, it is only a small factor in actually catching fish. Most game fish have large eyes which is an indication that they feed by sight. So while colors and certain shades are more visible, subtle differences are a key to fooling fish. With most baits I have a few of my own favorites based mostly off early experimentation and then performance. In short I like baits and colors because the fish are partial to that particular bait and color. One success secret is the addition of the color red to any bait. Some folks ask, "Why not a totally red lure?" Subtle is better than *in your face* blazing red. In extremely dirty water, a red lure is a great choice.

The color red in most instances in nature indicates something injured. For predatory fish an injured form of prey appears easier to catch and thus becomes a likely target. There are red worm hooks available. With topwater lures, even if you look at older baits, most had a splash of red somewhere on the lure. Artificial baits in shades of red or red combination colors are common in almost every model. Adding a small spot of red on the underside or throat of lures that do not have it is also very effective.

The color red maintains its integrity better than most colors. In deep water everything goes black anyway. Red in nature indicates something wounded, and to predatory creatures—including fish—incites the chase scenario. The gills of baitfish and even bluegill become red as blood rushes to various parts of the head during the escape attempt. This actually makes them more visible to other fish. Small alterations to your baits can make a big difference especially in highly pressured waters.

Guide Tip: For a different look, try spray painting a little red on the blades of some of your spinnerbaits. The hint of red appears sparingly while the blades turn. You can also sprinkle a little silver glitter on the blades before the paint dries. It simulates the look of a bait fish being *scaled*.

Guide Tip: When Texas rigging soft plastics, try adding a red bead between the slip sinker and the hook. You've added a subtle bit of color, and this also serves to protect your knot and additionally creates a clicking sound when the slip sinker smacks the bead.

44

Follow the Leader

Line leaders are fairly simple to set up. I employ a homemade leader to give an old bait a new look. Soft plastics can be deadly effective and rigged in multiple ways. Leaders make the baits weightless and weedless. Similar leaders used in salt water are sometimes referred to as shock leaders. On the freshwater bass application, because of the minimal amount of weight of the bait, it is cast on an open faced spinning outfit. The leader serves to avoid line twist. Twist avoidance is accomplished with the first component of the leader system—a high quality swivel which allows the line to turn freely. A section of line, six to 12-pound test monofilament or fluorocarbon is used. I prefer 10–12 inches of line for ease of managing the cast. I also like camouflage line for this technique making it less likely to be spotted by the fish. Depending on the size of the soft plastic I intend to use, I will vary the size of the hook. For straight tail floating worms or minnow imitators a 3/0 hook is preferable; for thicker bass tube type baits I opt for a 5/0 hook. The point of this is specific to fishing around aquatic vegetation, boat docks, wood, and shoreline cover. You can use stronger, heavier test and larger diameter line and get away with it because of the addition of the leader.

The soft plastic baits float and are rigged weedless, and the weightless quality allows for the baits to dart and slowly fall in a completely random action. One trick I use for the tube is to stuff a Styrofoam *packing peanut* into the cavity before *skin hooking* the bait. The Styrofoam keeps the bait buoyant and floating all day. This is also where the old time, seven-inch straight tail worm reemerges from the bottom of the tackle box. Tube colors the fish respond to are pumpkin/pepper, Gobi, and black neon. For the worms, insanely brightly colored baits are easy to spot after the cast, blaze orange, bubble gum, black, and white are all stored in plastic sandwich bags with a few sprayed with regular cooking oil. Any floating soft plastic bait easily wiggles. Throw the deepest cover with a small coat of lube.

Look for any surface green vegetation—pads, water weeds, submerged timber, and even boat docks all warrant a cast. Cast past the target, the perceived fish holding spot, and give the bait a twitch, pause, twitch, rest and continue until you get a reaction from the bass. The float, dart, dive, retrieve, and action incites strikes from otherwise inactive fish. This set up gives the appearance of an injured forage food source and the slow speed looks like an easy meal.

When working boat docks the side arm *skip* cast sends the bait under the dock and is deadly in the summer for the shade resting fish hoping to ambush anything that enters the immediate area. For the worms, I count on primarily two colors, white for clear water and bubble gum or pink for stained water. The minnow/shad/fluke style body is generally most effective for me in the pearl color. For the tubes, black neon or pumpkin pepper produce well. This technique is well suited again for working lily pads, cattails, hydrilla, coontail moss, boat docks, and around partially submerged trees. You'll find yourself looking for aquatic weeds that you previously avoided. The pattern gets stronger as the sun rises and pushes fish to any overhead cover.

A seven foot long medium heavy spinning rod allows for longer casts, a sure hook set, and the ability to play any size fish. Attached is a 6.3:1 gear ratio retrieve medium size spinning reel spooled with ten-pound test braided is my personal preference. Surface water temperatures of 60 to 80 degrees is where this tactic shines.

Heavy vegetation and thick cover, which are often the hideouts for trophy fish, are ideal because of the weedless and weightless capabilities. A good pair of sunglasses—not necessarily expensive; I use Strike Kings priced around $29 to $39—allow you to track the path of the bait, and often before you feel anything it looks as if the bait just disappears. Time to lean on 'em. Set that hook.

Just follow the leader.

Guide Tip: If you can't find a camo line, try marking one inch alternate increments of your line with a green or brown permanent marker to give the line a disappearing, less obvious look and minimal visibility. This is especially helpful with yellow high visibility braided line.

45

Low Tech Catch

In my book *I'll Be Tennessean Ya'* there's a chapter entitled, "I'm Playing Checkers While The Rest Of The World Is Playing Chess." The main point in the chapter is my common sense solutions to finding and catching fish. Personal preference for folks in kayaks leads to a large amount of customization and the options to go *bare bones* or *go gearhead* with the rigging and addition of electronics of all types and varieties. Either or anywhere in between is certainly acceptable.

While bass are typically my target, I chase crappie and bluegill during certain times of the year. Early spring when the crappie bite is good, catching and cooking is on the agenda. Soon after the bass go into pre-spawn, and they get my attention. As we move into the sizzling summer months, the bluegill spawn and will readily hit almost any undersized offering. There are also days when I just go *junk* fishing, casting at anything that is willing to bite.

For years I subscribed to theory that fish are not hard to catch—they are harder to find. Enter electronics, lending help to locating fish. Depending on your bass fishing budget, you can rig a super side scanning, depth determining, way point punch in, temperature gauging electronic gadget. My early resistance to electronics was a lack of finances. I developed a system to finding fish using visual clues, common sense, and a reliance on past performance. There's no doubt that off-shore anglers benefit from the revelations on the screen of their depth finder/locators. For me I use a set of criteria that work almost anywhere. Here's a peek at some of my favorites.

1. **Shoreline**—A scan of the shoreline in any body of water is a primary source of information. I look for irregular features ranging from rocks to docks, anything different. Bass are object oriented and will *set up* around anything in one to 20 feet of water and in some cases even deeper.
2. **In-flowing creeks**—Creeks that enter into lakes and even other moving waters like rivers are worth a couple of casts. Adding cooling water in summer, increased oxygen, and a natural hide for fish and forage make creeks productive.
3. **Surrounding shore structure**—A sloping shore means the slope continues. A bluff bank indicates deeper water and rock formations most of the time. A bare spot or the trunk of a tree most likely means submerged wood. Any or all of these can be counted on to produce at certain times.
4. **Bends**—In flowing water the outside bends catch the current, the inside bends redirect current. Either can be a gold mine. If the current is strong, fish of all species relate to anything that blocks current on the outside; the inside provides a place to sit behind the bend and wait for food to be deliver.
5. **Secondary cover**—*Big* bass time! Under certain circumstances fish will move to isolated secondary cover in the form of aquatic weed beds, downed wood, rock piles, or man-made attractors. Falling water sends fish to the next available cover, yep, secondary off-shore objects. Single sources of cover or a combination often hold the biggest *loner* fish.
6. **Points**—Long tapering points are often overlooked. They can be spotted jutting out from the shore, and they continue at measurable increments. For example a point goes—not always in a straight line—from a foot or two descending to 20 feet of water or more. Cast parallel or perpendicular to the point until the fish react.

Each of these possibilities lead to identifiable patterns, repeatable results and memorable catches. There are many more but this is a short list and gives a start. Another tip is the use of the rod and line to determine depth. A 7 ½ foot rod is fairly normal for me, I merely lower my line until it curls at the tip. The limp line indicates a bottom touch down. I raise the line and can pretty accurately gauge the depth of the water my boat is sitting in. One rod length—around seven feet, two rod lengths—15 feet. Anymore than that I'm in the wrong spot.

I'm admittedly not a deep water guy. When asked what do I do when the fish are in 20 feet of water or more, my reply is, "I stay home and watch cartoons."

I also use a small pool thermometer to find the surface water temperature. They're inexpensive, require no battery, and float.

Going low tech leaves a few dollars that might allow you to add other desired equipment. There's also a lot of self-satisfaction to finding and catching fish using your senses and intuitive skills.

46

The Right Bite

Have you ever wondered why certain fishermen will zero in on one or two lures while fishing for bass? Think about all the possible ways there are to catch largemouth, spotted Kentucky, and smallmouth bass. There are so many diverse water conditions, types of water, and various impoundments, rivers, ponds, etc. In my own case I'm drawn to specific techniques and baits because of the feel, or the visual created by the strike. I call it *The Right Bite*.

Spinnerbait
There are lots of different varieties available when you look at the spinners. Variations in weights from tiny ⅛ ounce to 1 ½ ounce bottom bumpers, a virtual rainbow of skirt colors, and let's not forget the infinite number of potential blade combinations with willow, Colorado, and Indiana blades plus, gold, nickel, brass, white, chartreuse, and others.

Years ago I met a lure designer and fellow fisherman while filming a *Bass Pro Shops* video in Mexico. Residing in Louisiana and fishing swamp water and backwater bayous, Eugene "Shoestring" DuBois invented a hybrid bait called the Tornado. It was a buzzer and spinnerbait all in one lure. The magic of this bait was the ability to *wake* it in retrieving it just below the surface, or you could *kill it*—stop the retrieve and let it drop—to make it helicopter down, or fish it like a conventional spinnerbait.

When discussing the ultimate spinnerbait strike Shoestring described it as a "dead thug." That's what he liked about it and what he wanted to feel.

In communicating my annual Canadian adventure stories, I've written about the smallmouth hitting spinnerbaits so hard they would immediately pull drag from the reel. That's what you live for if you're a caster of *scrap iron*. I rely, most of the time, on a ⅜ ounce Strike King Premier Plus spinnerbait with a nickel Colorado front blade and a #3 ½ gold willow blade on the back.

Crankbait

The bait I love to hate. Visions of a hooked bass, jumping alongside the boat and throwing a bait—usually a crankbait—have in the past, haunted me. I have learned to land bass consistently on two crankers, the Strike King Red Eye Shad in Sexy Shad, and Blue Gizzard Shad in ½ and ¼ ounce versions, and also the #3 Strike King Pro Model—my favorite color is #584 Oyster. There is something about casting out one of these plugs and starting it back with a stop & go retrieve only to be interrupted by a another stop—that of a bass crushing the imitation baitfish that got too close for comfort. Feeling that swimming motion through the rod and the sensation of the fish attacking the bait is pleasurable to many anglers. It's good, but certainly not my first choice.

Make sure to use a rod that is sensitive and has a forgiving tip. The reel should be spooled with monofilament line for the stretch that has the fish almost hooking itself. Too stiff a rod will not allow a decent hook set—a medium or medium light action is desirable—or you get the dreaded *one that got away* experience.

Topwater

Lots of options in this category, but the payoff is the same. The ultimate eye candy for fisherman is the demonic surface hit that a bass can provide. The appeal is ancient, and once you've experienced it you are drawn to working the surface for the next big strike. Smorgasbords of bass baits are available for this application. Popping lures, chuggers, buzzers, dog-walkers, floaters, and prop baits are just part of the list you can use.

The correct retrieve is the ticket to success on the surface. The speed and cadence controlled by the angler will determine how many fish you coax and catch. These criteria can also change by the minute due to weather and water conditions. Using a faster retrieve will work for aggressive fish—it's heaven when you find it. Unfortunately this occurs infrequently. The goal is to make the lure look like it is frightened and fleeing or injured. This, to a bass, creates a predatory response that is almost uncontrollable—the ultimate bite for a certain group of bass fanatics.

In choosing topwater lures, folks often describe the realistic color of the surface bait that they believe is the absolute best. I ask, "What color is the bottom of the bait? It's what the fish most likely looking up is going to see."

Feel Baits, Soft Plastics, and Jigs

Worms, craws, creatures, and oh yeah, the jig have a big following because of the many variations you experience with a strike that ranges from a subtle, almost imperceptible pick up to a slam and swim attack mode. While I'll cast a wide variety of Strike King soft plastic creations, the Rodent, the seven-inch Anaconda worm, an Ocho, the Flippin tube, or a Thumper worm, I always, always have a rod close by with a jig tied on. The jig bite is my drug.

Whether it's the line swimming off, a tap, a gentle tick, or strong tug, my heart begins to race when I sense the presence of a bass on the end of the line. The anticipation and questions that instantly come to my mind include, but are not limited to, the following:

- Is this the next trophy?
- Will the fish jump?
- How many fish are in the same spot?
- Is this part of a pattern that will lead to several more bites?

Then there's the hook set. The art of setting the hook on a bass that sucked in a *feel bait* is a thing of beauty. It's almost immediately followed by a surge from the hooked fish that offers the first clue as to the size and fighting potential of the prize at the end of your line.

Live Bait
Surprised? There is a lot of joy for me in occasionally using live bait. The opportunity to be transformed into a 10-year-old kid comes with watching a float dance on the surface knowing that at any moment a *bull* bluegill will take the worm threaded on #8 hook and pull that cork down. Feeling the tug of a slab crappie darting from a submerged brush pile sucking in a lively shiner minnow is just as exciting. The visual payoff of the float disappearing, seeing the line jump, and feeling the fish straining to retreat is all part of *the right bite* experience.

Just as each angler is different, so is the need for *the right bite*. A soft strike on a feel bait or the explosion of a surface attack means something different to the person on the other end of the pole. It may be connected to fishing as a kid, a special vacation trip, or landing the lunker of a lifetime, but regardless of the origin *the right bite* is all part of the joy of the outdoor experience.

Guide Tip: On surface lures remember the bottom of the bait is most visible to the bass. Don't get caught up in the top color concept.

47

The ABCs of Catching and Playing Fish

The reel is screaming, a massive pull on the end of the line, and your mind instantly goes to all the details you probably should have thought of before you made the first cast of the day.

For you, I offer a few of the A, B, Cs of playing fish.

A Always expect to catch a fish on every cast. How many times does it happen that you kind of *fall asleep at the wheel*, lose your concentration because of repetitive casts that have gone unrewarded? Fifty casts with a buzzbait then a giant explodes on it, and you respond by losing your religion. Stay in the moment—fishing focused.

B Bending branches and bend the knees on the hook set. Keep the rod bent with a fish on. The bend in the rod means you have it back and are applying steady pressure. Let the rod do the work—keep the drag set correctly to give on big fish. The little fish are easy.

C Consider all the variables. This is where most fish are lost. You picked the right bait, *but* did you tie a good knot? Was that hook sharp on your favorite bait? Was your hook set deliberate, effective? When's the last time you changed that line? Braid—no big deal. Monofilament—minimally should be switched out every six months and checked often. One nick created by a brush with a branch, a rock, or a dock piling makes it likely the strain of a big fish will cause a line break.

D Don't panic upon hooking a monster of any species. This is what you hoped for. If standing, you might want to sit down. Try plunging the rod down into the water. Why? Water pressure on the line beats air pressure, and the water resistance created makes the fish work harder while you play it and more difficult for the worn down fish to get away.
E Every time out learn something, look for the lesson. It may reinforce something you already knew.
F Fish often. On the water, experience is hard to beat. Fish at every opportunity and make mental notes of what you learn. Try new baits, new techniques, and new waters.
G Gather information from several sources to expand your knowledge of the fish—its lifestyle, habitat, food preferences, physical tolerances, capabilities, and anything else that can give you an edge on your favorite fish.
H Hit the rivers. The challenge of the ever changing moving waters are vital to accelerating your learning curve. With every possible scenario, rivers are great proving grounds. High water, low water, clear, muddy, slow current, fast moving, and irregular shorelines all provide lessons.

It's rare to get a big fish all the way to the kayak when you make a mistake playing your prize. Every error is magnified because of the power, weight, and fight of a trophy. Apply the A, B, Cs and you are more likely to land that big 'un.

48

Plan for Soft Plastics

With the impending summer weather, it may be time for a switch. A change in tactics can rejuvenate your fishing and catching in the months of June, July, and August. While advocating the use of certain baits at specific times and under certain circumstances, a seasonal switch can produce dramatic results for the versatile fishermen. Historically, my transition to soft plastic lures occurs when the water temperature reaches a range of 65 to 75 degrees. These baits for me are characterized as *feel baits*. After casting, constant contact is necessary for detecting the pick up, hence the nickname *feel bait*. You have to be able to feel 'em to fish 'em.

Post-spawn bass seem to be susceptible to the sight and movement of the multi-shaped creatures that are twitched, dragged, hopped, and made to glide through all depths of water. Because of the variation in size, shape, and color, there can be a lot of head scratching and over-stocking to assure adequate supply of soft plastic offerings. Post-spawn fish normally move to deeper water for a period of time but will frequent shallows and transition back and forth. It's also important to remember that none of the fish do the same thing at the same time. They will be in various stages of mood and habit through out the year.

My seasonal tackle box will contain the following; seven-inch curly tail plastic worms—these are for Texas rigging and use in one to 20 feet of water. I prefer a shallow water application normally because shallow water fish are usually aggressive feeders, but a large portion of the population will seek deeper water. As far as colors for Texas rigged worms, my preference would include black/blue tail, red shad, motor oil, and grey shade shad imitator. There is also a place for the old straight tail variety of worms. These will be used for a weedless, weightless, floating worm. While viewed as a pre-spawn and spawn lure, the floating worm is a good early morning, dusk, or a great bait for use around boat docks. As far as colors, white or bubble gum is all I need. A six foot spinning rod with the reel spooled with eight-pound test line is my choice. My rig starts with a swivel 12 inches above a 3/0 Diiachi Copper head worm hook. The swivel eliminates line twist.

Another solid choice for the warm water bass angler is a tube—the Strike King flippin' tube is my favorite. The identical Texas rig with a ⅜ ounce slip sinker and a 5/0 Copperhead hook is best. The green pumpkin color with the chartreuse tail is deadly in stained water and on Reelfoot Lake. White for clear water, and the black with red glitter has made for some memorable days also. The new Rage Tail craws are also a great option for Texas rigging and fishing heavy cover and under and around the dock. Simply stated, bass love to eat crawfish!

A forgotten but highly effective artificial is the curly tail grub. While not as flashy and hyped as other soft plastic, the three-inch pearl color, chartreuse, or smoke with silver glitter all catch fish anywhere. They are unbelievably effective for all species of fish. When cast and used in a natural swimming motion, a grub imitates a baitfish extremely well. My preference would be a ¼ ounce leadhead for feel, casting, and control but an ⅛ ounce head offers a slower drop and is at times irresistible to fish. Don't be surprised if you catch monster crappie while using these baits and methods.

Feel Bait Fishing Tips

- Keep three-point contact with your bait at all times. Use the rod tip, the handle, and the line resting over your thumb

or between your fingers for a third reference point to sense a bite.
- Hold the rod loosely in your hands. A death grip on the rod makes it harder to feel the subtle strikes. Relax your hands and fingers, and you'll feel more of what the bait and the bass are doing.
- Employ a longer rod for casting or pitching to get desired distance. You also can pickup the line faster and get a better hook set because of the additional length.
- Swim soft plastics. Regardless of what some folks believe, when first starting just cast the bait and lift the rod to create a swimming motion. This is easy; it looks natural and provides an arc and a falling motion which triggers lots of strikes. Other retrieves work, but this, day in and day out, produces hits.
- Concentrate. I never make a cast that I don't believe I'm going to catch a fish.
- Cover comes in the form of weeds beds, wood, boat docks, ledges, humps, drop offs, rock piles, and more. Get the picture? Fish structure.
- Keep your lure wet. If you cast and retrieve your lure twice per minute you'll make a 120 casts per hour. You can expect if you are the average fisherman to catch one fish about every 90 minutes. Sorry that's the average. Keep casting, stay focused, and be ready.
- Learn to cast accurately. The strike zone of a fish is greatly exaggerated. It's a fact the farther they move to eat, the more energy they expend. If they move too far to eat a small meal, it's a losing proposition. Put the bait close to the bass. It's why flipping works!
- You move the bait with the rod *and* take up the slack with the reel.
- Set the hook. When in doubt, set the hook. It's free! Set the hook!

Try these tips with these baits. Soft plastics work well and will forever, because they give off no negative clues. They are just another weapon in the arsenal of the successful fisherman. There are no magic baits, but you can make your own magic with the right bait, in the right place, at the right time.

49

The Hot Rods...and Reels

As you set out on your fishing adventures one of the decisions you make is which rods and reels to buy, take, and use. Fans of every type of rod and reel combination choose their favorites because of loyalty, past experiences, lure types, or even their bassin' budget.

Spincast
For beginners there's no shame in the game for spincasting. Press the thumb button and launch your lure—simple, inexpensive, and functional. Good for trophy size bass, but catfish might overwhelm the drag system on these reels. Generally paired with a 5 ½ foot rod, this might reduce casting distance, hook set, and ability to play fish. Other combos are more conducive to the task at hand. Retrieve ratio is also on the slow side.

Baitcasting
A little more complex initially to master, the payoff is the ability to *feather* your cast using your educated thumb to drop the bait in a precise spot. Baitcasters are also geared to help reduce the stress of using crankbaits, larger spinners, buzzbaits, and other cast and crank type artificial lures. Line capacity, strong drag systems, and specific adjustable controls on the spool also send many anglers in the direction of the *level wind* baitcasting reels. Retrieve ratios vary from the workman-like 5:3 to 1, good for

most chores, to the high speed 7:0 to 1, ideal for burning buzzbaits and lipless cranks. Coupled with a 6 ½ foot medium heavy rod, baitcasting reels are very popular with tournament anglers and those who fish often.

Open Faced Spinning
The most versatile is the spinning rig. Snubbed by many bass anglers, these rods and reels shine when the wind is up—no backlash to contend with. Lighter lures are the choice of fish and fishermen and longer casts are the order of the day. Generally geared for quick retrieves, and with a center drag system that can be adjusted while playing a big fish, spinning in fresh and saltwater should always have a place in any serious angler's boat.

Cane Pole
Turn the clock back and bring a cane or bamboo pole—typically a heavy line attached firmly to the top end—a few pinch-on split shot, and an all-purpose hook, say a #1 snuggly tied on. Bank fishing around shore line objects is a simple pleasure. Worms, crickets, minnows, or any other live bait might fool a fish.

Fly Rod
As much fun as any other rod and the purest form of presentation. A starter rod maybe a seven weight rod with a basic reel that holds seven weight floating line. Practice off the water casting a piece of yarn or a hookless fly. This outfit should allow you to cast surface popping bugs, mid-level streamer flies, and other bits of feathers and fur. Practice. Any species can be a target. Primarily viewed as a trout tool, the fly rod is excellent for all species of bass, bluegill, and many more types of fish.

The Four Functions of a Fishing Rod
1. The rod should be castable, you should be able to keep your bait in the zip code.

The Hot Rods...and Reels

2. You should be able to feel what the bait is doing at all times regardless of what type.
3. You should be able to achieve a solid hook set.
4. You should be able to play fish of any size. Always, always let the equipment do what is was designed to do.

Arm yourself with the best tackle you can afford, consider the space you have in your water craft, and the amount of money available to hit the water with today's *hot* rod and reel.

50

The Five Things I Always Do & The Five Things I Never Do

1. I **always** zip up my life jacket before I ever push my kayak off the bank. Having been flipped, slipped, and rolling my boat, canoe, or kayak, I never headed out on the water without a PFD—personal floatation device. Boating accidents occur everywhere, every day. The fact that you can swim isn't an excuse to not wear a life jacket. The Tennessee Wildlife Resources Agency slogan is "They float, you don't." Another cool water consideration is hypothermia. The 50/50/50 rule is this: in 50 degree water, if you are immersed for 50 minutes you have a 50% chance of survival.
2. I **always** have a game plan for what baits I will carry and how I will use them. A preview of weather and water conditions gives you an idea of where to go and what to throw. Seasonal conditions and species specific baits find their way to my tackle boxes. Experience will help a lot in formulating your approach and rod, reel, and lure decisions. A stash of lures that can be used with both a vertical and horizontal presentation should be included. Most of what fish normally eat do this. Spinners, cranking baits,—lipped as well as lipless—and jigs/soft plastics all fall (no pun intended) into this category.
3. I **always** have back up items available and loose items stored or tethered. What are the *must haves*? In my truck are an extra paddle, a spare life jacket—for me or anyone else—rope,

spare truck key, a light source, a first aid kit, battery backup for accessories that require battery power, dry clothes, an extra pair of shoes, hat, and sunglasses are all waiting in my vehicle. Tethered to the kayak—a dry box for my phone and another for my keys. A stout pair of needle nose pliers and a set of cutters. If you've never had to clip a treble hook out of some body part, you're lucky. Floating tackle boxes and bungee cords to secure rods are a great idea.

4. I **always** attach a pole with the American flag to my kayak. I don't feel the need to explain this one. Thanks to the folks and line boat builders at the Jackson kayak factory, most of my kayaks have also been custom color-themed red, white, and blue, USA!

5. I **always** represent and support those who have helped me along the way. I wear sponsor shirts and hats and use the products that they manufacture *and* that I truly believe in. Logos for my sponsors are firmly affixed to my Jackson kayak to help promote what they have to offer.

6. I **never** take chances in extreme weather conditions. High winds, extreme hot, or cold weather requires a bit more caution. When there are wind warnings and lake advisories, it is prudent to stay off the water. Consider wading or bank fishing. Sweltering summer days require hydration and cool clothing. In the cold, wool and wicking layered clothes are vital to comfort and more importantly survival. Even the most experienced paddlers should be wary of swift current and high or unfamiliar waters.

7. I **never** leave any evidence of my being at an outdoor location. I carry trash bags in order to pick up anything else I see. Protecting the resource is critical. I saw a sign in a wilderness area that read, "Take nothing but memories and leave nothing but footprints." Good advice anywhere you go.

8. Sorry, but I **never** reveal where my best fishing spots are

located. Stories or photos of *big* fish on Facebook, Instagram, online or in a magazine almost always peak the interest of a large section of the fishing folks. Eager anglers will boldly ask you to mark a map, give them directions, or even ask you to take them with you. Google Earth, binoculars, tackle store talk, or any clue they can glean is fair game for those seeking to claim jump your favorite fishin' hole. You also run the risk of someone removing every fish they catch and taking the trophy for the wall that they promised would never happen.

9. I **never** litter, take more fish than I can eat in one meal, abuse any piece of my equipment, or do anything to cast a bad light on our sport. We're all examples. We can choose to be good examples or bad examples, but either way we are examples.

10. I **never** withhold information from a fellow fisherman on the water and rarely let a young person leave without giving them some sort of fishing lure. For what it's worth, I'll tell or show people what I'm using. I literally lift my fishing rod and give them the close up look at it, a description, item number, and where they can find it. If it's soft plastic that's fooling fish that day, I will pitch a few over for people to use for that day. For the kids, I generally have a few single hook baits or a package of soft plastic tubes, curlytail grubs, worms, or craws to give them so they have their own tackle. Kids rarely forget a kindness.

I'm still trying to figure all this out, continuing to learn and apply what makes the most sense to me. Like most folks, my belief is that common sense is a great boundary to follow. We're not breaking any new ground when we say, "Pick up trash, even if it's not yours. Zip up your life jacket. Don't challenge the forces of Mother Nature," and on and on. When a question arises, my personal response is always the same—"The answer is in the question." Streamlining your strategy makes you safer, more efficient, and most likely will increase your catch, kill, and enjoyment.

51

Urban Angling

When you envision fishing, it probably takes you to a remote spot in a pastoral setting. Various fishing opportunities are changing, just like the world we live in. With high demands on our time, you might need to explore close to home or backyard bass trips. Picturesque wild trout streams still flow down from the mountains, and some remote lakes can be found, but there are emerging breeds of urban anglers discovering ample angling right down the road. Public lakes in parks, golf courses, local creeks, and streams are now surrounded by development and housing, while being advertised to enhance the eye appeal, these small waters can be the city dweller's tranquilizer.

With less time, and in some cases little disposable income, more people are opting for staycations—a vacation staying close to home—meaning previously ignored waters are receiving attention and new interest. Casting from a kayak, a canoe, or even the bank becomes the angling approach that creates the benefit of limited travel and reduces the need to burn several gallons of gas for a time consuming drive to a distant location or to tow a big boat.

Bait and Tackle

Urban bass anglers can gear up just like their big boat brethren and tests themselves against multiple species that are available in these neighborhood waters. Another advantage is that tackle selections can be smaller and nested easily in a tiny tackle box. Whatever you used in the past to catch fish will work in *city limits* fishing. Catfish readily eat a wad of night crawlers on a treble hook. Panfish of all varieties as well as bluegill, trout, rock bass, and more will smash small in-line spinners, tiny crankbaits or tiny tube jigs fished on a 1/16 or 1/32 ounce leadhead and light line. If you target bass finesse jigs, 1/4 ounce spinnerbaits, six-inch worms Texas rigged on a 3/0 hook are just a few of the baits that you should consider. Tiny top water lures work well in the spring and fall. The classic two-inch curly tail grub rigged on a 1/8 or 1/4 ounce leadhead catches fish everywhere. Experience tells me that pearl and chartreuse are the two best colors.

Rods and reels should match the lures. This type of angling lends itself well to open faced spinning gear and some baitcasting outfits or a fly rod. Try six-foot rods which are maneuverable and give you casting distance and also lure and fish control. Six-pound test line is ideal for these rigs. If baitcasting outfits are your choice, a six and a half foot rod and a lightweight reel balanced to the rod should be spooled with 10 to 14-pound test monofilament line.

Supersize Fish in Urban Waters
Don't be fooled into thinking that the fish that inhabit your local waters are all cookie cutters. Record books show many state record fish have come from farm ponds, quarry impoundments, small lakes, and streams. Many major cities were built on the banks of a river or a large lake, these places harbor big fish that seldom see a bait.

The Mississippi River runs from Minnesota to the Gulf of Mexico and has several major cities located on its banks. St. Louis, Missouri and Memphis, Tennessee, just to name a few, have a diverse population of fish. Similarly the Cumberland River also cuts through several metropolitan areas and boasts giant catfish, every major species of bass, crappie, and more. My personal bests include a 45-pound blue catfish within site of a major downtown.

A 10-pound largemouth bass, and a crappie over three pounds all came from waters within a few miles of well-populated cities.

All types of small boats are a great way to add an inexpensive, simple, easy to handle, highly mobile means to experience your neighborhood adventures.

Short drives coupled with wading, strolling the bank, or paddling trips might last just a couple of hours but could add up to more time to fish for urban anglers. Potential honey holes can be spotted during your normal travel activities. Check out local maps, Google Earth, and state-managed lakes. You might even get the chance to stop and wet a line on your way home from work.

There is wisdom to releasing your catch; this is the truest form of natural recycling. Water quality and forage food available to the fish will in large part determine the population and size of the fish in any body of water. Urban angling, fishing close to home, could become close to your heart.

Trophy Tip: Try throwing the quietest lures first, then graduate up in bait noise and disturbance—this minimizes the chances that you will spook the shallow water fish.

52

The Tackle Box Test

With all the possibilities on the types of fish and the ways to catch them, it's a wonder that fishermen don't go crazy or bankrupt. Once you begin to taste success in fishing it invades your mind, heart and soul. Truth be known though, the tackle box becomes the status symbol—along with rods and reels—that many are judged by.

One of my personal and favorite rules is *The One-Year Rule*. You can buy as big a tackle box as you want, buy as many baits as you can carry to stock your box, but if anything in there doesn't *get wet* or catch a fish it has to come out.

Tie It On, Catch Fish, Use It Or Lose It

Over the years I've fallen into the trap of *gotta have it* based off the recommendation of a Saturday morning TV angler, or from a tournament pro's quote in the pages of a fishing magazine. This leads to lots of lures and even more confusion.

My tackle box got smaller as I got better at finding and reading the fish. If you are a bass fisherman, you already know when you go out what you are going to use. You probably already have it tied on. Through the course of the day you might change lures 3 or 4 times. Let's peak inside my tackle box and highlight my selection of bass baits that have evolved over my last quarter century of casting for fun and profit.

The Tackle Box Test

The Lure of Lures

The baits that consistently catch fish for me have a few things in common. The logical stance is the triggering and attracting qualities. Suffice to say that the fish have to notice (attracting) any potential natural or artificial food source and have to be motivated (triggering) to *bite* the object of their attention. Sizes, shapes, colors, action, and swimming motion all come into play.

The exercise of minimizing your *tackle toter* starts with knowing what fish eat and what that thing looks like and swims like.

The Magic of Minnows

Minnow imitating lures will always have a place in my box. For my money, the A.C. Shiner, #300 C comes closer than anything else in mimicking the size, color, and swimming motion of the real thing. The side-to-side wobble is the factor that puts this bait over the top. The natural color of the shad pattern is a plus, while the daring/fleeing motion seals the deal. The speed and action is determined by the angler and makes all the difference.

Another minnow imitator is the spinnerbait. The blade size, shape, and colors help the fish decide whether to bite the bait or let it swim. Every tackle box needs a few. A ⅜ pounce, gold willow, silver Colorado with a white skirt is easily my #1 choice.

Buzzbaits can simulate schools of fleeing baitfish. A high-speed reel is advisable for the ease of retrieve and keeping the lure riding on the surface.

The survival of the fish is dependent on their ability to track down and catch baitfish and minnows. The least amount of energy any fish expends in catching food raises the eventual nutritional value. The shorter the chase, the bigger the payoff. Size-wise bigger from a potential food value is always better—if you have to move the same distance to catch a larger source it provides the biggest return. It just makes sense.

Crawdads

Crayfish, mudbug, crawdads—what ever you choose to call them, bass love 'em.

Bass and other game fish eat what's most available, in almost all cases that will be the minnows or shad that naturally inhabit their home waters. A major portion of their diet consists of the baitfish. Given a choice bass would choose crawfish over almost anything else—they are the candy of the underwater world. But bass, being opportunists, will eat whatever is most available.

Found all over North America, crawfish are important in a fishery that hopes to produce trophy size bass. For every five pounds of crawfish a bass eats it gains a pound—good for the fish and the fisherman. Knowing the lifestyle of these armored critters helps. They change colors seasonally, bury up in the winter, swim backward in bursts, and have soft and hard shell stages.

Crankbaits can match them extremely well in colors, but it's my belief that a jig matches their unique swimming motion better than any other artificial lure. The crankbait can move only a limited distance in depth and wobble. You can create a more random movement with a jig. Colors for me include, black/blue, pumpkin pepper, and a good crawfish color is brown/orange. I prefer $5/16$ ounce jig trailed by a #11 pork frog.

Odd Ball Baits & Techniques

Flipping and pitching are two techniques that have changed the face of bass fishing. The approaches are very similar, but the distances are the difference. Flipping is close range, while pitching is done from 15 to 40 feet. The jig is the lure most commonly viewed as the bait for these techniques. Realistically spinners, buzzbaits, swim baits, plastic worms, and craws all can be used. I use anything that does *not* have multiple hooks.

Fishing a drop shot rig is a great way to pull fish from open water. It looks odd with the weight on the bottom, next up is the hook, probably a #1, and finally a swivel. A small, four-inch worm is my bait of choice. I also use a soft plastic minnow. You cast out the rig and gently pull, twitch, and reel, wait for a *straight line pull*, then sweep the rod. This catches fish.

Another personal favorite of mine is the swimming worm. The set up for this one is making a leader about 12 inches long, with a high quality swivel on one end and #1 or a 186 Eagle Claw hook on the other end. I use a seven-inch straight tail worm threaded up the hook *and* line to form a 90-degree angle. When this is rigged and fished correctly, it swims through the water just like a small snake. The worm rotates and is weedless. Fish follow the lure and suck it in—sometimes they want it with a slight drop. This technique catches a *wad* of fish.

Peek into your own tackle box, try a few of these lures and techniques, and I'm sure you'll have less in your tackle box and more in your livewell.

53

The Science of Bass Fishing...and Catching

For the first few years of my fishing career, it was a struggle to catch many fish. There was the occasional, inconsistent success, but where were all those bass and trophy size fish that the magazine and lure manufacturers promised? Most anglers, myself included, fall into the trap of fishing the same spots with the same baits. The reason—"I caught fish here the last time." This logic leads to setting up what we call a *milk run*. You unload the boat, head straight for the point or creek you usually fish, and throw the bait you usually throw. This is followed by, "I caught one or two small ones here," and on to the next spot and the similar results.

Along with this train of thought is the frustration of not hooking any big bass. While dedicating time to watching the unlimited fishing shows offered by your favorite outdoor channel, reading everything you can get your hands on, and listening as the local legend speaks of 20-pound stringers, you still struggle with when and where to go, what to throw, and how to work that new bait.

I offer two ways to improve your catches, make them almost predictable, and stick some really *big* fish.

The Diary of a Bass Angler
Most great fisherman have a good memory for all the details surrounding their catches. Moon phase, time of day, the season, water temperature, color, wind direction, and much more. Once you begin

to recognize repeatable results, it becomes fun to memorialize your day in the pages of a journal. May years ago, after a respectable year of finding and catching fish, I put together my own version of a fishing logbook or diary. I wanted to remember where I found fish, what I used, and the conditions that lead to my success. In doing this you learn a lot about the lifestyle and movements of your quarry. You also realize that some of what you hear and read isn't necessarily *gospel*. Feeding, spawning, seasonal movement, and other intricate details of the fish's underwater world unfold as you re-count your trips on the pages of your personal record.

In my diary I mapped out the places I fished in order to lay out a grid system, which in turn identified hot spots for bass during certain times of the day and year. It became clear that a crankbait fished on this certain ledge in the fall would consistently produce fish. There were other areas that a jig would get hammered in the early spring and still other conditions that would dictate a floating white worm that would be the thing that would draw strikes from better than average sized bass in shallow water. All this unfolded as I reviewed the pages of my own diary. Learn the water, and you learn the fish. Learn the fish, and you catch the fish. It's really that simple. Two to three years of journal entries gives you a good snapshot of history.

You also find that you will learn what not to do. Trial and error creates a memory bank of these *doesn't work* scenarios. I recall a day when I came across another fisherman—it was early March but some unseasonably warm weather patterns had the water up to the high 50s. A buzzbait was tied to the end of my line, and the other angler chuckled as I cast the topwater bait around a fallen tree and began my retrieve. "A little early for a buzzbait, isn't it?" A split second later a four-pound largemouth attacked the buzzer. I replied, "That fish didn't think so."

You will learn how soon in the year fish will hit certain baits and when they'll stop, what retrieve speed works best, and the best color in clear or dirty water. All your questions will eventually be answered. Capture as much detail as you can. Your list, at a minimum should include the date, water temperature, water color, weather conditions, moon phase, wind speed and direction, lures used, catch times, the depth of water fished, and any cover that fish related to that day. I promise if you do this it will make you a better fisherman. It also works if your targets are crappie, bluegill, catfish, or most any other species.

Computer Assistance

Another potential aid in your development is a simple computer record of your fishing trips—a little more high-tech but fun and useful. If you are familiar with the Excel programs, you can easily set up a system that will allow you, with a few keystrokes, to calculate your daily, monthly, and annual catches. Even if you aren't well versed in computer use, someone can easily set this record-keeping program up for you. You can automatically calculate how many fish you average per hour and log the bigger fish by week, month, season, and total for the year. This type of record gives you a clear picture of how you stack up during certain times of the year and how well you do for any time period.

On the next page I've attached my records for this year. I had a slow year by my own standards. I generally catch a thousand bass a year. (I personally don't track panfish or other species) Because of my commitments to karate and volunteer work in the community I fished less this year but can still tracked my results. You can customize your records to include many other details; I opted for my favorites and the ones I see as most meaningful.

In summary, besides being fun, there is valuable information that can be documented for your own use. More than likely for years to come you will enjoy your journal entries and maybe even add a picture or two. Another plus is your family will also, for several years, get to peek into your personal thoughts and share in your fishing fun and facts.

Month	Caught per month	*Over 5 lbs.
January	7	0
February	23	0
March	57	2
April	68	4
May	71	5
June	37	2
July	38	1
August	44	1
September	97	3
October	82	7
November	86	9
December	35	2
Total	645	36
Hours fished	158	
Avg. per hour	3.9	

54

That 10%

There is a saying that goes, "10% of the fishermen catch 90% of the fish." If you buy into that theory, ask yourself, "Why would that be true?"

We're in the information age, where anglers are inundated with internet info, videos, reading material, cable TV shows, magazine articles, and more. Unfortunately some of the information is more a matter of opinion and not totally accurate. This misinformation can lead anglers down the wrong path and have them scurrying to the tackle box and the outdoor store to reload and try again. There are multiple fishing factors that have proven true over the course of the years and also things that have changed the sport which deserve a level of consideration.

What's changed? Fishing pressure over the last several years has skyrocketed. In my home state of Tennessee, older data from 2013 to 2014 shows license sales increased over 16%. In 2020, the year of *the virus*, license sales went up 20% more. More anglers, more fishing pressure, more fish caught, more on the water activity. The advancement in electronics has been astronomical. From archaic paper graphs and little round sonars that showed multiple lines indicating bottom and depth, to the high resolution screens that now offer a real screen shot of bottom, contours, cover, *and* fish it's a new watery world. Using the tools is essential to learning new water, determining water temperature, depth bottom changes, and the location of bass and the baitfish they depend on for food. But dependency on the electronic tools can block you from common sense adjustments and the puzzle pieces to honing your skills to fooling numbers of fish and big bass.

The exposure to social media, TV, and other informational outlets can create a jumble of doubt. One of the highly respected bass anglers ramps up the conversation saying, "We're catching 'em good on crankbaits." Fired up, the bass angling community goes into a frenzy. What kind—deep diving, square bill, lipless? What weight, on what kind of cover, in how many feet of water? Largemouth, smallmouth, spotted Kentucky bass? What's the secret color? Which rod, reel, and line? It could be the that the weather might change, a front moves in, three inches of rain falls, or a major change of wind direction or speed and things go haywire. All this requires a serious revisiting of the tactics not found on any screen or app. It's not panic time. Just take a deep breath and employ a common sense approach.

Bass Basics

The smallest compacted area that serves all the needs of the fish is a veritable gold mine. Oxygen needed to breathe, food to sustain their lives, cover as a security blanket and an ambush point, plus deep water close by as an escape route are all the components to keep bass consistently in an area. The fish will leave when the food source migrates, or when pushed by fishing pressure, falling water, or an increase in boating traffic. Most anglers have a fundamental understanding of the fish but fall short of comprehending their behavior, seasonal patterns, lifestyle, and their underwater world and the land that surrounds it. Once you grasp the details of what bass like, dislike, and how they react to certain stimulus they become more predictable in their reaction, location, movements, feeding patterns. And you learn how to minimize the search by anticipating where they will be. I've said it many times before, "It's not hard to catch fish; it's always harder to find fish."

That 10%

In weather extremes the strike zone of a bass decreases greatly. Very hot weather depletes the water of oxygen making it difficult for all fish to breath. Very cold water can dramatically slow down the metabolism of a bass. Both these circumstances require a slowdown approach and a few other possible adjustments. Location changes, lure size, and probably most important—retrieve speed. Artificial baits need to look realistic and move like the real thing. Anything appearing injured or easy to catch signals to a fish—attack, eat, and retreat to digest.

Studying the everyday motions of the shad, crawfish, frogs, and every other creature on the menu for a largemouth tips the odds in your favor. When you can mimic and match the look of your bait to simulate the natural thing, you'll catch fish every time out. Upsizing your offering positions you to fool a larger fish. It's nothing more than a return on investment. If a fish has to travel an equal distance to eat a small meal or the jumbo version, they always go big. The problem with a bigger bait is any defect in the look or presentation is magnified to a fish that primarily feeds and survives by use of its sense of sight.

Working heavy cover pays dividends. While many bass casters are fearful of pulling an $8.00 crankbait through a deep water, tangled brush pile, the deflection bite on cranks is awesome and extremely effective. The accuracy required to *pitch* a jig or worm into a matted mess of aquatic vegetation can frustrate many bass enthusiasts, but the payoff is the potential hook set on a hog. Likewise burning a buzzer or lipless crankbait over hydrilla beds is tiresome, until a monster crushes the bait. Similarly, working a frog threw a scum patch and waiting to feel the weight of the fish before setting the hook is tough somehow, and still there are swings and misses.

Tapping into experience, yours or someone else's, is highly recommended. When you just look at a spot, pick up another rod, and draw a strike on the first cast, that's the unbeatable combination of bass savvy, using every tool at your disposal, and most important the intuitive sixth sense that connects you to the bass. The feeling is undeniable. As important as anything is the understanding that no one ever conquers the sport. When you stick your thumb of a giant bass, even if just for a moment, you beat the bass at its own game. Congratulations, you're on your way to being one of the 10% that catches 90% of the fish.

55

The Underwater World of Fish

Below the water's surface there are lots of clues for any angler chasing almost any species of fish in fresh or salt water. It's rare for me to make a cast that I don't believe I'm going to catch a fish—part of that is confidence, part of it is experience, and part of it is understanding what makes each fish tick. A quick look at a fish gives you an abundance of knowledge about the lifestyle of these creatures.

Many gamefish feed by sight. Large eyes equals, "I feed by sight." Spotting the real or fake food source—artificial lures—and closely scrutinizing it for details that say "chow time," fish, once convinced, move in for the meal. The way their eyes are set off to either side of the head also allows for a wide field of vision, likely around 270 degrees of vision, which speaks to the level of importance that the sense of visual appeal plays in the feeding of each such fish.

Watch for natural signs. Feeding shore birds or even gulls are a tip off as to the presence of schools of bait fish. Bug hatches related to moon phases are also recognized as potential feeding areas.

Another subtle clue is the upturned lower jaw of bass, crappie, and others. The upturned jaw facilitates feeding in an upward fashion. Feeding in the tilted eyes and body up position is a critical factor in effectively and consistently fooling fish. If you are using lures that run below the fish, it's a lot less likely that you will draw as many strikes. For example, throwing a topwater bait to fish suspended at 20 feet in 30 feet of water isn't a recommended tactic. It's more likely a deep diving crankbait is the ticket. In the same scenario a shaky head worm or swimbait will draw the interest of a bass who will move to the lure and possibly get a follow which may eventually turn into a hit. Conversely, a shallow water—one to five feet—dwelling fish is susceptible to a topwater or a shallow swimming presentation.

I've been questioned about my belief and statement of the magic of the depth range being three to eight feet. My records indicate many of my trophy size catches come from these depths. In truth those fish are actually, in my opinion, easier to catch because they are there to feed. Another key factor is that many fish—bass, crappie, bluegill, and others—are object oriented. Put a submerged tree, rock pile, stump row, or boulder in the same depth, and fish migrate to it naturally. Find an area where there is three to eight feet of water, distinct cover, and an available food supply, and *bingo*, there more than likely is a fish or possible a school of fish present.

Another lesson: many of the targets we cast to are schoolers—find one and many times they have friends. Crappie are notorious for schooling up tight around downed partially or fully submerged trees. Man-made fish attractors can hold great numbers of fish. They come to these places and stay for the previously stated reasons.

Most fresh water fish search of four very specific criteria.
1. Oxygen—Part of the survival of fish is the intake of oxygen. If they can't breathe nothing else matters. Extreme water temperatures in the summer months create low levels of oxygen and the possibility of a complete die off and loss of every fish in the waters. It's why small pond owners often install aeration systems on their mini-waters.
2. Food—To sustain life fish must eat. To reach trophy status they must eat a lot of the right things. Most crappie eat minnows. Giant crappie come from places that have a good population of shad. Crappie—at least the large ones—graduate from minnows to shad and the occasional crawfish. They

grow quickly and thrive under these circumstances. Similarly bass that have a variety of forage but have crawfish available grow fast and fat.
3. Cover—Gamefish migrate to cover.
4. Deep water—Deep water provides an escape route which makes a fish feel a little safer.

If you find these *honey holes*, commit them to memory and visit them each time out.

Other species snitch themselves out by their appearance also. Catfish are a great example. At first glance you notice small eyes, whiskers (barbells), and hidden is a unique tasting system. The eyes in this case say, "I can see but it's not my primary sense for finding my food and avoiding predators." The sense of smell is the first line of the hunt for food. Staging downstream near cover, catfish get a whiff of possible food and move to it. Once located, cats hover over the potential meal and literally taste with the thousands of taste buds they have located on their underside. All of these sensory capabilities are used in unison in the survival of the catfish.

These are just a few examples of what goes on beneath the surface of the waters we paddle and pitch baits in search of a big fish and great stories. Apply a common sense approach, keep a mental or actual notebook, and use your ability to assimilate information to make your kayak fishing adventures more successful for seasons to come.

Guide Tip: A compact area that serves all the fish's needs will hold populations of fish year after year. If the food source leaves or there's a catastrophic weather event they may temporarily relocate.

56

Continuous Improvement

After more than 60 years of fishing, I'm still working to get it right. Thousands of fish have taught me lessons, but each trip out either teaches me a new lesson or reinforces a previous one. Here a few lessons learned:

Don't Give Up
I've fished from every kind of water craft there is, walked the bank, waded in some close-to-home places as well as some distant exotic locations, but the back story is initially I caught zero fish. For months as a kid I went *fish free*. So I *was* learning—yep, learning what *didn't* work and what *not* to do. Persistence pays off. Learning the waters and applying your knowledge consistently eventually leads to patterns and techniques that will produce.

Tackling the Issue of Tackle
Jigs come in weights from a diminutive 1/16 ounce finesse model to over an ounce used to punch matted vegetation. Pick a color and there's a bait to match it. Spinners come in safety pin styles, in-line versions, in weights from lightweight to mega metal. Blade configurations in the thousands—willow leaf, Colorado, Indiana, turtle shell and more. Then there ares crankbaits purported to dive more than 20 feet and the super shallow models, Square bill, oval bill, no bill, rattling, silent, and sizes from micro to magnum. You

don't have to have one in every size, color, and technique specific type. Start slow with basic baits and build.

The Right Rods
Who has at least six? Raise your hand. You know you do!

After realizing I can only use one at a time, I began to collect lengths, actions, and technique specific poles. At last count between spinning, baitcasting, fly, flipping, pitching, cranking, and all-purpose rods, I count a few over 100 resting in various spots in my home. When I launch my kayak normally I have four or five rods accompanying me. For panfish and lightweight lures, a spinning combo is almost always on board. Artificial offerings in the 1/16 ounce to 1/4 ounce range are used to catch bluegill, crappie, and even bass. In windy conditions—the bane of the kayak angler—a larger set spinning set-up is handy for small spinners, minnow plugs, soft plastics, and mini crankbaits. Two bait casters sit close by—one heavier for pitching jigs/soft plastics and the other used to work spinners and crankbaits. That leaves room for a specialty rod—maybe a flyrod or a favorite topwater pole. It's the person behind the rid more than the rod itself.

Gearheads Versus Team Low-tech
If you fish farm ponds and small creeks and have a *Superduper XR 3900 split screen 35000 megawatt fish-o-matic* depth finder, you might want to rethink your goals and check your bank balance. In my world the addition of any extra equipment creates the possibility of failure. *disclaimer: *I absolutely love low-tech super simple in all forms of life.* If the latest and greatest enhances you experience, by all mean go for it. My constant concern is that people allow themselves to be separated from their senses in technology overload.

While I canoed through the Canadian wilderness, I didn't use a birch bark canoe, but I proudly minimized the gear I carried and used a lot of common sense, a paper map, a healthy dose of respect for the environment, and an understanding my own limitations.

My interests lie in the water temperature—taken with a $6.00 pool thermometer— and depth—determined by lowering line until it reaches the bottom and then measuring against the rod. If it's battery operated or mechanical, I recommend having a redundant solution or a backup plan.

Fishing Conventionally Catches Convention Fish
Read that again. Whatever is being touted as the next *game changer* isn't always the best choice. Old standby lures and techniques don't quit working; people quit employing them. My tackle boxes are peppered with *golden oldies*—baits that have been around and caught fish for over 50 years. For example, when night fishing, a black Jitterbug from the Arbogast bait company has probably caught millions of bass. Because it no longer is viewed as *sexy*, people quit using them. If everyone is throwing the same thing in the same waters, it's my belief fish get conditioned to the sight and sound of that artificial lure. This is why live bait rarely fails and is illegal in bass tournaments. Blend a little new with some of the old and experiment until you're convinced—either way.

Ramp Up Your Observation Skills
Try being in tune with falling and rising water levels. Make note of the moon phases. Are there water birds feeding? They go where the food supply lives. Study the effect of current on the fish—it dictates where they stage. Know the surface water temperature. Spawning, feeding, and migration all are direct results of water temperatures.

Pick Up on Patterns
Simply stated: the first fish is luck, the second we call a clue, the third is a pattern. Are the fish schooled in eight feet of water? Are they on the shady side of cover downstream side of fallen trees? Are there a school of crappie in a submerged tree, and are they hitting a vertical presentation as opposed to a horizontal retrieve? Look for

repeatable results based off the pattern, and understand patterns can change with the rising sun, change of wind, and certain times of day. Be cerebral and flexible in your approach.

Once you hit the water be aware of the lessons offered to you each time out, and you will be on your own journey of continuous improvement.

57

The Moment of Truth—The Hook Set

Watch any fishing TV show and regardless of the species being targeted, the most critical part of boating any catch is the hook set. The first hand witnessing of a lost bass also creates incredible tension in the boat. Any major mistake in technique generally results in a lost fish—and the bleeping out of the words that follow the frustration of losing a fish. There are line break-offs and other circumstances, but in my experience, faulty hook sets by far cause more losses than any other factor.

Let's analyze the sets and try to refine your own hook sets to get that fish to you hand.

For fishing certain type baits, spinners, crankbaits, Carolina rigs, and others, the hook set required is *the sweep*. Most critical are the components involved. Rod, reel, line, and bait all have to work in concert to make sure you get a solid set. As you retrieve any lure, rod position is important. A sideways position gives you room to make a wide sweeping motion, but it all starts with where the rod is in reference to feeling the take. One big mistake is to point the rod directly at the lure/fish. A slight offset to either side allows the fish to inhale the bait and puts you in position to sweep sharply and bury the hook point. This is tougher with multi-hook lures like crankbaits. I've lost bunches of bass while using cranking baits, until I realized that the rod I was using had too stiff a tip and would not give as the fish struck. Essentially you want the

The Moment of Truth—The Hook Set

hooks so sharp that when the fish takes the lure they get stuck, and then the sweeping motion provided by the angler finishes the job burying the hook past the barb.

Getting a good set requires many factors—a sharp hook, a rod that has the appropriate action—in this case a medium action rod—and either fluorocarbon (no stretch) or monofilament line that counts on the rod and hook set to produce a sure set. The only job of the reel is to take up excess line and then control the fish with the proper amount of pressure and drag. Interestingly enough, this the same method for buzzbaits, other topwater lures, and even Carolina rigs dragged along the bottom.

Many anglers compensate for less the spectacular hook setting technique by using braided line. Biggest problems with braid are line slip on knots and the difficulties when hung up. Because it's virtually impossible to break braid, it must be snipped off with sharp scissors or another cutting tool. It is also hard on rod guides. You can't convince me that rod guides physically stand up or are made to accommodate monofilament, fluorocarbon, *and* braid all the same way.

With *feel baits*—soft plastics, jigs, tubes—which are my personal favorite for bass and crappie, there is a completely new dynamic for the hook set. The similarity is the need for the rod, line, and hook point to work in unison for a solid set. Because there is only one hook and point, I believe there is a huge advantage. Single hook baits can facilitate hook sets that put up to 11 pounds of pressure at the hook point. This means you can drive that hook point through any part of the mouth and jaw of your fish.

Rod position is the key to the goal of feeling, setting, and gripping the fish at the end of the fight. When retrieving these types of baits it is vital to never let the rod get past the 10 o'clock position. Any lower and the fish is in charge, and the ability of the angler to feel the hit is greatly diminished. Any higher than the 10 o'clock position, and you have no space for the proper hook set. This would require you to lower the rod and thereby lose contact with the fish, lose valuable time, and possibly, because of the change in tension, make the fish spit the lure. The feel bait hook set needs to be swift and technically correct. Elbows in, arms extended slightly, rod dropped to the nine o'clock spot, and a slight amount of slack in the line. If your arms are extended out completely it decreases the shock power of the rod, line, and your entire ability to slam the hook home. Arms in close to the body is where you have the most potential power, I usually use the example of opening a stubborn jar, you hold it in close not out away from you. The dip in the rod to nine o'clock creates room in conjunction with the slack to add momentum to the set.

Think of it this way—when you hammer a nail, you wouldn't set the hammer on the nail, you raise it back and slam it down. You are doing the same thing with this hook set except slamming back instead of down. That's the mechanics of what you are doing to accomplish a solid set on a feel type bait. This is made more difficult with lighter line or a lighter action rod. Medium heavy to heavy actions work best for bass and medium action for walleye and other game fish. I enjoy the feel and fight of crappies on light to ultra-light rods, but must admit I am holding my breath when the huge slabs hit.

How about no hook set? There is such a thing. I was introduced to circle hooks years ago. With an odd shape and look, they are deadly for fishing live bait or in many live bait fishing applications. If you sweep the rod back with a circle hook you loss the fish every time. Because of the construction and design, you merely reel the line in after sensing the pick up by the fish. Turn the rod away from the fish, then count to seven and start to reel. The hook slides up and buries in the corner of the fishes mouth snuggly. It is such a deadly set that it usually takes a needle nose piers to remove the hook. Mortality rate for circle hooked fish is extremely low and valued by strict *catch-and-release* minded anglers.

You might consider videotaping your hook set techniques. Make sure you line is fresh, your knots are good, the drag of your reel is

The Moment of Truth—The Hook Set

set properly, and work to make your hook set technically sound and you will be rewarded with many more fish throughout the year.

58

The Rules of Fishing

After many decades of fishing there have emerged my own personal rules of fishing. They each have a specific purpose and are good for the fisherman, the family, the environment, and in some cases even the fish.

Fishing Is Supposed To Be Fun
Too many times we are influenced by the words and pictures of authors, speakers, and TV personalities. The emphasis on one species or a type of boat sways a large group of people to be like someone else. In reality, you should fish in a way that allows you and your family to derive the most amount of enjoyment. Case in point, while I love to fish for bass, when the bluegill spawn is on you will find me working a sponge spider on a 5 weight flyrod. The bass equipment is set aside for the pure fun of seeing these midget heavyweight fish *suck down* the little bugs. The slurping sound a bluegill makes as the white spider disappears and the fight they put up is unmistakable, especially after you've heard it and felt it 40 or 50 times in one afternoon. The solitude of a pond and the fight put up by the *bull* gills will make you go several days in a row. When the crappie are schooled up and thumping jigs on a ultra light spinning outfit, not only is the action fast but the reward of frying freshly caught slab crappies is enough of an incentive to abandon the largemouth—if for only a few weeks. Lesson: don't

be lulled into imitating somebody else's passion. Fish for the fun of it. It's a truly joyful experience.

Never Leave Fish To Find Fish
During bass tournaments many anglers believe they're missing out, and someone else is loading the boat. Stay with the bass in an area and on a specific pattern. Switch baits, boat positions, and depths before you blast off to another spot. Fish will feed and shut down but rarely leave an area. Try fishing deep to shallow—uphill, or shallow to deep—downhill. Experiment with various baits at different depths. Use search type baits and techniques—a Caroline rig, spinnerbaits, or crankbaits all fit the bill. After relocating the school, you can fish any lure you want knowing at least you're throwing in the vicinity of the bass. If the bite slows down, give yourself a set amount of time to try to wait out the next feeding cycle. In many instances repeated casts are necessary fool the biggest bass.

Extra Equipment Is The Key To Being Ready
Ding, Ding, Ding! Thanks for playing the game, but *no*, the angler with the most stuff is not the most prepared and probably not the best fisherman. As you gain experience and confidence, the volume in your tackle box will shrink. You already know what catches fish and for the most part what you're going to use. Years ago I was going fishing with a friend. Some confusion arose about who was going to load my tackle box into the boat. Upon my arrival I came to the realization that in the haste to load up and go my box was left sitting at home on my back steps.

My partner for the day asked, "What are you going to do?"

My reply—"I'll use the three baits I have tied on and do just fine."

With the baits I had tied on to three rods—a spinnerbait, a jig, and an A.C. Shiner (silver black back) minnow plug I caught 41 bass. Another valuable lesson—the more you have between your ears, the less you need in the tackle box.

The Rules of Fishing

Catch & Release Or Hook 'Em And Cook 'Em
The ancient interest in hunting and fishing came about with the idea of a natural harvest of food rather than being recreational. Hunting does not allow for shoot and release—unless you use a tranquilizer gun—but fishing does afford the opportunity to fool the fish, admire it momentarily, and return it. In research done for a magazine article I wrote years ago, the owner of the Creek Chub Lure Company told me the highest sales they ever had was during the Depression. People were fishing for food and not for fun. In the 60s and 70s it became fashionable to release your catch, especially for bass fishermen with the idea of protecting the resource—kind of a recycling of fish. This gave a better image to tournament fishing and also meant the population was being managed rather than depleted.

While the concept is sound it is also good to manage populations of all species with selective harvest. Crappie and bluegill will over-populate a smaller body of water. Because of the timing of the different spawns, if proper numbers are not maintained, one type will overrun the waters. Simply stated, it's all about balance. There exists what is known as *the ten to one rule*, for every ten bluegill you take you can keep one bass. This maintains a population balance. I rarely keep bass but personally only keep smaller legal fish and release anything over 16 inches—about 2 ½ pounds. It's OK to have a fish fry!

Fish as Often as You Can
One sure way to get better at almost anything is to do it often. You learn lessons each time out. When asked, "When do you go fishing?" my response is usually, "Only on the days ending in *y*." Go during the day, at night, in the rain, hot, cold, windy, clear water, muddy water, and any combination of the above. You learn lessons from catching fish, and you should learn lessons on the days you don't catch fish. Be aware of everything around you, and commit to memory the conditions that led to catches of

numbers and trophy size fish. Listen to learn and teach to those who are struggling.

Fishing has allowed me to do so many unbelievable things. I've gotten to travel, go places, and experience things I would have never imagined. Dream big!

59

Look, No Batteries Needed

Each person for the most part carries all the tools necessary to launch and land—launch the boat and land fish that is. Ever watch a fly fisherman wade a stream? Did you notice the absence of a depth finder? With the possible exception of a cell phone, most decision-making is done via the use of senses—utilizing past experience, knowledge from multiple forms of education, and common sense. The same sense of senses can be employed in your fishing approach.

With *old school* beginnings, my early fishing exploits certainly left a lot to be desired from a success standpoint—randomly casting, hit and miss, the occasional catch, and a fair amount of frustration. Decades ago there was very little available in terms of technology. In my own case, I often found myself bassin' on a budget. My number one complaint about the world of electronics, on and off the water, is that people can and often times do become separated from their senses. For example, many people find doing simple math in their head difficult or have lost the ability to recognize common spelling or grammatical errors. Granted tech gizmos can be helpful as tools for assistance but should not be used as a stand-alone devices. What about when they may not be available or are not functional—batteries die, and at the worst possible time.

In my on-the-water exploits seeking out bass, crappie, catfish, trout, bluegill, and more I try to use all the available information

I can pick up using my human senses, knowledge gained through educational materials, and previous experiences. Things like fishing moving water, because current is a critical component. Most fish avoid current in one of two ways: they station themselves behind objects that block current, or redirect it for comfort and *fast food* delivery. Most gamefish will face into some level of current, using their hydrodynamic shape to their advantage. Positioning themselves behind objects minimizes their need to fight the motion of the fast flowing waters. Another way to dodge the water flow is to descend to the bottom column of the area, resting away from the push in calm lower level depths.

To recognize an object that is breaking the current is done with just your eyesight. Employ this tactic to find and fool creek, stream, and river bass.

Determining Depth
Bass move shallow the majority of the time to feed or spawn. Simplicity is available. Unless you're an avid deep-water ledge angler or fond of working a jigging spoon over a point in 40 feet of water, depth can be figured out by using the paddle or your friendly fishing rod. For water less than seven feet, your paddle can be plunged down to the bottom and provide a pretty fair idea of how much water is below. Up to 14 feet, I generally drop a leadhead jig or Texas rigged soft plastic bait down until the line curls indicating touch down on the bottom. Pull the line up and measure it against the rod—most of mine are seven feet long, it's noted on the base of the rod—and you can easily tell anything from seven to 14 feet. Being a power fisherman—spinners, crankbaits and jigs—any more than 14 feet means I'm in the wrong water. My catch records show the majority of my big bass come from three to eight feet of water.

Recognizing Cover And Bottom Contours
Cover, in most instances, can be recognized by a visual scan of the

area. A branch poking through the surface—there's a tree below. Big branch equals big tree. A point extending out means a gradual depth change and a defined bass highway. A gradual slope or drastic slope of shoreline more than likely means a continuation of the same. Most bottom contours call for the bottom drop the bait down method.

Patterns
The first fish is luck, the second is a clue, and the third is a pattern. Be aware of all the conditions water and weather related. First fish tells you depth, cover, and how aggressively they are feeding. On those rare days when you catch multiple fish on the same bait, in the same area, and on the same retrieve speed, make a mental note of everything you are doing. Rare are the days when bass are *choking it* and that bite continues for hours. Patterns change and require an adjustment, which could come in the form of different size baits, a more subtle color shade of lure, slower speeds, and more, essentially a pattern within a pattern.

Optical clues
Inflowing creeks, submerged trees, bridge pilings, boat docks, rip rap forming banks on dams all are easily seen with sunglassed eyes. I do like normal shades for shallow water and sunny days, or amber lenses for dreary or low light conditions. Sunglasses also protect you from errant casts by you, other anglers, or a swing and a miss on a fish. *Incoming!* Spotting birds feeding on baitfish as well as bass busting schools of bait are additional clues worth noting. Weed beds, log jams, secondary points, changes in bottom or shore composition are all good, easy to spot, and worthy of a cast or two. For finding water temperature, I picked up an inexpensive floating aquarium thermometer—problem solved.

A Few Hand Tools
My tendency is to trust my sense of touch. After thousands of

pick-ups, hits, strikes, and bites ranging from subtle to smashes, you develop and sometimes even anticipate the signal. That signal is transmitted through the line, to the rod, to your hands, and eventually to the brain. For maximum feel I like braided line. For buzzbaits, spinners, crankbaits, and topwater plugs my choice is monofilament.

While the line is critical, the fishing rod is even more so. Casting, feeling the bait and the strike, setting the hook, and playing the fish all fall to the rod and the holder. With the fly rod being the only exception, my boat floor is covered with rods that are there because they are light yet strong, sensitive, and supply the proper punch for a sure hook set. Especially for the braided line, the efficiency and sure cut of a Line Cutterz ring is a welcome change from clippers.

In summary, some old timers say they can smell bluegill spawning beds. Listen for the surface feeding bass, see fish move in shallow water, feel the *tap-tap* of a plastic worm being inhaled. And as for taste—that comes after the catch and cleaning of a mess of crappie!

That covers all the human fishing senses. You don't have to stow your electronic devices—just don't separate yourself from your senses. Tune up your senses for some uncommon success.

60

The Three Best Baits

Nothing invokes more questions than discussions surrounding fishing and catching fish. The old, "what did ya' catch it on" quiz is almost a sure thing when coming back to the dock, showing off a stringer full, a loaded livewell, or viewing pictures of previous catches. Ask ten fishermen, and you'll probably get ten answers. Based on my experiences, here are my personal picks for our favorite freshwater species.

Bass
Of course we would start here. During seminars one of the suggestions is to learn to fish crankbaits, spinnerbaits, and jigs if you want to consistently catch bass any where, any time. Largemouth bass regularly feed on creatures that can swim both vertically and horizontally. Each of these baits offer that potential. Another key to catching bass is to keep your bait in their strike zone. Crankbaits can be reeled down to a desired depth and stopped and will slowly float up—one gentle crank of the reel handle, and they're back in the same depth. Spinners can be controlled by retrieve speed and rod position. Once you slow down or stop, they will begin their descent. Jigs, which I believe put you in position to catch bigger bass, fall into the same category. You lift the rod to swim the bait and stop to get it to drop. In many instances, the bass will bust it on the fall.

- Crankbait: Strike King KVD 1.5 in Chartreuse/Black back, # 535
- Spinnerbait: ⅜ oz. Strike King Premium plus, gold willow, nickel Colorado blades with a #209 Blue shad skirt. *I alter the bait by adding this skirt. It adds volume to the spinner and is a good match to the natural color of shad.*
- Jig: The Strike King Denny Brauer Structure Jig ⅜ oz. in black/blue.

Bluegill

The favorite fish of young and old alike. Found all across the country in any kind of water, bluegills are plentiful, fun to catch, and great at the table. At home in lakes, streams, and ponds these little scrappers are, at times, simple to catch. Hand size bluegill on an ultra light rod and four-pound test line make for a fun time on the water. Liberal limits and so many ways to catch them make the pugnacious creatures the target of anglers everywhere. Almost any rod and reel set up will work for bluegill. Closed face reels, like the Zebco 33 or open-faced spinning reels attached to a 5 or 5 ½ foot rod work nicely. Another great way to catch a bucket full of bluegill is the fly rod.

- Live bait: Nightcrawlers on a #10 hook with a tiny split shot weight six inches above the hook and a float six inches above the weight is a great rig.
- Crankbait: Since they first came out the ⅛ oz. Strike King Bitsy Minnow (535 black back/chartreuse) earned a place in my tackle box. These little babies run true and catch 'em good!
- Flies: Get about six of them, all the same, a white sponge spider. Present the sponge spider on a five weight fly rod and get the cooking oil and cornmeal ready.

Crappie

Each year 35,000,000 fishermen set out to catch crappie. Off the

The Three Best Baits

bank or in a boat of any size and description, this fish has a passionate following. Because they are excellent eating fish, and once found schooled up, can be easy to catch, the crappie has fans all across the nation. Moving seasonally, crappie will hover around structure and can be drawn to an area by sinking man-made brush piles. Natural habitat is submerged wood and fallen trees. Legendary Kentucky lake catches were measured in the hundreds. The limit now in most of Tennessee is 30 crappie, which are a minimum of 10 inches long. *Slabs*, as they are known, range up to two and three pounds with lots of fish in the one-pound category caught regularly.

- Live bait: You can free line or fish them under a float, live minnows are ideal crappie bait. A similar set up like the bluegill rig use the #8 or #10 hook, a split shot, and with or without a float. The float can keep the minnow out of the brush and also indicate a strike.
- Soft Plastic: A leadhead ranging in weight from $1/64$ ounce all the way up to $1/4$ for windy days is desirable. As far as the lure, my first choice would be a the #0095 Monteleone Silver tube from MidSouth Tackle followed by chartreuse tube with red glitter. Right behind that would be white with silver glitter, and last, a pearl colored curly tail grub.
- Crankbait: Believe it, in the late summer all the way through fall, crankbaits catch crappie. I discovered this by accident and use them now on purpose. A Strike King #3 in Oyster (584) or Bad to the Bone (502) will catch numbers and some monster size crappie in August—prime time October and November.

Catfish

Wide spread and highly prized for their willingness to bite, fight, and taste, catfish have a large following all across the world. Thirty pounders are no longer rare, and much bigger fish swim rivers and lakes in the south.

- Live Bait: #1 is River Herring or Skip Jack, whichever name you prefer will catch catfish day in and day out. This bait is oily, greasy, stinks, and will flat out catch blue and flathead catfish. Caught in the same waters as the catfish with small jigs or cast nets, skip jacks are great. Bluegill can also be used, but check your local regulations for use of any live bait as restrictions vary from place to place.

- **Commercially Prepared Bait:** Catfish Dynamite Bait by Strike King is proven to draw the fish out and make them bite.
- **A Good Ol' Gob Of Nightcrawlers On A Circle Hook:** Those are my three best baits, match any of yours?

61

What About Winter

Winter looks different geographically. In the extreme areas like the frozen north the water is hard—as in, ice—and in Florida a cold front drops the surface water temperatures into the 70s. Somewhere in between water temperatures may vary from 45 degrees to the low 60s. For many kayakers winter fishing, from December through March, can be tough. Here's a few ideas to make your kayaking winter weather adventures safe and successful.

Winter Wardrobe

From my head to my toes, staying warm is important. I rely on boundary boots from NRS for my footwear. I use a small lightweight sock inside the boot and have found in cold water and weather conditions my feet stay warm and dry. *Wool* and *wicking* are the key words for my paddling apparel. To retain your body heat, wool undies and waterproof pants and tops are excellent and worth the cost. I have an Immersion Research dry suit that's incredible for my cold weather kayaking. If you can tolerate gloves, there are fingerless models that work, but I personally feel like they *dampen* the feel I depend on to sense strikes on my *feel* type baits.

Life Jackets

Regardless of the season, I wear a life jacket. I have an Astral V-eight for summer and another Astral Ronnie Fisher for winter wear. Freedom of movement for paddling and pitching is important. I chose orange for summer and lime green for winter—both are visible to other boaters on the water. I'm a fan of function over form, lots of pocket space and comfort.

Boat Choices

Stability and comfort come at a price—so does a bad decision in the winter. A conventional bass boat is multipurpose. Pontoon boats provide lots of leg room and loads of space, but they're not built for high speed moves. V-hulls are favored up north and in the wind, but you can make a case for many styles of boats. While I've spent many hours in a canoe, I wouldn't suggest it for winter fishing.

At the top of my list is always safety. My normal ride is an old school Jackson Big Rig—next, the MayFly. My reasons: stability—wide kayaks allow me to stand and fish easily—open decks, and lots of foot space in each is more than adequate. On my list next are the next generation of Big Rigs, the HD model and FD. Both are a mammoth 40 inches wide! Maximum stability comes with additional width. In pedal boats I still pack a paddle, mine is the Bending Branches Pro Angler Carbon Fiber, weighing in at a mere 26 ounces. *Each of my non-pedal kayaks is equipped with the custom casting brace.*

Bring on the Baits

Bait choices vary according to the species you target. My criteria for choosing artificial baits are surface water temperature, water color, sky, and wind speed. Each of these is a factor in the feeding mood of the fish. Bass, crappie, walleye, and others are equipped naturally with super senses in the eyesight category. Appealing to their sight gets the bite. Hearing and picking up vibration are good, and a minimal sense of smell complete the list. Each freshwater species is somewhat the same and still in ways different. Catfish will confound you if you use bass baits and techniques. Any bait that is still and stinky gets the nod for winter whiskered fish. Some of the most successful winter walleye fishermen will use jigging spoons—I'm not a fan—while other drift live minnows and night crawlers. For bass, finesse jigs—⅛ to ¼ ounce—trailed with soft plastic craws are great.

For winter jigging, spinning rods and reels spooled with eight-pound test braided line in conjunction with a four-foot fluorocarbon leader is perfect. Flat sided or lipless crankbaits and a small selection of spinnerbaits are also likely to draw a few hits. Jerkbaits excel in winter water. Cold and clear finds a jerkbait tied to a bass type baitcasting outfit. A baitcasting reel geared at 6.3:1 and 12-pound test monofilament line, a seven foot medium action rod all make of a great set up.

Fish With A Partner
Be aware of hypothermia, carry a thermos of chicken broth, and go with the mindset you may be fishing for five bites all day. Safety, safety, safety.

62

What Does It Weigh?

One of the most frequently asked questions by anglers is, "What does this fish weigh?" A bump board gives you an accurate length as one means of measure—most kayak bass tournaments are formatted to use inches caught. An identifying card is distribute to the tournament competitors, fish are laid on the bump board—mouth touching the front plate—the identifier is placed in close proximity to the fish, and a photo is taken to verify the catch.

Still, anglers can be plagued by the pounds and ounces of their catch question. Here is a simple and reasonably accurate measure for bass. Take the bump board or tape measure reading, and try this formula: If your bass measures 20 inches long, use your phone calculator with this equation: multiple 20 (inches in length of the fish) times 20 which equals 400 and then again multiply by 20, which gives you 8000, then divide by 1600, this yields an accurate estimated weight of 5 pounds. Substitute any number using the same equation, and you will get an answer that is very close.

In fairness for a bass that is *potted up*, the type that is described as a *football* you can add ¼ to ½ pound. For those skinny, long, spawned out bass, a reversal is in order. You may in the spirit of truth, subtract an equal amount. You will find this method to be very accurate if you do a side by side check employing the equation and accurate digital scales. *Remember use the length as the mathematical measurement.*

What Does It Weigh?

For fish that will be released, it's a good idea to wet the bump board as to not remove the necessary slime coat from the bass. For the long range survival of any fish to be released, never touch the eyes or the gills of your catch. In the summer months when water temperatures soar, hook and play the bass in as quickly as possible. The length of the fight endangers the hot water fish due to a buildup of lactic acid in their system The reaction is similar to the bass of a full body *Charlie horse*, and the fish will be doomed. Please measure your fish quickly to reduce the stress on your fish to ensure a successful release. Bass, especially big ones are too valuable of a resource to be enjoyed once. Make a trophy experience possible for the next angler by handling your fish ethically and releasing them to spawn and fight again to thrill a future fisherman.

Formula
Length X Length, take the answer and again multiply by Length, take that answer and divide by 1600. This gives you a very close weight in pounds and ounces for your bass.

Trophy Tip: before you place a fish on a measuring bump board or any surface wet it first to reduce the chance of removing the fish's protective slime coat.

63

Why the Fly

With evidence of being around for hundreds of years, used in both freshwater and salt water environments, fly fishing has an appeal for almost anyone. Flicking flies can be accomplished from the shoreline, waist deep in a stream, or from any kind of water craft including the kayak. Current kayaks actually give you the advantage of reaching waters inaccessible to other types of boats. Some kayaks are more stable than a canoe. Also kayaks afford you the option of presenting flies from a sitting position or while standing.

While I have my own viewpoint, I also enlisted the perspective of Tony Evans, former boat/kayak builder for Jackson Kayak. Evans also is a fan of the fly rod, and he crafts custom rods—including fly rods—and even takes the time to tie his own flies. With experience on streams, the ocean, and every type of water in between, Evans has a passion for the complete fly fishing world.

First you must overcome the misconceptions. We've been influenced by media to view fly fishing as for just for trout. Of course movies like *A River Runs Through It* and images in magazines, on the web, and on TV typify and reinforce the targeting of rainbow and brown trout to take the fly. The truth is your local farm pond, an urban creek, your close-to-home lake, some exotic locations or even a salt water site can all be successful with the *magic wand* aka the fly rod.

You can pick up a starter rod and reel inexpensively. For less than $100 you can find a basic outfit—rod, reel, and line—that can be yours. Evans offers rods for the more serious angler. Some might view *custom sticks* as expensive. You can order a custom rod in the price range of $150 to $300 or up depending on detail, rod components, and amount of customization.

Why
Tony Evans explains his reasons for kayak fly fishing. "The artistry of the casting, working the fly, and reading the water is itself fun and a challenge for me. Small assortment of flies, a basic rod and reel will get the job done. Another thing is the rod is easy to transport and can be disassembled."

My own reasons: "Simplicity—the rod delivers the fly, the reel merely holds the line, retrieve is accomplished with the downward stripping of the line; yep simple."

Tie or Buy
My opinion: "There's a fly pattern to match any natural food source."

Tony Evans says, "A good tier can imitate any fish food source with natural or synthetic material, not just wood, fur, or feathers. Buy a small assortment to make sure you're going to stick with it." Evans continues, "Try to buy from local experienced fly tying folks and get their advice"

I did try tying my own for a while and realized it's much easier to pick one off the shelf than tie one, and it requires a certain degree of patience and spare time to be a fly tier like Evans. You can also get exactly what you want by going to an individual as opposed to a factory tied fly. I realized rainy days and severe winter would be okay for me to sit and create artificial bugs, but if it's nice enough to fish I'd rather be casting flies than tying them.

Imitating Life Forms
If it exists in nature it can be copied at a fly tying vice. The fly

fishing and tying community observes the indigenous creatures and tries to match the look in order to fool fish. Limited only by their imaginations, they can go easy with a *wooly worm* or go intricate with crawfish, a reticulated frog pattern, or some exotic creation.

Deer hair is hollow and floats making it excellent for topwater flies like a deer hair field mouse and many more fake fly rod baits. Bug hatches like the infrequent cicada or the annual mayfly are effective for fish gorging on the creatures that hatch seasonally in profusion. Natural and not so natural material included are fur, feathers, wood, tinsel, yarn, or sponge. If you can visualize it, it can be produced and likely fool a fish.

Fly Friendly Kayaks

As with choosing any kayak there are several determining factors. What type of water are you going to be on? How will you transport your boat? What's your price range? Stability and specific fly fishing requirements also are key considerations.

Tony Evan weighs in: "Room for you equipment is important, also an open deck for the fly line at your feet. Initially sitting to launch your flies is better. Once you get some experience you may want to try to stand—life jackets 100% of the time. Standing makes it less likely you'll snag on your back cast. I keep a fly rod in my kayak year round. If I'm sitting I keep a towel in my lap to avoid line tangling around my feet."

My preference to stand is similar to Tony's, but also because I can see more clearly and get a sure hook set from the standing position. We agreed on the potential paddling kayaks that best suit the fly guy/gal. The Kilroy, Liska, certainly the MayFly, the Bite, and my personal favorite, the original Big Rig or the HD model.

Don't fear the fly rod. Many prospective fly fans worry about the mechanics of working the fly fishing equipment. In the era of everything electronic, the cell phone is a great way to capture your early casting classes. Video the casting practice from the side and watch the line on the back cast and all the way through the forward

Why the Fly

delivery. To avoid the hook barbs, simply tie a piece of yarn or a *hookless* bug to the end of your leader. For the sake of simplicity and cost effectiveness, I use monofilament or fluorocarbon a foot shorter than the rod for my leaders. If on your cast you hear the sound of a type of cracking whiplash snap, you're bring the line forward too quickly. To correct this count "one thousand one, one thousand two, one thousand three," let the line *lay out* and then start the line toward the target. Always let the equipment do the job—power comes from the rod.

Fresh or Salt

"Using the fly rod can be applied on anything from a little farm pond or a vast section of the ocean, targeting anything from trout to tarpon," Tony says. "Don't limit yourself to trout."

There are even fly rod tournaments for carp and musky. In our home state of Tennessee, tournaments are held each year for these and other species. Evidence of this is Evans' personal best catches: a Cobia on the Clouser fly that measure 32 inches, a largemouth bass that scaled 5 pounds 7ounces on a white *game changer fly*. My own bests include an accidental catch of a 25-pound carp on a Cicada pattern and from a numbers standpoint, over 100 bluegill in one day. I live for the bluegill spawn when they're easy to catch, and a few sponge spiders and maybe a wet fly or two will net you several dozen chunky bull bluegill.

One trip to Tampa Bay chasing tarpon produced some good memories of sight fishing for the big salt water creatures but no hook ups. While trout certainly can be brought to the side of the kayak, so can bass, crappie, catfish, musky, and many other species. My own preference is freshwater because the ocean just looks like a big horizon. Tony chimes in with, "Trout don't live in ugly places."

To get started, check local fly fishing groups, do some internet research, find a fly fishing friend for some guidance—and maybe borrow some equipment—and then jump right in. Soon you'll know, *Why the Fly*.

64

Summer Midnight Monsters

Summer time and the temperatures are rising. You might hear people say it's too hot to fish. Largemouth bass have an incredible tolerance to water conditions. When water is in the low 90s, almost bath water, they do slow down but prior to that they are eating machines. Weather almost always affects the fisherman more than the fish. Keep in mind fish are in survival mode—you are in recreational mode. They adapt to their environment. The fish simply adjust and do whatever they have to do in order to get by.

Movement and Metabolism

Fish learn to seek comfort. In extreme weather situations, cold or hot, fish will do things that naturally aid in their survival. In very hot weather, there is less oxygen. Oxygen depletion is the reason many pond and small lake owners install aerators. The water is pumped and sprayed, and oxygen is added to the water. Fish breathe easier, and survival chances are increased. When there is less oxygen present and the same amount of fish using up the oxygen you get a mass die off. This is much the same as several people in one room at the same time. A limited amount of fresh air for a large group of people, the oxygen is used up, it gets harder to breathe, and people struggle.

Limited movement and activity is the order of the day for most creatures, they attempt to conserve energy and feed on whatever is most available. Cooler water provides relief from the heat and has a higher probability of drawing more food sources. Fish of all types will search for cooler water in the form of shade, underwater springs, inflowing creeks, and streams.

Bass digestion is based off the water temperature. Optimum range for digestion is 72 to about 80 degrees. They are, at this point, eating machines. The fallacy that you can't catch big fish now is dispelled. The *need to feed* is one of the reasons you can catch trophy size bass now—they have to eat to maintain or gain weight. Water extremes—very cold water or very hot—create in bass a slower digestion process. This is the primary reason fish feed less in the dead of winter and summer. Less physical activity requires less energy and decreased feeding.

Hot Water, Hot Fishing

During the sweltering days of summer, as water reaches surface temperatures of 80 degrees or more, I rethink my strategies. As for bass fishing, night time haunts include boat docks, weed beds, or on ledges, humps, points, or submerged wood. Lure choices are guided by the bass' lifestyle and capabilities. Understand the bass are looking up, and their eyes collect light better than that of the angler. Black is best, they minimally see the silhouette of baits on the moonless nights. A list of lures that work for warm water, after hours bass include the old standard black Arbogast Jitterbug black bladed spinnerbait, the bass like the Strike King Midnight Special, dark skirted buzzers and big, 10-12 inch models of Texas rigged black plastic worms.

Topwater prop baits, minnow plugs and dark colored crankbaits all should be in the after-hours tackle box and considered for bass action. Night fishing is effective also because presentation flaws are not as obvious, heavier line can be used, and there is less boat and water traffic at the time. On the darkest, new moon, or cloudy nights employ noisier artificial baits and steady retrieves.

Don't be surprised if you find big bass in thin water. After hours bass adventures can start an hour or so before dark and go into the wee hours. A pre-dusk start gives you time to let your eyes adjust to the change in light. Bass also normally go into a feeding period as the light source changes. Bass' eyes adjust to the loss of light faster than those of minnows and shad; this gives the bass a decided advantage for 15 to 30 minutes and naturally triggers the night bite.

Nighttime can be the right time to land a lunker. Try a slow, steady retrieve to make the lure easier to see and catch. The correct lure choices can turn a hot summer night into a fisherman's dream day.

What Else

Lurking in varying depths are other species susceptible to the late night bite. Catfish certainly qualify. Giant cats roam the waters day, night, in rivers, lakes, and all year long. It's a waiting game with the channels, blues, and flatheads. Previously live bait like shad, skip jack, bluegills, or a heaping helping of nightcrawlers are all definite possibilities to be affixed to single hooks, treble hooks, and the popular circle-style hooks. Where there's current, a cast upstream from the suspected holding place allows the smell to call the catfish from their downstream hideout as the water carries the scent/smell of your bait.

Hook sizes should match the intended target. Where crappie populations are good, there's a band of crappie anglers who work their baits through the night for these schooling highly prized table fare. Once you find crappie and establish a pattern you can catch dozens. Night fishing for walleye, bluegill, and many other species is popular across the country.

Night Fishing Factors

Not just for night fishing, the moon phases also play a part in consistently catching fish. Day or night bass will bite better during the new and full moon phases. Minnow and insect hatches coincide with the moons. More food, more fish. Consider launching just before dawn or right before dusk. There are fewer fishermen pressuring the fish, shorter lines at the ramp, possibly no skiers or Jet Skis, and the solitude the dawn and dusk offer.

Summer vacation pressured bass seek relief form the chaotic activities during the late night hours. They lose their fear of noise and move freely about. Shorelines and any normal lake objects like launch ramps, rip rap shorelines, boat docks, and more are great nighttime targets. Safety guidelines include the proper lights on your boat, signaling apparatus, GPS or lake maps, a cell phone, and trip planning information for those at home. Zip up that life jacket and enjoy the cooler temperatures, minimal lake activities, and great fishing that is all part of the quest for a midnight monster fish.

65

Ultimate Organization

Where is that—?

Ever been out or even just preparing for a fishing trip and wondered where certain essential items were? You know you had it, but the exact location eludes you.

The solution—organization!

Because when the bass or crappie or others are biting, you don't want to waste time turning the tackle boxes upside down to find the hook, sinker, leadhead, or the correct bait to fool the target fish of the day. I got tired of digging through tackle box trays and scrounging through interlocked hooks to find the exact item I was sure would be the most effective for catching my limit or a lunker.

The frustrating on-board search for the best bait can be eliminated. During winter or rainy days is an excellent time to inventory, organize, and replenish those pesky mini to magnum tackle boxes. It starts with accessories, goes to various categories of lures, and even get species specific. I'm so OCD I do all three. I even have back up boxes.

I have a passion for bass—not just any bass but big bass. My confidence level rises with *feel* type baits—soft plastic worms, craws, tubes, and jigs all fit the category. I already know colors and sizes that have delivered the trophy fish and will likely not stray away from that list. Packs of plastics and pre-trimmed jigs, worm style

Ultimate Organization

hooks, and any other additional necessities are all arranged to be easily identified and accessible almost immediately. Hooks have all been sharpened with a small diamond file and placed in a well-marked tray to eliminate any confusion. Likewise slip sinkers, beads, and *hitchhikers* are all there for the always popular Texas rig. The plastic boxes range in size to fit the capacity of the items I deem necessary for that day's trip.

When I'm crappie or bluegill fishing, 90% of the time small soft plastic tubes are tied to the end of my line. I'm using a 6 ½ foot open face spinning outfit spooled with four-pound test, and then, depending on the wind, I choose the leadhead that makes the bait castable, allows for the size tube, and gives the best drop speed for the conditions. Clear water, no wind—$\frac{1}{16}$ ounce leadhead. Slight breeze, it's a ⅛ ounce head. Windy weather calls for a ¼ ounce model for casting and contact with the bait. In various colors of water, I might choose a painted head—normally it's the standard unpainted lead look. The multi-compartment box allows for easy selection of the lead and also the baits. Normally for me three weights of heads and a half dozen colors rest under the seat of the kayak. For accessory boxes I even tape the lead weights and hook sizes to the back of the tackle box tray.

The bass boxes get a little more complicated. The previously mentioned jig box is a given—another small 12-tray box is split between topwater plugs and crankbaits. Skirted baits like spinnerbaits and buzzers also deserve their own box. A super producer bait or color is always present with a redundant model. For soft plastics, I carry a day's supply plus 25% so I won't be caught shorthanded but also as to not be overloaded.

I will move baits in and out of my regular boxes but refuse to carry tons of tackle. Three one-sided tackle boxes (Plano #3600) and packs of proven plastic are my constant kayak companions. Back up boxes are stored in my *tackle room*. These are larger versions of the kayak carry-on boxes. Visible inventory levels are monitored to keep a healthy number (don't ask) of *go to* lures on hand. I maintain insane amounts of all-time favorite colors in case they are discontinued or the company goes under.

If I go pond hopping or make a quick trip, I go with one tiny tackle organizer knowing I'll probably only be using three or four lures, possibly one rod—no more than two. I allow myself a backpack occasionally to hold a spool of line, pliers, a small bottle of water, and a few other items.

With a little time and effort you can *tame your tackle* and achieve the ultimate organization.

66

Keys to Kayak Crappie

Of all the beloved species of freshwater fish, crappies almost always invoke a broad smile and the quick suggestion of a fish fry. Scattered throughout North America, Cajun French call them *sac-a lait*. Others refer to them as specks, speckled bass, and many more titles. The white and black crappie varieties are fun to catch and are sought after for the table. In many environments including rivers, lakes of all sizes, ponds, and streams, the crappie can be caught in a number of different way, with many kinds of tackle and techniques. Some states raise crappie in their own hatcheries and place fish attractors in public waters to draw fish and fishermen.

Crappie tend to school and are partial to cover in the form of submerged wood. Shallow in the spring, *spawners* will seek out water temperatures in the 60s to nest and feed aggressively prior to reproducing. Post-spawn crappie will generally move to deeper water, points, creek channels, and off-shore cover. During the summer months, boats of all sizes and descriptions employ a technique called *pulling*, essentially trolling for deep water schooled fish. Speed control is very important then. In the fall crappie migrate to shallow water haunts and begin to feed heavily in anticipation of winter. Caught through the ice in the dead of winter makes it evident that they opportunistically feed year round.

The crappie-seeking kayaker has some distinct advantages for the open water fish and also those hugging the jumbled jungle of submerged trees besides the maze of branches they love to stage in. Crappies can be finicky and reluctant to bite, but a kayak drifting into their diminished strike zone can present live minnows or artificial baits to the lazy fish. A vertical presentation allows for an extended stay in the shortened strike zone of the inactive crappie.

I use a seven foot spinning rod and open face reel spooled with six-pound test line, or a fly rod with an undersized push button reel can be substituted to drop a bait straight down. Once the line reaches the bottom it will curl. I then lift the bait on two-inch increments until I find the holding depth of the fish. They'll let you know! Repeat until the bite slows and then move to the next area and water logged tree.

When a bait hovers in front of the fish, it becomes almost irresistible. When they are actively feeding, a horizontal casting and steady retrieving motion with the occasional pause and twitch will generally pull the fish away from cover to strike the invading imitation. The ultra-light spinning rod and reels make this fun.

A six foot kayak friendly set up with the reel spooled with four-pound test monofilament or six-pound test braided line is ideal. The braid has a rod's length of six-pound test fluorocarbon leader. Experiment with speed and default to slower when the fish are reluctant. Either way it's possible to *fire up* a school of crappies.

The kayak allows you to pinpoint presentations and get *right in amongst 'em*. The silent approach and entry inherent to the *yak* into their territory is a huge plus.

Developing an individual system for inducing the black and white versions to bite can be simple or detailed. Years of experimenting brought me to a few crappie conclusions.

- A majority of the diet of the crappie is comprised of minnows and smaller bait fish. Big crappie also will grow bigger, faster when shad are available, and they gorge on the shad. Mimic or match the minnow/shad, and your well on your way to fun or a fish fry.
- A supply of soft plastics is desirable. I maintain a crappie

specific box. Compartments of small tube jigs, curly tail grubs, and minnow-shaped artificials have all earned their way into my box. Having alternate shapes, sizes, and colors can sometimes save the day.

- Crappie Colors—I match bait colors with conditions: Water color, Sky color, Wind velocity. Clear water, bright sky, minimal wind call for lighter shades. My favorite the 0095 Monteleone silver tube from MidSouth tackle. It gives off a shine like that of the real thing and is my *go to* choice. The same bait fools bass, bluegill, and even catfish—that tells me it appears real to all types of predatory gamefish. In stained water, cloudy sky, and a ripple of wind, I chose a chartreuse or chartreuse combination color. Dirty water, dark sky, and windy conditions the crappie and I try darker shades and combo color like black/chartreuse. Many anglers rely on plastics in purples, pinks, red, white, and glitter added models to land their limits.
- LOL = Lots Of Lead. Because of the nature of crappie fishing and where they hang out it's critical to carry a good supply of lead heads. The weight of the lead that I use is based off a few criteria. Most important is the wind. In zero winds I have used $\frac{1}{16}$ ounce lead heads. The lighter the lead the slower the fall, this can be critical to the listless fish. My most used lead is the $\frac{1}{8}$ ounce in slight breeze which allows for a consistent feel of what the bait is doing. In heavy winds I will reluctantly go to a $\frac{1}{4}$ ounce and normally use a curly tail grub or larger minnow body. The other determining factor is the current in moving water. It's imperative to maintain contact with you bait regardless of the fish you target.
- Alternate Baits—undersized crankbaits, small spinners—safety pin and In-line—along with Ned rig or tiny finesse types of plastics are all potential crappie catchers. Live bait, minnow rigs under floats, tight lined or set ups similar to drop shots are also possible presentations.

Wide spread, willing to bite, and great sport, kayak crappies are likely to become a fan favorite with you once you develop your own system and use the kayak's qualities to deliver those crappie to your grip. Experiment with baits and techniques. Soon you'll be slamming some *slabs* in your home waters.

67

Working the Weeds

For fishermen, access to remote locations and shallow water is a gigantic advantage. Part of the puzzle for those seeking out fish is finding the most distinct factors that will hold all types of gamefish. Close to the top of the list are several types of aquatic vegetation—I always describe them as weeds. Emergent, above the surface, and submerged varieties both hold fish especially in the warm weather months. Below the surface, cabbage weed, coontail moss, hydrilla, and others allow bass to hide in ambush and dart out at the appearance of various types of forage. The emergent brand of bass hideouts are cattails, pepper grass, duck weed, and my personal favorite, lily pads. There are the larger size and the others I refer to as dollar pads because they are about the size of a silver dollar—remember those?

The draw on aquatic vegetation is it offers three of the basic bass needs. It supplies cover, oxygen, and it in brings in potential food sources. Overhead cover during hot weather is beneficial to bass. The water temperature in the shade is slightly cooler. The shade also offers an ambush point. From a scientific standpoint bass, bluegill, and crappie have been equipped with eyes that are oriented upward. The appearance of minnows, bugs, frogs, snakes, mice, and more creeping along the greenery rings the dinner bell for bass.

The silent glide into the watery world of *weeds* adds a dimension to the stealth mode of paddlers. The flick of a fly rod with a surface popper is addictive—you can also pitch plastic rigged weedless in and around the cover. Gaining popularity is *frogging*—throwing hollow-bodied frog baits in the middle of heavy vegetation and watch as the bass blow through to attack the intruder. For larger models of the fake frog, I employ a seven foot heavy action baitcasting rod and reel spooled with 30-pound braided line to wrestle fish from the middle of the pads.

A floating worm rig is equally exciting. I build a leader consisting of a 12-inch length of line with a high quality swivel at one end and worm hook, generally a 3/0 model tied with a Palomar knot to the other end. The swivel keeps the line from twisting. I throw this on an open face spinning reel attached to seven foot medium heavy rod, I prefer spinning because of the light weight rig. The worm, a seven-inch straight tail type will slither through, over, and around cover. Colors for me are limited to white and bubble gum—OK *pink*. The hits are explosive and make the whole proposition fun.

Another deadly tactic is a floating tube. I take a hollow soft plastic tube, make a leader similar to the floating worm rig, and before *skin* hooking the tube I insert a Styrofoam packing peanut in the bait cavity. Cast on either spinning or baitcasting this lure will stay buoyant all day and can be maneuvered through the heaviest cover. A little shot of cooking spray oil keeps any bait zipping through vegetation. When working watery fields of weeds, once I get to the edge I pause for the fish have followed my lure to the very end of the weed patch. Often bass and other will *unload* on a bait resting or slowly drifting down. Stay alert for this hit.

All game fish use aquatic vegetation for one reason or the other. Musky are found along weed lines, bluegills will move into weedy waters to take advantage of bug hatches, crappie will after spawning move to off-shore isolated wood *or* weed beds. These are just a few examples, but greenery plays a part in the everyday lives of many species.

The first sign of green vegetation in spring, into summer, and all the way through the die off in late fall should send the anxious anglers toward those areas where all these types of weeds exist. After all, "The bass is always greener on the other side of the fence."

Guide Tip: As fall approaches I toss a deep diving crankbait to try to get it into subsurface aquatic vegetation. The purpose is to pull up any type of weed to see if they are green and growing or *browning up*, the indication they're dying. Green = good / brown = bad. Simple and effective.

68

What's All the Buzz About?

In bass fishing, there is a category I call *situational* baits—specific baits that work under certain weather, water conditions, or seasonally. Let me introduce you to the buzzbait. The appeal for bass is its reputation as a raucous, whirling, gurgling surface intruder. For the bass angler, there is the anticipation of a heart-stopping hit from a determined bass trying to kill/ingest that noisy, shiny, fleeing, alien creature.

Bass on Buzzers

Buzzbaits catch any size bass. Buzzers aren't necessarily a *numbers* lure, but most times I use them to target trophies. A super-size bass will hit with a water-splashing explosion, a silent sucking vortex, or somewhere in between and then head for cover or deeper water. While most of my time is in pursuit of largemouth bass, the sight of a smallmouth attacking a surface lure is undeniably one of the greatest thrills in fishing. Buzzbaits can draw ferocious strikes. Besides all species of bass, northern predatory toothy fish like northern pike and the musky are prime co-conspirators to try to steal your buzzers.

A key to success on buzzers and almost any topwater bit is retrieve speed. I always use a steady retrieve, but I will adjust my speed until I find what the fish responds to. This can change by the hour or by the day, but ultimately it *will* change. Make adjustments to the speed and consider the *crash*. Crashing the bait amounts to throwing over, in or around cover, and running the buzzer into the cover—this often generates a *deflection* bite, and the predictability just adds to the excitement. On a personal note, when my buzzbait is traveling through what I imagine is the sweet spot, I've noticed I'm holding my breath. The tension and heart-stopping hits will have you doing that.

When

Most anglers start throwing buzzers too late in the season. Regardless of your region, tie one on as surface water temperatures reach the high 50s and remain stable. As temps rise into the 60s and 70s, bass eat more often and digest quickly. This fact sends them back to the hunt for their next prey. Spring, summer, and fall have the potential payoff for the angler willing to consistently cast a buzzbait. When bait fish in the form of shad, creek minnows, or even bluegills are schooled, bass are most vulnerable to the appeal of buzzbaits. Fall, when bait and bass are schooled up, can provide a buzzing bonanza.

Bass adopt a wolf pack mentality and herd bait to the surface. It's then a buzzer will draw repeated strikes from the aggressive bass. Even if you are casting spinners, worms, or crankbaits for bass and see the surface eruption, keep a rod ready to throw the buzzer into the middle of the fray.

Where

Most likely buzzing waters range from literally inches to double digit depths. Key considerations are water color, wind velocity, and available cover. In clear water single small blades are preferable; as the waters takes on more stain from run-off or rain, up-size the blade size or try the twin bladed models. The double blades make it easier on the angler to keep the bait on the surface and allows for a slower retrieve. Wind matters because it changes the amount of sunlight that penetrates the water, and since bass feed by sight, they are looking up seeing minimally at least the silhouette of artificial lures. When the sun is bright and the water clear, largemouth bass will move into heavy overhead cover. This sets up a unique scenario. Throwing into the slop or edges will often bring the bass through or out of the vegetation.

Another possibility is the use of a hollow body frog in the area. There are also soft plastic baits that mimic frogs and giant shad that are equipped with paddle tails and legs—these are also possibilities for the surface feeding fish. When searching for buzzing opportunities consider submerged wood, weed beds, boat docks, chunk rock, and shoreline objects as potential hangouts. With their location often predictable, a well-placed cast beyond the cover sets the stage for a buzzer catch. Cast beyond the object to keep from spooking the fish, and minimizing it's time to view the bait essentially forcing the fish to strike or miss out on a substantial meal. Big bass don't pass up many meals or a well presented lure of any type.

Endless Possibilities
There are several varieties and different configurations; there are the double bladed buzzers, buzzers with clickers, one blade models, plastic bladed versions, and there is always the option of altering your bait. Adding a small willow leaf blade behind the buzzing blade, or pulling the skirt and adding soft plastic minnow or frog bodies are potential alterations.

Try bigger or even colored blades for aggressive fish or lure-shy fish. Skirt colors vary but matter little; they are more of a fishermen's preference than bass' preference. One big plus with these lures is that they allow for the use of heavier line, braid or 30-pound test monofilament, because in most instances the line is well above the surface during the retrieve and not likely to be seen by the bass. A 6 ½ to 7 ½ foot medium action rod with a high speed bait casting reel is preferable for casting and retrieving buzzing baits most effectively.

What's All the Buzz About?

Buzzbaits appeal to the predatory nature of bass. Experiment with different baits; vary your retrieve speed until the fish tell you what they want. You'll know you have it right—the water explodes and through the spray you see a heavyweight bass dancing on top of the water. My personal best: a ten and a half pound largemouth buzzer bass!

Buzzbaits—it's what the buzz is all about.

69

Catching Fish on the Crossover

Peering through the trays of your tackle box you might wonder which bait is best. You consider the color, size, and certainly the success you have had previously. Plus there's the pressure of the strong suggestions in all forms of media, as well as your fishing friends' boasts of recent or maybe even past catches.

A test and testimony might well be which artificial lures have been around the longest. You probably also think about the season of the year and the current weather and water conditions. While all this may be true, some of the all-time best baits—those that have stood the test of time—are what I call crossover baits.

I bet in the years that you've been fishing, you've caught some fish *accidentally*. Don't be shy. We've all done it. To me it's a good sign that you're casting for bass, and a big slab crappie grabs your bait. Or maybe you were working a jig around heavy cover, and a catfish sucked in your jig. How about a spinnerbait that was intended for a largemouth, and a big pike or walleye ambushed on the way back to the boat. After a little contemplation I believe it's a good sign that multiple species are willing to hit a bait regardless of the intended target. Heck, I'll take just about anything that is willing to strike my bait.

It's been my own experience that often while hoping for one type of fish I set the hook on a total surprise species. On a small middle Tennessee River system, I was paddling and pitching plastic

Catching Fish on the Crossover

in search of some late spring crappie. With a few fish already to my credit, I tossed a tiny tube out and began an erratic swimming retrieve back when I sensed a not so subtle *thump*. I leaned back only to realize whatever this was exhibited power that could never be mistaken for a crappie. With my reels drag singing, I prayed that the knot on the four-pound test line would hold and that the ultra-light rod had enough backbone to play whatever this was. For several minutes we wrestled each other—I was making up line, and the mystery Moby took it back. The fact that it never jumped had me rule out a trophy bass. Time slipped by and at 40 minutes into the spirited fight a giant carp rolled by the side of my Jackson Big Rig. I did manage to get a grip on the *bugle mouth bass* and asked a bank bound angler to snap a quick pic for me. I wasn't as proud of the catch as the ability to land a giant on the super light set up.

On other occasions I hooked walleye on spinnerbaits while working points and off-shore areas for smallmouth. Launching buzzbait produced several northern pike, and some oversized catfish ate jigs and bottom bumping soft plastics. Every die hard crappie fisherman has a story about the big bass that hit a tube or grub on light line around a brushpile.

Baits that have appeal to multiple species are effective because they mimic the attributes of the regular forage foods of all types of fish. There's very little in the underwater world that won't devour some unsuspecting creature that ventures too close. A lot of the excitement occurs because in the hands of the angler, when you make any lure look real, something will hit it.

Crossover baits that are most likely to be attacked are crankbaits because they run from inches to over twenty feet, have visual and audio appeal, and with all the colors available might easily give the look of a minnow, shad, bluegill, or crawfish. Multiple designs of body style, bill shape, colors, and rattling capabilities offer a universal appeal to almost any species. Also the spinnerbait, because of the flash and vibration emitted by the shiny spinners, can easily be seen as a shad—a major food source for almost every fresh water fish. An unending size, skirt, and blade set-up makes spinnerbaits likely to get slugged by any size and type of fish. Panfish like bluegill, rock bass, and red eye, and giants like pike and musky all strike spinners with equal vigor.

Don't discount the in-line spinners—they're a staple for all veteran anglers. Soft plastics qualify as the most likely to get hit by anything with eyes and a mouth. The inherent action of a soft plastic worm, a grub, craw, tube, or swim bait all call out, "Come and get me."

There's no limit to the potential for a soft bait. Colors, sizes, shapes, tails, appendages, and a wide selection of rigging options makes this the ultimate category of crossover baits. Soft, silent, subtle, and with the capability to mimic worms, craws, snakes, frogs, and creatures not even natural to the water, soft plastics are ideal for the trophy hunter.

The best baits, those that prove to have universal appeal to multiple species of fish, have to be high on the list. I call them crossovers.

Trophy Tip: While considering size and color, think about the profile of the artificial bait. A big bite properly presented is tempting to a big fish. Bass eat lots of bluegill—look at the profile a bluegill offers.

70

Shad-Oh

You name it, a largemouth bass will eat it. If it fits in their mouth and they can catch it, it's a meal. Any creature in or around the water is fair game. Snakes, birds, frogs, bugs, even baby bass—and they love crawfish. But what they end up dining on more than anything is shad. Gizzard and threadfin shad make up a majority of the diet of all species of bass. When I keep fish to eat, I do the amateur autopsy and check the stomach contents. You're liable to find anything in their stomach cavities, but most often its crawfish or shad. Bass love crawfish because it's high energy food—I've often referred to them as Red Bull for bass. Once cold weather hits, the crawfish will bury up, but shad are around all through the year. That's exactly why bass eat more shad than anything—it's the most available food source.

Huge numbers of shad populate most major lakes and river systems with the shad spawn during the summer months after the bass and in water temperatures above 65 degrees. The shad can be the key to the catch for bass anglers since studies have revealed that up to 75% of the bass diet is shad.

Adult shad, if they make it that far, can be up to 20 inches long, weigh three pounds, and are loaded with Omega 3 fatty acids. Bass as well as catfish and other game fish will gorge themselves on this particular forage base food source.

Many baits mimic the shad and produce numbers of fish. My

choices are spinnerbaits, crankbaits, soft plastic swim baits, and buzzbaits. In my opinion matching the color is more important than matching the size. In choosing a bait, I almost always upsize—the logic being, if you're competing with thousands of shad, you have to make your bait stand out. For this reason I go to a larger lure. A typical spinnerbait blade is the #5 willow leaf blade. It's good, but to draw the attention of a big bass, I switch my blades to #7 willows.

The profile of crankbaits is also important. I prefer and have had the most luck with the square lipped models—the Strike King 1.5 and the 2.5 in color #584 Oyster is a hit with the bass—to crank into cover and get the deflection bite from the lure hitting almost any object. On the lipless cranks, same color or chrome and blue in the ½ ounce version, or the downsized quarter ounce model. On tough days, try the Red Eye Shad, also from Strike King. I throw the buzzbait to try to simulate a small school of fleeing shad. I like to change the skirt to a #204 blue shad skirt to give the most authentic look to buzzers and spinners.

Retrieving the bait is critical to make the shad imitators appear to be making a break for it, injured, or just in a panic. A swimming motion that goes into a stop-and-go with a change of pace is generally the most effective. Giant school of shad, especially in the fall, will draw the interest of bass who follow like a pack of wolves and attack the large gathering of shad. Another fall trick is to change the blade on your spinner to a straight white Colorado round blade.

As the waters get cold and drop below the 40s, shad will in many instances die off. The flutter and fall of a dying shad is hard for bass of any size to resist—the white bladed bait matches this. A retrieve that allows this bait to helicopter down and look helpless pays off. A white swim jig with a soft plastic minnow body trailer is also a great late season bait.

For most of the lures, a stout monofilament or even braided line should be spooled onto a baitcasting reels—most of mine are Lew's with a mid-level retrieve ratio. The baitcasters have the guts to battle big bass and stand up well to larger lures and a heavy schedule. I cast and catch on 7 ½ foot medium to medium/heavy rods. If it's possible I prefer standing while fishing. *Life jackets 100% of the time.*

While I keep a jig handy for those bass searching the rocks for crawfish, I always have a rod rigged for baits that look like shad. What are they feeding on? Shad…oh.

71

Weather or Not

It's a 70-degree, balmy late spring day; the moon phase—full; a slight breeze—perfect weather to be out and drifting in your boat, kayak, or other water craft. That happens about three days out of the calendar year. The rest of the time it's a battle against whatever nature throws at you. We paddle and fish when we can. Sometimes you fight the natural forces more than fish. Here's how I try to get along with Mother Nature.

Wind

The worst scenario for paddling and pitching baits is the wind. Gusty winds take away or minimally make fishing jigs and soft plastics very difficult. You're dependent on keeping contact with your bait to sense a strike, and the wind will put a substantial bow or slack in your line and destroy the feel of what's happening at the business end of the line. I do two things to combat the wind:

- Rule #1—Tie on a spinnerbait. The spinner is ideal to throw into the wind-blown bank where now the feeding cycle has begun. The bottom is churned up, small bits of natural food are stratifying, and the bait fish, minnows, and crawfish feed on the tiny bits.
- Rule #2—I paddle up into the wind and then turn to put the breeze at my back and use it as a natural trolling motor. Next I make small periodic corrections with my Bending Branches

Angler Pro Carbon paddle to cover the *fishiest* looking spots. Keep the rod low and parallel to the water's surface to minimize the wind's effect on your line, and you can still work the feel type jigs and plastic.

Murky/Muddy Water

Where many anglers freak out at *dirty* water, I look forward to it. On the downside, if you are in a small stream, creek, or river, current comes with rising water due to rain. On the plus side, the location and positioning of the fish is dictated by current and color. Another advantage is the limited vision of the fish—you can make a close up presentation without spooking them, ideal for flipping soft plastic and jigs in their *house*.

Bass will stage behind any cover that breaks and redirects the flow, and relate strongly to any immovable object. In highly stained water they set up close to cover and approaching them becomes easier. Logical holding places are submerged trees, boulder rock, boat docks, and shallow points which redirect the current and create swirling eddies where fish will often time rest and wait for the waters to drift food to them. Willowleaf spinnerbaits deliver extreme visual flash. Jigs mimic the crawfish dearly prized by all the species of bass; buzzbaits for surface feeding fish, and rattling cranking lures ring the dinner bell with the audio signal—these all work when there's *mud in their eye*.

Temperature Extremes

Different, but the same. Really hot or really cold, the metabolism of a bass goes into slow down, also minimizing their activity levels including feeding. They're a lot tougher to catch when they're in a neutral or negative feeding mode, and they are reluctant to move. The strike zone of a lethargic bass shrinks considerably and requires a change in tactics and possibly a bait change.

The solution? Sloooowww doooowwwn.

Minnow imitating baits in the form of plugs, plastic versions, a downsized spinner, and maybe the in-line models, or a tantalizing topwater are all likely to draw the interest of the hot and cold bass. When and species of bass are lazy they are less likely to chase anything any amount of distance. You have three jobs now—make your bait selection look real, make it look easy to catch, and make a good hook set. Under the most adverse circumstances, a small bait coupled with a slow retrieve will generally produce enough action to make it a good day.

Your "Bank" Account is Empty
Cruising the bank or shoreline in fear of getting skunked is OK, but there comes a time—in the heat of summer and in the midst of winter—when the bass abandon the bank. It's always a comfort zone to cast at visible shorelines and the objects dotting the banks. Take a deep breath and move to secondary, off-shore objects and distinct bottom contours. Bass will set up here when water levels are falling and food sources *dry* up, or relocate.

Fish move seasonally in and out as weather and water brings bait into different waters. After two or three days of any naturally occurring activity, it becomes a pattern. Recognition of this helps you to find the new hiding spots. Fish will move in or out, but a drastic change in conditions can cause them to relocate again. Lake water is more stable and thereby more predictable as to water level consistency, but moving water gets the nod as to the majority of the bank and shoreline all being alive.

Hitting a Moving Target
When all else fails I go *junk* fishing. Switch species to the almost always accommodating bluegill, white or black crappie, white bass, or any class of catfish. Smaller versions of the bass baits are likely to fool a few fish. Small open face spinning rod and reel combinations are fun and effective. Try an ultra-light or light 6 ½ foot rod spooled with four or six-pound test. They're ideal.

Another consideration is dunking some live bait in the vicinity of alternate species. Red worms, nightcrawlers, crickets, or minnows all work well.

Don't wait for the picture perfect day to push off in your kayak. Use caution, but test yourself against the weather and the fish under adverse conditions. You'll find that fish can be caught under any circumstances.

72

Stream Secrets

Flowing freely across the continent, rivers, creeks, and streams all hold the promise of adventure, fishing, and fun. If you can navigate moving water, breakdown the puzzle, and fool a few fish you're on your way to learning stream secrets. Lakes and ponds are flat waters. They are great places, but there's little change to the landscape and minimal current to challenge the kayak anglers. On the other hand, flowing waters rise with the rain, fall with the drought, and experience shoreline change from eroding banks and the power surge of the swollen streams.

While being capable of holding multiple species of fish, streams offer a diverse fishing experience. Standard species generally include bluegill, sunfish, and several species of bass, crappie, catfish, walleye, trout, musky, and more. You have the choice of targeting a certain fish or going after whatever is willing to bite.

With irregular shorelines, streams give indications of location based off the bends—inside and outside—which are ruled by current. Fish can position themselves to wait in the swirling eddies for food sources to be delivered. Add structure and objects and the positioning puzzle becomes simpler. Fallen trees, boulder rock, gravel bars, and aquatic vegetation all are potential hangouts.

Year round activity characterizes streams. Because the water is in motion, streams are warmer than lakes in the winter and cooler in the summer. The fish respond likewise and remain active for longer periods of time and in some cases throughout the year.

Food sources can be a wide variety and plentiful. Typical streams are a smorgasbord of fish forage. Normally evident are minnows of several types, shad, crawfish, frogs, mayflies, snakes, and many other meals for the inhabitants. Fish thrive on the abundant food sources and in many cases feed on each other in the form of fry or adults.

Current can be the bane of the kayaker or the friend to the fishing fans. The presence of current—aside from adding another key ingredient, oxygen—makes fish location easier for the experienced *river rat*. The stronger the current, the more likely the location of the fish seeking to avoid the push of the fast moving water. Fish of all types will stage on the downstream side of objects that deflect and redirect the current. Knowing this, you can use the drift of the lure as an effective presentation to the fish.

The stream tackle box is a miniature version of its big water cousin. Most of the same lures that lake fans cast are likely to fool steam fish. Mimicking the normal food sources is highly recommended. Small soft plastics, worms, craws, and minnows are a good choice for stream fish. Medium size and mid-level cranking lures in a couple of colors deserve a spot on your box. Shad and crawfish patterns are almost a sure thing, and a few should the square bill models. The square bill crankbaits excel when cast past cover and bounced off submerged wood, rocks, docks, and weed beds. Save room for some spinnerbaits and a few topwater plugs.

If you're a lover of wildlife, streams are frequented by everything that walks, climbs, swims, and flies in the area. Nature photographs are almost too easy on stream trips. Don't discount a hunting trip from your kayak. Silent and stealthy are good qualities for fishing *and* hunting. *Check your local regulations for the rules governing your own state.*

While the launch ramps at lakes are crowded, in many instances you might be the only boat on some streams. Often the shallow

Stream Secrets

waters that welcome a kayaks that drafts in inches of water is impenetrable to big boats. Solitary and serene streams are the scene of many memories.

Stream secrets are revealed slowly but are worth the wait.

73

Trophy Bass Tackle Box

It is always interesting to me when I get to look into the tackle box of another angler. It begs the question of why they want they have, what's the story behind it, and when do they use it? Tales always exist of the $25 crankbait that never leaves its spot, and the lucky topwater plug which has very little original paint left on it, and the spinnerbait with the rusty hook that helped fool their first five-pound fish always seem to come out in the conversation with very little coaxing.

While intriguing, it helps to have a few tried and true baits but also a few new editions for the fish that have become *lure shy*. There are also some artificial lures that seem to catch wads of bass but seldom trick a trophy into biting.

Big bass are wary and will snub anything that looks or sounds phony. The mere fact that they can be inquisitive doesn't mean they will inhale just anything that swims by. Two main qualities of any artificial lure are *attracting* qualities and *triggering* qualities. The attracting qualities seem to appeal to the fisherman more than anything else. Bright color or a highly realistic paint scheme has many folks ready to *add it to the cart*. Attracting qualities are large sizes, bright colors, noise making capabilities, and mechanical motions. Triggering qualities, which are much more important, are overlooked because they are subtle. They consist of natural colors, easily swallowed shapes, silent and random swimming motions.

Other aspects of lure choice that are critical are the ability to be presented and retrieved in a vertical *and* horizontal fashion. Almost everything a bass eats has the ability to move this way. Plan on loading the boat with big bruiser bass now. Here are some essentials for your tackle tote.

Crankbaits

The most successful fishermen have learned to lean on cranking baits. On the tour there are many new *crankensteins*—the folks who throw diving baits from blast off until weigh in. While they certainly catch fish, they can be hard to master correctly, and other lures are more likely to put the big one in the boat.

Cast out and crank back will catch fish, but there are downfalls to this logic in some instances. Cranks shine off-shore or along shoreline objects. Generally they are most deadly when fished around cover and for suspended fish. One of the two best search baits—spinnerbaits being the other—hard floater/diver crankbaits allow you to cover water quickly and locate fish but are not viewed as the best bait to fool a *wallhanger*. If you're trying to fool deep water fish, and a big bass is your target, try a large crankbait like the Strike King 5XD and 6XD which earn rave reviews from the legion of ledge fishermen.

Shallow water power fisherman should try the popular and deadly Strike King 1.5 or the HCKVDS 2.5—part of the silent series and has the square bill to deflect off cover. Try changing the front hook out on both baits—use a red replacement hook (Daiichi) using the same size as comes with the bait (usually a #2 or #4). Red triggers the predatory instinct of all species of bass. Lipless crankbaits also deserve some consideration for spring time and around summer grass beds.

Spinnerbaits

The curse of catching bass by merely casting and retrieving dupes many into thinking this is the best way to work a spinner. It works, but a few small changes position you to catch Mr. Big. The reason they work is they closely imitate the look and motion of the baitfish that comprise a huge percentage of a bass' diet, the shad. Bass eat more baitfish because they are more available, not because they like them more.

A little more work but worth the effort is determining the best blade configuration for the water conditions. My recommendations: clear water—Colorado blades and lighter colored skirt. For moderate stain or murky water—in most places a willow/Colorado combination allows for the best of most worlds, some vibration and a little extra flash. Make the willow leaf blade gold and the front Colorado blade silver. One is bound to be more visible to the bass. The willow provides maximum flash, and the Colorado displaces water. Skirt color—consider a chartreuse and white combination. I prefer ⅜ ounce for feel and the ability to accurately cast the bait. For short striking fish, try trimming the skirt or adding a trailer hook. For muddy, dirty water, a double willow leaf has max flash and draws lots of attention from the sight feeding bass around most types of cover.

Feel Type Baits
Soft plastic worms, craws, tubes, and jigs could well be the best category of lures to help you land the bass of a lifetime. In referencing the triggering qualities, this group is loaded with them. They appear easy to swallow, can be silent, the action is random, and provided by the angler, the speed of the lure which is the most critical factor to tempting a big bass into striking any bait.

Feel baits can be a little more difficult to master, but the payoff is the possibility to always being in position to take a true trophy. The single hook makes the hook set more sure and reduces the possibilities of the fish throwing the bait. The slow retrieve entices fish of all sizes but in the case of the jig gives the illusion of crawfish—bass' all-time favorite food—moving along slowly making it easy to catch. Crawfish are high energy food. The addition of a trailer also creates a wide variety of looks and colors. The Strike King Rage chunk or craw model in #50 Okeechobee Craw and #229 Roadkill have produced dozens of lunker bass for me. Also popular with feel bait fans are the larger versions of the plastic worms and tubes. Almost without exception the vast majority of fishermen use the Texas rig, a conical shaped sinker above a #4 or #5 worm style hook. Check out the Daiichi Copperhead hook—it has a small spring attached to the eye of the hook which keeps the bait straight and holds it on tightly. My preference for slip sinker weight and jig is ⅜ ounce. Using the same weight spinner, jig, worm weight, and any other lure makes for a similar feel and casting consistency when you change rods.

Odd ball baits

The lures that fall under the heading of situational baits but offer the chance at heavyweight bass are buzzbaits, floating straight tail worms fished weightless and weedless, dog walking surface baits, surface frogs, spoons, swim baits, and suspending jerkbaits.

Stock your tackle box with some of each of these lures, practice your casting, think speed control to match conditions and mood of the fish, fish heavy cover, and make sure your equipment is in top condition and your reward could be the biggest bass of your life.

74

Kayak Casting Accuracy

When the bass bite is insanely good you can throw anywhere and get a hit. Unfortunately this window of opportunity is rare and limited in duration. Common sense in casting and presenting your bait says that the shorter the distance a fish has to go to eat, the more likely you are to get a bite. Big fish don't get big from chasing food sources for a long distance—it's a return on investment type of logic. Certain weather and water conditions can decrease the size of the strike zone of a bass. Severe cold fronts, muddy water from recent rains, and extreme heat are a few of these factors. This is when casting accuracy is at a premium.

What are the casting mechanics that will help the kayak angler fool a few more fish? Here's my recommendations.

- Balance in equipment is important. I try to use fishing rods of similar length and action so they all feel the same when I pick them up or more importantly when I make a switch—normally a seven foot rod, medium action. A huge advantage in the *balancing act* is the same weight bait! I tend to lean towards ⅜ ounce versions of jigs, spinnerbaits, Texas rigged soft plastics, shakey heads, buzzbaits, and more. They provide the same feel and make accuracy more likely.
- I prefer to stand in my kayaks—and I wear a life jacket 100% of the time. Each of my Jacksons is rigged with a casting brace that allows me to stand and switch paddle and rod

without much effort. Standing facilities target recognition from a visual perspective. The hook set is also more easily accomplished from a standing position. If you are relegated to sitting the high position is better if possible.
- From a mechanics standpoint, start with the same amount of line from the rod tip to the lure each time. Doing this makes for a consistent feel and increases the chance for the pin point location of the lure. Reel set up, same line, same spool tension, and even the weight of the outfit are pluses.
- For most single hook baits, jigs, soft plastic worms, craws, and bass tubes I almost always employ the underhand pitching technique. Pitching allows for silent lure entry, low profile casts into confined spaces, and is sneaky quiet. If not pitching, try a low trajectory launch of your lure.
- Sloppy casts alert spooky fish, especially in clear water environments. Low light early and late in the day will mask poor cast and presentation to a degree but rarely result in trophy size fish.
- Casting practice off the water with new equipment or techniques is highly recommended. Start with a large target and work your way down.
- Consider casting past your assumed fish holding spot or object to avoid scaring your potential catch. Multiple presentations from different angles sometimes results in setting the hook on bass species of all sizes and types.

A bad cast in the best spot probably won't get the job done, but an accurate cast—even to an ugly spot—coupled with a realistic presentation could lead to the fish of a lifetime.

75

Submerged Secrets

As winter draws closer, many waters are subject to what is commonly known as a drawn down or taking water levels to *winter pool*. Generally complicating things for fish and fishermen, there is an upside to this man-made phenomenon. Hidden gems in the form of bottom contours, isolated structures, distinct objects, and secondary structures make an appearance and should be memorialized through committing to memory or digital photos. While sophisticated electronics can pinpoint certain fish attractors, rivers constantly change and evolve. Some smaller waters and rivers may offer a tiny, nondescript clue that could produce a trophy bass or stringer of crappie to the kayak angler.

Subtle things can prove to be a gold mine. A change in bank composition such as a single stump—my personal favorite—could be 15 feet off the bank on a creek channel or in a river bend is *money*. Debris stuck on the inside bend of a river, creek, or stream, or something as minor as the materials supporting a boat dock all could be the missing puzzle piece. I have one favorite stump normally covered by about 12 feet of water that is a part of my normal run when fish my home river.

For moving water, understanding the flow of the current is key. In this case a small rock point—almost imperceptible—could be the holding spot for a big bass. A carefully cast square bill crankbait, a jig, or spinnerbait from the upstream side of this spot—bass face into the current the majority of the time—is a likely start to a predictable pattern that can be used to catch a limit of fish.

A sloping sand bank is a pretty safe bet to accommodate spawning bluegill in big numbers. A submerged tree could be a crappie *house*. Ledges, drop offs, off-shore humps, and other bottom contours are also more visible when the water is pulled down. Boat docks and their specific structure can also be investigated.

This a good time to make a mental note of the materials used and the configuration of the dock supports. Wood, concrete, PVC, and any combination could be important. Wood harbors algae which draws in bait fish *and* game fish. Concrete warms up and retains the heat from the sun and draws early spring fish. Cross beams under the dock supply ambush points for bass, bluegill, and crappie. I've caught several fish pitching jigs and soft plastic directly under docks of all sizes. Paralleling docks with square bill crankbaits will draw a deflection bite from the dock inhabitants. Spinnerbaits and buzzbaits also pull fish from the security of the shade and cover of boat docks. Don't dismiss the small docks or fail to pick apart the big docks with multiple slips.

Be prepared for some surprises. I've seen sunken vehicles—probably stolen—damaged boats, farm implements, and many other odd sights. Viewed as bizarre to us, they're used as cover by fish.

While the winter draw down can create difficulties in launching a kayak or limit access because of the low water, it's time well spent. While you're searching for the spring/summer secrets hidden in deeper water, if bait is present, you're likely to land a few fish while you explore. The time you spend now will pay dividends as spring approaches, and water levels come back to normal. It's time to discover the submerged secrets on your favorite fishing holes.

Acknowledgments

This book, this labor of love took 60 years to write. Six decades of river research, playing in ponds, searching big lakes for all sizes of fish. This book—a collection of tips, tactics, and suggestions—is for the kid with a cane pole and a can of worms who is fishing the local creek bank; for the tournament anglers casting for cash; for hopeful trophy chasers and someone wanting to string a few fish for a fish fry; and everyone in between.

My thanks to anyone whoever pitched a topwater plug around a watery field of lily pads, the first few folks to throw the new-fangled plastic worms in submerged brush piles, those who took the common sense approach to finding fish, and the next generation staring at multiple pixels on electronic devices. Over the years I've seen the people who fished for food, those who fished for fun, and a few trying to make a living catching these creatures. As long as there's fish there'll be fishermen and fisherwomen—that's the way it was intended.

We've been intrigued by the freshwater, saltwater versions, different sizes, shapes, and the places they live. They call us to local spots and faraway places all in the name of getting another bite. The promise of a trophy is always just around the bend, on the next trip, and in our eternal hopes and dreams. There's no cure for the fish fever—just a dose of belief that on the next cast, just one more cast, and you'll get another bite.

So, here's to you, my fishing friends—no secrets, nothing held back. These are the lessons I learned in ***60 SEASONS, A Fishing Guide***.

To those friends who have gone before me and blazed the trail, Pioneer Bill Dance, Outdoor Communicator Homer Circle, BIG bass expert Doug Hannon, Steve Parks inventor/innovator of Ragetail soft plastics, Outdoor Industry Icon Tommy Akin, to Debbie who fishes with me day, night, hot, cold, or rain and has taught me patience and appreciation—and suffers through my repeated fish tales quietly. To my daughter Angie who fished with me for her first 20 years. To author and fishing friend Michael Vines who inspired me to write a book. To Jimmy Yates for your friendship and opening the gate to new adventures. To Garry Mason for the recognition and creating a coaching example, Brenda Valentine who carries the outdoor message with a gentle strength and country wisdom, Earl Bentz who quietly continues an example of quality boat building. To Tony Evans who will tie my flies and listen to my stories. To those who gave me the opportunity to appear on television, be heard on the radio, to tell my stories on the pages of periodicals small and large about places I've visited and the adventures I found there. To those who allowed me to stand in front of audiences all over the country and teach (and learn) about this sport we love. To all of you—my eternal gratitude.

Thanks to all those who gave me the platform to communicate the experiences of my trips from farm ponds all the way to foreign countries. Thanks for decades of devotion, the chances to share the passion I have for the entire outdoors, the resource, and the joy I found in fishing. To longtime friend and radio royalty Bill Cody and sidekick Charlie Mattos and WSM for the air time. To all of you past, present, and future that will enrich my life and add to my mental scrapbook, my sincere thanks.

To my sponsors, Strike King Lures, Ragetail, Lew's Fishing, Bending Branches, MidSouth Tackle, A.C. Shiners, Jackson Kayak, Astral, Charlie Brewer's Sliders, K9Fishing, Blue Bank Resort, National Marine Manufacturers Association and many more.

Acknowledgments

To my Fathers—my Heavenly Father, thanks for taking me to the most magical places, introducing me to the most extraordinary of Your people, bestowing gifts, talents and the opportunity to use them, being the ultimate fishing Guide, shielding me from harm and allowing more incredible memories than anyone could ask for in three lifetimes, and for leading me beside still waters and your magical moving waters. To my earthly father teaching lessons that I could apply on land and the water, for modeling hard work, perseverance, and an uncommon passion for family, flag, and country. Thanks for the blueprint on living the American Dream.

To those who live to see a bluegill make a popping bug disappear, have a big bass inhale a plastic worm or try to annihilate a top water bait, or the crappie catchers waiting for the next thump on their tube, for all those chasing walleye, musky, trout, catfish, or just little sunfish, and all the stories that go with the catch or even the fish tale about the one that got away. Keep on casting, flicking flies, trolling, or still fishing waiting for that float to disappear

I'm sure there's someone who deserved all this more, but I promise, there is no one who appreciated it more.

Also Available From

WordCrafts Press

Never Run a Dead Kata
by Rodney Boyd

The Riptide
by Jacob M. Carter

Country Music's Hidden Gem
by Billy Rae Stewart

Devotions from Everyday Sports
by Tammy Chandler

www.wordcrafts.net

www.ingramcontent.com/pod-product-compliance
Lightning Source LLC
Chambersburg PA
CBHW010921230426
43673CB00032B/494/J